The Italian Nationalist Association and the Rise of Fascism in Italy

The Italian Nationalist Association and the Rise of Fascism in Italy

Alexander J. De Grand

University of Nebraska Press • Lincoln and London

The publication of this book was assisted by a grant from The Andrew W. Mellon Foundation.

Publishers on the Plains

UNP

Library of Congress Cataloging in Publication Data

De Grand, Alexander J. 1938–
The Italian Nationalist Association and the rise of fascism in Italy.

A revision of the author's thesis, University of Chicago.
Bibliography: p. 229
Includes index.
1. Italy—Politics and government—1915–1922. 2. Italy—Politics and government—1922–1945. 3. Fascism—Italy. 4. Associazione nazionalista italiana.
I. Title.
DG568.5.D48 1978 320.9'45'091 77–24633
ISBN 0–8032–0949–5

To Mary Ellen De Grand

Contents

Preface

Fascism is one of those political phenomena which defies precise definition. Social scientists have argued about its content for more than fifty years. This study of the Italian Nationalist Association will not presume to offer a general answer to the question, "What is fascism," but it will propose the thesis that Italian nationalism, as elaborated between 1903 and 1923, was one of the crucial ingredients in the mix which eventually became fascism and that its influence steered fascism in the direction of traditional conservative authoritarianism. Although Mussolini and many of his close associates came from the revolutionary Left and early fascism had radical currents, the conservatives in Italy were so well organized, both economically and politically, that they exercised decisive control over fascism during the 1920s, limited its radical implications, and made Italian fascism quite distinct from the Nazi variant which Hitler created in Germany after 1933.

Initially, the Italian Nationalist Association was part of the conservative response to socialism. It grew up in the climate of crisis at the beginning of the century as the Italian liberal parliamentary state gave way before the rise of mass politics. Later, after World War I, the Italian Nationalists took on the mission of channeling the Fascist movement along a course which would represent no challenge to the established order. The Nationalists were always conscious of their elite role and deliberately formulated their programs and chose tactics to insert themselves most effectively into the political system.

The study of the Nationalist Association covers the years from 1903, when the first Nationalist periodical, *Il Regno*, appeared, until 1926, when a combination of industrialist pressure outside the government and Nationalist influence within Mussolini's ministry resulted in the creation of a conservative and traditionalist authoritarian institutional structure for fascism.

I would like to thank those who were kind and helpful to me during the preparation of this book. Professors S. William Halperin and William H. McNeill supervised its early stages as a dissertation at the University of Chicago. Professor Jack Roth of Case Western Reserve University helped me formulate the project. Professors Marion Miller, Charles Delzell, and, especially, Claudio Segrè read the manuscript and offered many valuable suggestions on style and substance. I would also like to thank Professor Renzo De Felice of the University of Rome, whose unfailing generosity made every visit worthwhile, and Signora Luisa Federzoni and Signora Elena Argentieri for sharing their memories of Luigi Federzoni and his friends. As are all who work in Italy, I am indebted to the directors and staffs of the libraries and archives: the Sala di Consultazione of the National Library in Florence, the Archivio Centrale dello Stato in Rome, the Museo del Risorgimento of Milan, the Biblioteca Comunale of San Giovanni in Persiceto, and the Biblioteca Alessandrina of Rome.

The Foreign Area Fellowship Foundation extended a dissertation fellowship for 1965–67, and Roosevelt University provided me with a faculty research grant in 1972. Both made trips to Italy possible when there was no other way. I would also like to thank the editor of the *Journal of Modern History* and the University of Chicago Press for permisson to use the material in chapter four which had appeared in the *Journal of Modern History*.

Finally, I owe a special debt to my wife, Linda De Grand, who used her talents as historian and critic to improve the work at every stage.

The Italian Nationalist Association

Introduction

THE ITALIAN Nationalist Association has, by and large, been treated peripherally in the history of fascism, yet it was an important political force. The Nationalists formed part of a new authoritarian reaction which was to dominate so much of the history of the first half of the twentieth century. As a political movement, it bridged the gap between the last decade of the nineteenth century, when the term "reaction" began to take on its modern significance, and the post-World War I years, when fascism developed in Europe. Until the 1890s, the "reactionaries" had been champions of some past aristocratic regime which had been swept away in one of the liberal or national revolutions of midcentury. After the decade of the 1890s, however, in France and in Italy "reactionary" began to assume its modern meaning of rejection of mass or democratic society.[1]

That decade of the Dreyfus affair and the defeat at Adua was crucial to the history of the extreme Right in the twentieth century. For the defenders of tradition, the decade was a disaster. In France, the recovery of radicalism after the suppression of 1871 became more marked and, on the extreme Left, socialism moved beyond its initial organizational stage. Even worse, the efforts to form a solid conservative front failed. The *ralliement* (the abortive movement sponsored by Pope Leo XIII to promote a reconciliation between church and state) to the Republic by French Catholics ended, along with efforts begun by Jules Méline in 1892 to form a conservative, protectionist, clerical alliance in a series of scandals which culminated in the Dreyfus affair. In Italy, the conservatives went down to a similar series of clamorous defeats. Between 1893 and 1896, Francesco Crispi sought to use social unrest in Sicily to strike at the entire socialist movement. Such strong-arm tactics were to be accompanied by a dose of imperialist adventurism in Ethiopia. When an ill-prepared Italian expeditionary force was defeated at Adua in 1896, Crispi's government collapsed, and Italy was plunged into four more years of continuous crisis. In 1898, under Luigi Pelloux and Sidney Sonnino, the conservatives made a last-ditch stand by attempting to erect a constitutional barrier against further evolution in the direction of parliamentary democracy.

These efforts to block the advance of democracy by forging a conservative alliance on the basis of tariff protection, military expenditures, and colonial expansion were premature. The revolutionary threat was not serious enough to warrant such a violent suppression of the nascent popular movement. Moreover, within the ranks of the bourgeoisie the old split between clericals and anticlericals was far from healed. More attractive than conservative authoritarianism was the reformist alternative offered in Italy by Giovanni Giolitti after 1903.

The failure of the conservatives to stem the popular tide during the 1890s had enormously important consequences, not the least of which was the expansion of socialism and democracy in the optimistic and idealistic indian summer of the old European order before World War I. Equally important were the possibilities which the conservative defeat offered for the development of a new Right. The experience of the 1890s convinced many young conservatives of the inadequacy of traditional authoritarian solutions and of the need to find an ideology to encounter the socialist movement. Such an ideological response involved the concepts of nationalism and the organic nation. As it took shape, the new nationalism completed the process of separation between nationalism and liberalism which had been in progress since Bismarck appropriated the nationalist program for his own conservative ends. These neoconservatives considered the nation to be the supreme and most natural expression of the community. Within the framework of the nation they called for a hierarchical and corporative social order to take the place of the existing liberal parliamentary one. To bolster the social order, neoconservativism also demanded reconciliation between the national bourgeoisie and the Church. In foreign policy, it called for a shift from class struggle within the nation to an aggressive, imperialist foreign policy. Thus, the new authoritarianism was a multifaceted response to socialism, democracy, pacifism, and liberalism.

The most famous of these movements, the Action Française, developed in the aftermath of the Dreyfus affair and the triumph of radical republicanism in 1900. Under the brilliant leadership of Charles Maurras, the Action Française elaborated a cultural-political alternative to liberal democracy, but it never found its way to the center of political life. Its intellectual contribution to the development of the new Right has been amply documented, but especially after the movement was condemned by the Catholic Church in 1926, the Action Française became a marginal political force, which found itself flanked on the Right by more dynamic and overtly fascist parties and movements.[2]

The Italian Nationalist Association had much the same original impetus. It began (like the Action Française) as a reaction to a humiliation suffered by the nation. In the Italian case, though, the precipitating incident came in foreign, rather than in domestic, policy. The differences between the defeat at Adua and the Dreyfus affair indicated substantial differences between the two movements, but the coincidence in time between the formation of the Action Française and the first Nationalist review, *Il Regno,* led many observers to the conclusion that the Italian Nationalist movement was simply a copy of the French original.

In fact, similarities between the two movements resulted from the fact that both were part of a common European reaction. The younger generation, which had lived through the trauma of the Dreyfus affair and the Italian crisis of the 1890s, and the generation which was just coming of age in 1900 were both tired and impatient with the political and philosophical baggage they had inherited from their parents. Not only were they profoundly antipositivist and antimaterialist, but they were also antiparliamentary in their political psychology. "Antiparliamentary" came to represent opposition to a whole gamut of objectionable things, so much so that it became a by-word of politics between 1900 and 1922. First and foremost, it meant a movement toward life, action, and dynamism and against debate, compromise, and endless corruption. As one French representative of this new mentality remarked, the Dreyfus cause was never so beautiful as before its victory. Converted into a parliamentary triumph, it was sullied forever. Antiparliamentary symbolized much more. It was a defense of virility and of aristocracy that parliament destroyed by a system of universal suffrage in which the major aim was to be elected and to stay elected. To be against parliament meant to be for selection of the best, for freedom from artificial and confusing political positions. Parliament meant opportunism, bargaining within a closed world of the capital and its power brokers. On the other side was the mystical, the ideal world in which lines could be drawn. War represented action which was the opposite of parliament, that was why the young were so enthusiastic for any kind of conflict, from class struggle to international violence, and why, in 1915, they hailed Italy's entry into World War I as a great victory over parliament.[3]

From Maurice Barrès and Charles Maurras, Charles Péguy and Georges Sorel, Gactano Mosca and Vilfredo Pareto elements of the new nationalist ideology were drawn. The important point is not to trace influences, practically impossible in this case, but to see exactly what the Italian nationalists took from the vaster movement and how they made it uniquely Italian. The latter process is what counted, for if the Italian Nationalist Association had been only the copy of the Action Française which its detractors liked to say it was, it would never have gained its enormous influence in Italian politics. Out of the stock of ideas which were floating around Europe, both French and Italian nationalism took over a theory of the organic nation, of a corporative and hierarchical vision of society, and of politicaly inspired religion which used the Church as a bulwark for the existing social order.

Yet the differences between the two movements were equally, if not more, important. Italian nationalism was essentially imperialist. Not only was the defeat at Adua the precipitating event for the whole movement, but the Italian nationalists also used imperialism as the pivot around which they worked a transformation of both foreign and domestic policy. A fundamental premise of the Action Française was that the French tradition was completed and needed only to be defended. The Action Française's racism was, in part, derived from Maurras's feeling that foreign influences had corrupted classic French culture. Italian Nationalists responded to what they considered to be the incompleteness of the Italian nation-state. For them, the heroic process of the risorgimento had yet to be concluded. Italy had neither attained her true borders—the Brenner, Trieste, Dalmatia—, nor an adequate colonial outlet for her surplus population. Unlike France, Italy was poor in resources yet rich in population and of necessity looked outward to seek a solution. Even more serious was the fact that Italy was still divided internally. National unity had not yet created a strong sense of Italian identity. Here again, unlike the French, the Italian Nationalists had no past to draw on. The Action Française became fixed in an obsolete vision of prerevolutionary France. The Italians used Rome and the glories of medieval and renaissance Italy, but they realized that these had little meaning in the modern world. Thus, Italian nationalism was forced to seek its alternative to democracy and to parliament in some future system. In so doing, the Nationalists designed an economic and social policy which was attuned to modern, large-scale, centralized production.

Perhaps the greatest difference between the two movements lay in an external fact, beyond the control of either nationalism. The structure of Italian politics offered great opportunity to a party willing to fill a vacuum on the Right. In the Italian case, what was called for was a certain degree of opportunism and freedom in self-definition. Whereas the Action Française moved within a regime already marked by a higher degree of party organization and by a system of universal suffrage which had been in existence since the beginning of the republic, in Italy, the Liberal party, that vast and amorphous force which was the legacy of the risorgimento, dominated the political landscape. In a parliamentary regime of small, single-member electoral districts and limited suffrage, regional and personal loyalties between the deputies and their electorates counted far more than ideology. Italy had only one nationally organized mass party, the Italian Socialist party, and did not enter the era of universal suffrage until 1913. Therein lay the opportunity for Italian nationalism. To work within the ranks of the national bourgeoisie was not only possible but also offered hope for real political influence in a system which had not yet taken final form.

From the beginning, the Italian Nationalists were extremely conscious of the need for flexibility in defining their program. They moved with great skill to position their group on the far Right of the Italian political spectrum, but unlike the German "revolutionary conservatives" of the Weimar period, they took equal care to avoid any taint of mysticism, paganism, or absurd economic ideas which might have set the Italian nationalist movement against the modern economic development of the country. Even the German National Peoples party (DNVP), which resembled the Italian Nationalist Association in its flirtation with fascism, had strong racist, mystical, and anti-Semitic tendencies that set it off from its Italian counterpart. The Italian Nationalists largely avoided the quagmire of racism to concentrate on their primary mission of offering to the Right a modern, authoritarian alternative to the liberal democratic order.[4]

The Nationalists refused to accept the institutional development which Italy had taken between 1903 and 1915 under Giovanni Giolitti, Italy's great liberal prime minister. Giolitti's policy of controlling pressures for reform by a gradual liberalization of the political order necessarily meant the expansion of the parliamentary system to include Catholics and a part of the organized proletariat. Recognition of the right to strike and the granting of universal suffrage went hand in hand with an attitude of conciliation toward the Catholic Church. Careful doses of tariff protection for industry, a moderate but politically useful armaments program, and the perpetuation of the south in a kind of permanent state of political underdevelopment completed Giolitti's complicated and risky political gamble.

The Italian Nationalists were convinced that Giolitti's effort would fail and that the institutional framework which he had established in parliament and through the traditional system of electoral patronage would be insufficient to contain the forces unleashed by economic change and increased potential for class struggle. The Nationalists operated on the firm conviction that the political system of liberal parliamentary Italy, based on compromise within the relatively narrow elite and on an inadequately organized party structure, would collapse. This certainty allowed them to develop an alternative which they could offer to the bourgeoisie in time of crisis. Their rejection of the political institutions of parliamentary and liberal Italy was often misunderstood by more traditional conservatives, who during the crisis after the murder of the socialist deputy Giacomo Matteotti in 1924 hoped that Luigi Federzoni, the Nationalist leader and interior minister in Mussolini's government, would step in to remove the Duce in the name of a conservative restoration. Federzoni, of course, had no such intention. Fascism, as it had developed up to 1924 and as the Nationalists felt that it would develop once they held the controlling positions of interior and justice, was just the regime they wanted.

In this regard, the Italian Nationalists are even more interesting in the history of conservative politics because of their combination of social and economic orthodoxy and absolute ruthlessness in the choice of political weapons. Throughout its history from 1910 to 1923 the Italian Nationalist Association (ANI) remained a relatively small, elitist party. Its leadership understood the limitations which a small membership implied and sought to counteract them by an alliance with popular or mass movements which might be infiltrated or controlled from the outside by a well-organized and self-assured minority. Thus, the period of Italian neutrality in 1914 saw the Nationalists side-by-side with democrats, republicans, and revolutionary syndicalists in the battle for intervention on the side of the Entente. The Nationalists continued this policy during the war in an attempt to gain a measure of control over the pro-war Left. After 1918, the phenomenon repeated itself as the Nationalists attempted to find their mass base in the various veterans' movements and finally in fascism. The Nationalists not only prepared the way for fascism, but were also among the first conservatives to experiment with the new techniques of political violence, which became common after the war but which the Nationalists helped develop before 1915.

Mussolini's seizure of power in October 1922 was not a triumph for the Nationalist movement, nor was the fusion with fascism which took place in early 1923 a significant gain. The real triumph of the Nationalists came in 1924 when Federzoni assumed the interior ministry and a few months later when Alfredo Rocco became minister of justice. Between January 1925 and the end of 1926 much of the institutional framework of the dictatorship was established, and the Nationalists, with very clear ideas of the type of regime they wanted, had a predominant influence on the shaping of the Fascist state. Even though they were removed from positions of influence after 1926 and spent the later years of the regime on the sidelines as disappointed critics, Mussolini could never escape the legacy of Rocco and Federzoni. The two Nationalist leaders gave to fascism its statist, authoritarian rigidity, which drained life out of the Fascist party and centralized power in the traditionalist state bureaucracy. Without the Nationalists' legitimist cover in 1924 during the Matteotti crisis the regime might never have survived. It was a harsh justice which forced them to stand aside as a regime that they helped create but no longer controlled dragged Italy to the wars which destroyed the *grande Italia* of their dreams.

One

The Origins of the Italian Nationalist Association

Corradini and *Il Regno*

It was a curious beginning for a political movement that day in September 1903, when Enrico Corradini met Giovanni Papini in Rosalie Jacobsen's sitting room in Florence. Madame Jacobsen's passion was to introduce, by mail or in person, the various literary figures of her acquaintance. On this day, she happened to invite to tea Giovanni Papini, the young editor of the *Leonardo*, a literary and philosophical review which was just getting under way, and Enrico Corradini, a playwright and critic, who she thought might enjoy meeting one another. On the way out, Corradini mentioned that he too was about to launch a new venture, something quite different for him, a political review, which he hoped would act to restore Italy's consciousness of herself as a great nation. Papini, fresh from his reading of Pareto and Nietzsche, was immediately impressed and responded favorably when Corradini asked him if he would like to become an editor.[1]

Corradini's decision to enter politics marked a major change of direction for a man who began his career as a secondary school teacher and literary critic. Enrico Corradini, the father of the Italian nationalist movement, was a kind of Tuscan original. He was born on July 20, 1867, at Sanminiatello, a small village near Florence, and studied at the *ginnasio* of Empoli and then at the Istituto di Studi Superiori in Florence. On finishing his education, he taught for a time, but literature was his major interest, and with some friends he began the review, *Germinal*, in 1891. After that short-lived venture he passed to a new journal, *Il Marzocco*, which he helped found in 1897 and directed until 1900. The *Marzocco* became an important literary force and, as editor, Corradini made his name in the world of letters of turn-of-the-century Florence. The Italian defeat at Adua in 1896, which Corradini felt marked an abdication from Italy's imperial destiny, kindled a growing, all-consuming interest in politics. In 1900, Corradini left the *Marzocco* to become an editor on the *Gazzetta di Venezia* and then, because of his desire to return to Florence, he became correspondent for the *Corriere della Sera* in that city. Evidently none of these positions satisfied him, and, with a recklessness about money which marked his early career, he decided to begin his own periodical. Papini, who knew him well at that time, was never sure how he managed to live. A bachelor of simple habits, Corradini was not at all the romantic, decadent literary figure made popular in Italy by the poet Gabriele D'Annunzio. His private life remained obscure. His passions for politics and for Italy seemed to be sufficient. Intense and charismatic, he was able to convey these twin passions to others in articles and speeches. Never much of a playwright or novelist, Corradini was a clear and forceful writer with a gift for finding just the right expression.[2]

On November 30, 1903, Corradini and Papini put out the first issue of the *Regno* from a dark, dank, two-room, ground-floor office on Via dei Ginori, in Florence. Financing for the publication came from some friends of Corradini. It was a shoestring operation which seemed destined to have a brief life. The moment, however, was favorable, and the *Regno* lived longer and had far greater influence than anyone in those gloomy rooms could have expected. Florence around 1900 was the center of a cultural revival. Young intellectuals from all over Italy gathered in the cafes and on the staffs of small reviews to argue interminably over the new ideas which were being elaborated in Italy or imported from abroad. Jamesian pragmatism, Croce's idealism, the new mysticism of Péguy, Mosca's critique of parliament, and Pareto's theory of elites—all ideas, no matter how incompatible, were used to attack the old positivist certainties of the nineteenth century. New publications abounded. The *Leonardo* of Papini and Giuseppe Prezzolini, *Hermes* of Giuseppe Antonio Borgese, and Corradini's *Il Regno* were among the most important. It was enough to catch the spirit of the times, to question the established truths, and to write with passion and conviction.[3]

Out of the confused and contradictory intellectual climate of the turn of the century the *Regno* selected five themes which became the basis of the early nationalist ideology: social Darwinism, romantic imperialism, pessimism about the ability of the Latin peoples to compete with Germans and Anglo-Saxons, contempt for democracy, which was viewed as rule by the weak, and an emphasis on will over reason and violence over restraint. The groundwork for this new ideology of nationalism and imperialism was laid by Mario Morasso, a pre-Futurist and romantic imperialist, whose passion for machines and power led him from the *Marzocco* and the *Regno* to the editorship of the magazine of the Italian Auto Club just before his death. In his articles for the *Marzocco* and in his book, *L'imperialismo nel secolo XX*, Morasso developed two fundamental ideas of the new nationalism: a glorification of imperialism and an anticipation of the theory of the productive bourgeoisie. Modern civilization, Morasso believed, was not evolving toward democracy but toward a system more than ever based on force and violence, which took the form of a struggle among nations for markets and among men for advancement and mastery in a technologically oriented society. Just as the nineteenth century had been the century of socialist and humanitarian ideas, so the twentieth century would be that of force and conquest. The democratic system only tended to obscure this reality. At the basis of the new power system lay the mechanical revolution. Greater and greater efforts would have to be made to bring new sources of energy under control. The new masters of the world would be men like Krupp and Morgan who controlled that power. Morasso was pessimistic about the ability of the Latin nations to participate in the imperialist battles. Italy, he thought, had one advantage, her people's fertility, which made her, along with England, one of the world's great colonizers. If Italy could overcome the decadence of the democratic political system and bring her political life into harmony with the new realities—imperialism, nationalism, colonialism, and technological power—then she might avoid the fate of the other Latin peoples. Morasso's fascination with industrial progress and his reversal of the modernization equals democracy thesis became important elements in Corradini's thought and entered as a central component in the new nationalism.[4]

The group which collaborated on the *Regno* was a microcosm of bourgeois intellectual dissent in Giolittian Italy. Two figures, Giovanni Papini and Giuseppe Prezzolini, stand out. A generation younger than Corradini, they looked to Bergson, Croce, Pareto, and Mosca for guidance. In 1903, the same year in which Corradini published *Il Regno* and Croce began *La Critica*, Prezzolini and Papini initiated their own review, *Il Leonardo*. Elegant and elitist, *Il Leonardo* sought to shock the materialistic bourgeoisie out of its supposed mental and moral complacency. Common enemies brought Corradini, Papini, and Prezzolini together. Corradini's invitation to Papini after tea at Madame Jacobsen's automatically opened the pages of the *Regno* to Prezzolini, Giuseppe Antonio Borgese, Maffio Maffii, and Emilio Cecchi. Additional support for the *Regno* came from Gabriele D'Annunzio. A contingent of conservative liberals soon joined up. These Young Liberals, as they were called, believed in free trade, economic individualism, and strong government as the cure for Italy's ills. Their collaboration on the *Regno*, never an entirely happy one, offered an early contrast between the classic conservative solutions and the new imperialist nationalism. In fact, the coalition of personalities behind the *Regno* was a difficult combination from the start. Corradini believed in the primacy of foreign policy. Prezzolini sought a solution for Italy's ills in the revival of the bourgeoisie as a ruling class. Papini, whose career took him from the *Regno* to futurism, fascism, and Catholicism, was at that time closer to Prezzolini. The Young Liberals seldom strayed from their hopeless ideal of free trade and rugged individualism. The *Regno* experience, despite its many problems, allowed the basic themes, which later became associated with Italian nationalism, to be developed for the first time. Out of the debates over imperialism, protectionism versus free trade, socialism, and the role of Catholics in political life, there emerged a first draft of the program of the Italian Nationalist Association.[5]

Corradini and his friends made imperialism the basic tenet of the *Regno*. They proclaimed to the ruling class of Italy that it could only regain the initiative against socialism by engaging in an active, imperialist foreign policy. War would bring into being forces antithetical to democratic civilization and its socialist offspring. An imperialist war served a dual purpose in Corradini's ideology. Its emphasis on heroism and violence diverted the middle class from the false values created by liberal optimism. Moreover, it established a new justification for national solidarity. A reinvigorated bourgeoisie would take its rightful place at the leadership of the nation as it engaged in the imperialist struggle. Imperialism became vital for the future of the nation and for the survival of the bourgeoisie as a ruling class.[6]

All of the *Regno's* collaborators shared an admiration for the successful imperialism of Joseph Chamberlain and Theodore Roosevelt, but Corradini went further than most in rejoicing over the victory of Japan, a poor country which transformed itself into a modern military nation, over Russia in 1905. Tsarist Russia, although conservative, was corrupt and inefficient and could never be a model for successful imperialism. Corradini's admiration for English and Japanese imperialism brought out another dimension in his thought. Imperialism had to win mass support in order to succeed. This failure was the real defect of Russian imperialism.[7]

For the *Regno*, which dealt with foreign policy continually, the contradiction between the Triple Alliance and anti-Austrian irredentism (the movement to liberate Italian areas like the Trentino, Trieste, and Dalmatia, still within the Austrian Empire) presented a ticklish problem. The imperialists viewed the sentimental fixation on *Italia irredenta* ("unredeemed" Italy), as nothing more than an instrument to be used in the imperialist struggle. No formal commitment to the Triple Alliance could overcome their hostility to Austria, but admiration for German power and an equally strong contempt for France made Italy's choice of allies palatable. Only the overriding goal of expansion remained constant. On the specific issue of unredeemed Italy, the *Regno* refused to limit itself exclusively to the question of Trento and Trieste. It demanded that Italy pursue an active policy of territorial expansion in the Balkans and in the Mediterranean. In practice, rather than incite the irredentists, the *Regno* used tension with Austria (such as the riots between Italian- and German-speaking students at the University of Innsbruck) to demand increased military expenditures.[8]

The issue of free trade versus protection revealed the latent tension between traditional liberalism and imperialism. In 1904, the fight for free trade was still being waged by noted economists like Luigi Einaudi, Vilfredo Pareto, and Maffeo Pantaleoni, but it was the protectionist side which won governmental favor. The liberals in the *Regno* group saw this situation as one more reason to oppose Giolitti. For Corradini, however, the issue was complicated by the logic of imperialism and by his admiration for the protectionist imperialists in England and Germany. Despite liberal protests, the *Regno* took a far from orthodox position on free trade.[9]

Economic issues tended to merge into the third theme of the *Regno*'s ideology, antisocialism. Opposition to socialism and to democracy was the cement which held the whole *Regno* group together, yet, even here, important differences arose. Corradini's manifesto, "Per coloro che risorgono," in the first issue of the review, set the antisocialist theme with great clarity. The enemy was international socialism, which through the class struggle worked to break up the "great ethnic and historic harmonies which are the nations" in order to subject all other classes to one single class. Corradini's concept of the nation left little room for either socialism or liberal democracy. The state was a living organism, separate from and superior to the individuals who composed it. Internal struggle represented a danger to the vitality of the organism and a dispersion of its energies. Liberalism, with its doctrine of individual rights, opened the door to just such conflicts which, given the weakness of the Italian state, automatically led to anarchy. The socialists, using democratic, pacifist, and antimilitarist propaganda, hoped to weaken the will of the ruling bourgeoisie. Only imperialist nationalism offered a program of recovery to the middle classes, while liberalism left them with no hope of resistance.[10]

Prezzolini offered the *Regno*'s other broad critique of socialism and democracy. Using the political and sociological theories of Pareto and Mosca, he argued that the whole system of representation, free elections, and popular suffrage concealed the fact that the ruling elite perpetuated itself. Democracy was the work of an organized minority rather than the expression of the will of the people. A mass electorate simply broadened the possibilities of manipulation. To give the worker and the bourgeois the same weight in elections handicapped the middle class, which contributed proportionately more to the state but received no equivalent advantage from the democratic system. Democracy resulted in a corrupt and self-serving political class, increasingly separated from the productive forces of the country and entirely devoted to electoral manipulation. Nor was socialism any better in Prezzolini's eyes. A vested interest, with its bureaucracy, political hierarchies, cooperatives, and newspapers, it offered no alternative to the existing system but accepted its worst features.[11]

Vilfredo Pareto played a direct role in the formation of the antisocialist program of the *Regno*. In a letter to Prezzolini, he argued that socialism, a sort of secular religion, could only be met by another religious view, which the *Regno*'s nationalism might provide. Pareto, however, remained pessimistic about the ability of the middle class to reverse its decadence and to check the advance of the socialists. The negative conclusions of the sociologist offered a challenge for the young Prezzolini. He conceded the corruption of a large part of the bourgeoisie, but he believed that it could be reversed by an aggressive counter-program, such as that put forward by the *Regno*.[12]

Relgious policy was the final area in which the nationalist doctrine began to detach itself from traditional liberalism. The Nationalists of the *Regno* refused to be drawn into the old conflict between church and state over the seizure of Rome by Italy in 1871, which seemed to have been resolved by the passage of time and was of lesser importance than the danger posed by socialism. During the elections of 1904, called by Giolitti after the general strike of September, the *Regno* left no doubt of its position. It was the duty of conservatives to unite: "If the bourgeois bloc must be formed, the Catholics must also take part."[13] Catholicism was also important as a manifestation of Italian imperialism. When an anticlerical nationalist group was formed in Rome, the editors of the *Regno* declared that hostility to religion had nothing to do with nationalism "since the Catholic Church is an essentially Roman and Italian creation." Corradini contrasted the submissive and pacifist nature of primitive Christianity with the hierarchical and authoritarian structure of the Roman Catholic Church, which had inherited the imperial and civilizing mission of the Roman emperors. Naturally, the Nationalists totally rejected any idea that the essence of the Christian religion was a message of justice and peace.[14]

In the end, however, the *Regno* of 1903 was a limited phenomenon. As a political movement, it was deliberately elitist and made little effort to organize outside of Tuscany. Moreover, the group was divided along ideological lines. From 1903 to March 1905, Corradini edited the *Regno* with a strong imperialist bias. After March, the review passed into the hands of the liberal Aldemiro Campodonico, who shifted toward a more orthodox liberalism. The original group of collaborators began to disperse. Some of them, Corradini, P. L. Occhini, Campodonico, and Alberto Caroncini, temporarily joined forces in the Italian Nationalist Association of 1910; others, like Prezzolini, Papini, Borgese, and Giovanni Amendola, became friendly critics of imperialist nationalism.

The *Regno* offered a first attempt at an elaboration of the new nationalist ideology and began to disentangle it from traditional liberalism. The weaknesses of the *Regno*'s position were clear. The early imperialism seemed too literary and abstract for Italian conditions. It was out of place in the early years of the Giolittian era, when Italy was still smarting under the colonial defeat in Ethiopia. Furthermore, there was no effort to find a mass base for the movement or to bring it into contact with the powerful conservative economic and political forces of the country.

EMIGRATION, SYNDICALISM, AND THE REVIVAL OF NATIONALISM

When the *Regno* ceased publication in 1906, neither it nor the Nationalist movement left many traces. It took three years before the experience could be resumed on a new basis. Three factors paved the way for the Nationalist resurgences after 1908. These were the economic slump of 1907, the Bosnian affair of 1908, and the growing awareness of the emigration problem. The depression of 1907 and 1908 reduced opportunities for investment in Italy and increased the attractiveness of expansion into the Ottoman Empire. The coalition of industrial and political interests which was to back the imperialist venture into Libya and intervention in World War I began to form, with serious consequences for Giolitti's hold on Italian politics. Moreover, the elections of 1909 saw further gains for the Socialists and increased pressures on the badly organized Liberal party.[15]

Even more important for the immediate development of the Nationalist movement was the annexation of Bosnia Herzegovina by the Austrians, in 1908. This move had several important consequences. First, although the Italians had no right to ask for compensation under the terms of the Triple Alliance, the Austrian action served to convince many Italians that their country could gain little from acquiescing to Austrian expansion. This feeling weakened confidence in the government's policies favoring the Triple Alliance. Second, there were hopes that Italy might profit from a Turkish boycott against Austria. These hopes dissipated, and the Bosnian incident left a sense of rancor in Milanese industrial circles, which aided the irredentist revival in 1909. Finally, the Bosnian crisis had a profound impact on irredentist opinion. There was a decided shift to the nationalist Right after 1908. In fact, some have argued that it was from the Bosnian crisis rather than from the defeat at Adua that the origins of the Nationalist movement can be traced.[16]

Of as much immediate importance for the rise of imperialist nationalism as irredentism was the growing public awareness of the problem of emigration. Concern with Italian emigration finally allowed Corradini to link his imperialism with a major social issue and to appeal beyond his narrow group of political allies. A lecture trip to South America in 1908 and another to North Africa brought him first-hand experience of the consequences of mass emigration as it reached its highest point in the years before World War I.[17]

The idea that Italy should have her own outlet for emigration was popular even in socialist and syndicalist circles. What seemed to set Italian imperialism off from that of the richer nations of Europe was precisely the desperate poverty which drove the Italians to find new homes in foreign lands. Surely, the argument went, these poor Italians, mainly southerners, deserved to remain in their homeland or, since that was impossible, in a colonial extension of Italy. This rationale for expansion was summarized in the slogan "imperialism of the *povera gente,*" or "poor people's imperialism." Writers as diverse as Corradini, the syndicalist Arturo Labriola, and Giovanni Pascoli, Italy's most famous poet after Carducci, were attracted by it. Pascoli's role was especially important. In his writings, socialism and the desire for Italian expansion combined in a potentially attractive political synthesis. Unlike the elitist D'Annunzio, Pascoli did not ignore the existence of a social problem. Italy's weakness led to foreign economic exploitation of its citizens: "The Third Italy [after Rome and the revival of the Renaissance] is in large part poor as before [unification] and, where it appears richer, alas, the work is always Italian but the wealth is almost always foreign." As early as 1900 Pascoli suggested shifting from the class struggle within Italy to the struggle against other nations. He called for the creation of a patriotic socialism based on national solidarity rather than on class conflict.[18]

Pascoli's socialism and imperialism of the *povera gente* were mixed with another sentiment common to the poets and writers of the postrisorgimento generation: that of the unfulfilled greatness of Italy. Here Pascoli had much in common with the Nationalists. Like Corradini, he spoke of "free Italy, completely free," with the "Mediterranean for the third time Italian."[19] Pascoli expressed the rancor felt by his generation for the defeat at Adua when he wrote, in 1896, of the "long stubborn thought of revenge."[20] Later, in his famous speech "The Great Proletarian Has Stirred" on the occasion of the Libyan War, he made a plea for colonial expansion justified by the poverty of Italy and by the wave of emigration to America. A victorious colonial war could give Italians new pride in themselves as colonizers and civilizers of backward nations. This use of the poor migrant as justification for imperialism made Pascoli an important precursor of the Nationalist movement. By popularizing the myth that colonies would resolve the southern problem, he helped translate the statistics of emigration into everyday language.[21]

Corradini immediately sensed that the emigration issue could be expressed in national and corporative terms, akin to the language used by revolutionary syndicalism. His novel *La patria lontana* and a series of articles written on his return from Latin America revealed the new additions to Corradini's imperialist ideology. His writings of this period were based on the premise that emigration offered a basis to work for the convergence of revolutionary syndicalism and nationalism. The fate of the Italian emigrants was merely a reflection of the greater exploitation of poor by richer nations. Exploitation on the level of class was less important than the similar exploitation on the national level. If syndicalism was the struggle of the working class against the bourgeois state, nationalism was an analogous struggle of Italy, a proletarian nation, against the plutocratic nations of Europe. Class loyalty was merely transferred to the nation as a whole in Corradini's appropriation of revolutionary syndicalist rhetoric.[22]

If imitation is the highest form of flattery, Corradini carried his wholesale raid on the enemy camp a bit further. The syndicalists, he argued, understood the fundamental truth that man was by nature violent and that violence was necessary for the acquisition of power. In his somewhat distorted vison, syndicalism was an elitist movement which sought to create worker aristocracies to wrest power from the bourgeoisie. Similarly, Corradini's nationalism hoped to stimulate a new attitude in the bourgeois ruling class. It would be the mission of a revived bourgeoisie to convince all Italians that the nation was an economic fact of life, no less real than social classes. Through the nation an entire people struggled for a greater share of the world's riches. To succeed in this struggle, the goals of each class had to be subordinated to the ends of the community and internal conflict redirected outward in the form of war.[23]

Corradini's merger of syndicalist and imperialist themes reflected a general mood, especially among young middle-class intellectuals. The revision of traditional ideological categories, which had taken place since the beginning of the century, continued. Socialism, liberalism, patriotism were given new meaning. The younger generation, sensing the insufficiency of traditional oligarchical liberalism, sought new ideological combinations, without regard for logic or coherence. Many people acknowledged the need for reform, but the inspiration for this crusading spirit was contradictory: a desire to modernize, coupled with an intense rejection of and contempt for the masses. A number of local initiatives and publications manifested this new mood. Weekly papers like the *Tricolore* of Turin, the *Grande Italia* of Milan, the *Carroccio* of Rome, the *Nave* of Naples, and the *Mare Nostro* of Venice sprang up after 1908 and prepared the ground for the relaunching of the Nationalist movement. The experience of the *Regno* was transmitted directly through several of these publications, as the vague concept, patriotism, was redefined into a new synthesis of domestic and foreign policy. Imperialism, syndicalism, and irredentism were elements which might be encompassed within the patriotic ideals. It was a question of appropriating an expression, of taking advantage of a mood among the younger generation, who by education and background tended to identify with and respond to an appeal to the nation and who sought an ideological response to the challenge of socialism.[24]

In the effort to develop a theoretical framework for the new nationalism, the *Tricolore* of Turin probably best reflected the position of Corradini. This paper, first published in April 1909 by two young followers of Corradini, Mario Viana and Riego Girola, attempted to fuse syndicalism, conservative liberalism, and imperialism. Like Corradini, Viana saw syndicalism as a means of shifting the class struggle to international politics. His real interest, however, was the application of syndicalism and imperialist nationalism to internal politics. Syndicalism offered a possibility of breaking the hold of socialism over the working class, while keeping ultimate control in the hands of the bourgeoisie. The middle class had only to allow the syndicalists to bear the brunt of the struggle against liberal democracy and reformist socialism. Viana accepted the syndicalist call for class struggle as a challenge to form an equally aggressive middle class, actively identified with the interests of the nation.

Anticipating some of the later Nationalist theory, Viana realized that modern capitalism demanded cooperation from the workers. To insure this collaboration, the hold of the Socialist party over the unions had to be broken and the worker organizations brought directly under the control of the state. Viana hoped that an alliance might be forged between the bourgeois and worker elites.[25]

This curious amalgam of Sorel, the Action Française, and Corradini drew some syndicalists into a dialogue with the new Nationalist movement. It was done primarily through two marginally syndicalist papers, *Il Viandante* of Milan and *La Lupa* of Florence. More important than any intellectual illumination which emerged from the exchange was the recruitment of several young men, who later became leaders of the Nationalist Association, from the ranks of revolutionary syndicalism. Tommaso Monicelli, at that time editor of the *Viandante* and later editor of the *Idea Nazionale,* Roberto Forges Davanzati, and Maurizio Maraviglia, two of the most important Nationalist leaders, came to nationalism during that period.[26]

Although the imperialist nationalism of the *Tricolore* group represented the strongest support for Corradini in the heterogeneous nationalist front, irredentism was still the sentiment around which a patriotic political movement could be formed. There was, however, an underlying conflict between the traditional irredentist position, with its concentration on Trieste and Dalmatia, and the new imperialism, which looked beyond the unredeemed territories in the Austrian empire toward the Mediterranean and Africa and toward potential conflict with France. In the Milanese weekly *La Grande Italia,* traditional irredentism and the new imperialism worked in an uncomfortable alliance. The *Grande Italia,* which began publication on April 25, 1909, was for a time the most important paper of the new movement, but it was far more inclined to traditional irredentism than Corradini and his friends liked.[27]

In preparing the ground for what later became the Italian Nationalist Association, the *Grande Italia* was seconded by another paper, which was founded in Rome at almost the same time by Vincenzo Picardi. The *Carroccio,* of March 1909, brought together a loose coalition of anti-Giolittian moderates and conservatives. Its foreign policy position sought common ground between irredentism and the imperialists who tended to support the Triple Alliance (as a temporary expedient), although economic nationalism generally made the *Carroccio* hostile to the expansion of German capital in Italy. The Nationalists of both the *Carroccio* and the *Grande Italia* shared a desire for a stronger Italy, for a more ardent patriotism, and for a harder line against socialism.[28]

These weekly papers of limited circulation were not the only means of propagating the ideas of the new nationalism. The young nationalist intellectuals had the right credentials to enter the world of politics and journalism. By background and education they belonged to the bourgeoisie, which dominated Italian political and cultural life. Even their nationalism was seen by their elders as merely youthful enthusiasm. The major newspapers were open to them. Francesco Coppola, who later became editor of the Nationalist *Idea Nazionale* and was the most controversial of the new nationalists, argued in the pro-Giolittian *Tribuna* of Rome in favor of an integral nationalism, patterned after the ideas of Charles Maurras. Even more important to the new nationalism were the *Resto del Carlino* of Bologna, which featured Corradini's articles, and Sidney Sonnino's *Giornale d'Italia*, a Roman paper and voice of the conservative Right. Luigi Federzoni and Domenico Oliva, who eventually became Nationalist leaders, served on its editorial staff. Oliva was a theater critic and writer from the older generation. Federzoni became, after Corradini, the most important of the Nationalist leaders.[29]

Supremely confident, talented, and handsome, Luigi Federzoni was the true political leader of the Italian Nationalist Association. Born in Bologna in 1878 of an old, patriotic, Emilian family, his early training destined him to follow his father into a literary and academic career. Giovanni Federzoni, a Dante expert, professor, and friend of Carducci, very much wanted his son to pursue the same career. However, the younger Federzoni was drawn, not to literature, but to journalism and to politics. He did take from his father and from Carducci a sense of the hopes and disillusionments of the risorgimento generation. Federzoni was a rare Nationalist, whose career was all of a piece. Unlike Forges Davanzati, Alfredo Rocco, or others who passed from radicalism or syndicalism to nationalism, Federzoni was from the outset a conservative traditionalist. He was not a theoretician like Corradini but a political tactician, whose sense of the possible and whose traditional monarchist sentiments curbed the more sweeping aspirations of some of his fellow Nationalists.

After a brief and unsuccessful career as a novelist, Federzoni opted for journalism, much to his father's disappointment. Using the pen name Giulio De Frenzi to mollify his father, he wrote first for the *Resto del Carlino* and then for the *Giornale d'Italia*. By 1910, he was known in irredentist circles for his articles on German expansion in the Lake Garda region and for several duels with Socialist opponents. His contacts with Catholics were excellent, perhaps because of his political and religious orthodoxy. Although he was closer to the classical conservative position than the other leaders of the Nationalist movement, political instinct led him to side first with Corradini and then with Mussolini. It was this last choice which brought him not only political success but also defeat and exile after 1943.[30]

The Congress of Florence

By early 1910, enough interest in nationalism had been generated to warrant a formal organization. Corradini first proposed a congress, and from the beginning he and his allies (Federzoni, Forges Davanzati, Maraviglia, Coppola, and Gualtiero Castellini) worked to direct the budding movement to their ends.[31] For the promoters of the congress, unity was paramount. The various patriotic groups of irredentists and imperialists had in common their opposition to current policies. For this reason the letter of invitation to the congress was a carefully balanced compromise meant to have broad appeal without presenting much of a counterprogram. Even direct mention of the monarchy was avoided so as not to lose the support of the few republicans who might wish to attend. Overt control by the imperialists was held to a minimum. Corradini was, however, determined not to let control of the congress slip from his hands. He urged Castellini, a young convert from irredentism who acted as secretary for the group, to pay special attention to Viana and his *Tricolore* Association of Turin for "they must form our majority at the congress."[32]

To prepare for their future position, the imperialists also made plans to publish their own newspaper as a rival to the irredentist *Grande Italia*. These plans were kept strictly secret to avoid raising an issue which might have disrupted the congress. By autumn, the project was far enough advanced for Federzoni to write to Castellini that the paper would be established in Rome rather than in Milan or Florence and that he would have equality of responsibility with Corradini.[33]

The first Nationalist congress finally opened in Florence on December 4, 1910. Three hundred people attended, including representatives from the major patriotic societies. Scipio Sighele, a noted sociologist and irredentist leader, was chosen president, and the other offices were apportioned with an eye to balance among the factions. The facade of unity crumbled almost immediately, however, when the small republican contingent left because of the congress's overwhelming monarchical sentiment. There was no room for republican nationalism or irredentism in the tradition of Giuseppe Mazzini in the new organization.[34]

The congress attempted to reach a broad consensus on the important issues of imperialism, irredentism, and free trade. Irredentists and imperialists were united only in their dislike of Giolitti and of socialism. Corradini's speech "Proletarian Classes: Socialism; Proletarian Nations: Nationalism" was a watered down version of his theories of national syndicalism. Instead of stressing imperialism and war, he spoke of the cultural and economic revival of Italy, the southern problem, and the need for a more active colonial policy. There was nothing objectionable about this approach except to his own imperialist supporters, who had hoped for much more. Federzoni was just as cautious to strike a balance between proponents and critics of the Triple Alliance when he suggested that Italy should be aware of the potential conflict between herself and Austria and should remain strong enough militarily to take an independent position in the Triple Alliance, if necessary. Sighele, on irredentism, followed the same moderate line but, whereas Sighele spoke of the Italians in the Austrian provinces, Corradini broadened the definition to work against the French, in Nice and Corsica, and against the English, in Malta. In Corradini's program, irredentism remained merely one part of a larger colonial policy.[35]

Further equivocation on basic issues came after the report on economic policy, given by the protectionist Filippo Carli. Carli's pragmatic, neomercantilist approach was a shrewd appeal to industry's growing desire for expansion. He criticized dependence on foreign products and investment and urged industrialists to play a more active role in politics. His protectionist stand seemed to follow the logic of nationalism by subordinating economic policy to the requirements of war and imperialism, but it was expressed too bluntly for the free-trade liberals. Carli's protectionist bias led to a wave of protests and a retreat on the final resolution (drafted by the ever-diplomatic Federzoni), which put off any decison on economic policy to a future congress.[36]

The final resolution on domestic policy, drafted by Corradini and Maraviglia, reflected the consensus that Italy was weak because the government constantly yielded to socialist demands for reform. The Nationalists called for a reversal of priorities so that internal policy would become a function of a strong foreign policy. The political form which extreme bourgeois patriotism eventually took was conditioned from the start by this strong opposition to socialism and to Giolitti.[37]

Before adjourning, the delegates approved a motion which set up a permanent organization, the Italian Nationalist Association (Associazione Nazionalista Italiana—ANI). The terms "association" and "movement" were consciously used because most of the members were still unwilling to give up their Liberal party affiliation. For the time being, the Nationalists were content to remain a pressure group within the ruling party.[38]

Comment on the congress varied from expressions of support from the extremely conservative Milanese paper, *La Perseveranza*, which favored any new antisocialist organization, to the disappointed comments of Corradini's followers. In an interview after the congress, Mario Viana remarked that he had been let down on the issue of imperialism by Corradini. Similarly, the Nationalists drew criticism from the syndicalists, who also had been attracted by Corradini's ideas. Only Massimo Rocca, an anarcho-syndicalist who later passed over to the ANI and to fascism, saw how attractive nationalism could be, if it followed the lead of Corradini. What disappointed the imperialists and syndicalists satisfied the irredentists, who envisaged a party above politics, a sort of moralizing force in Italian life which would keep alive the cause of Trento and Trieste.[39]

Although the moderates felt that they had won a victory, the real triumph belonged to the authoritarian imperialists. They managed to mold generic patriotic discontent into a concrete political movement. If the congress did not give them full satisfaction, it was because they did not push the issues that far. Unity was vital until the new organization became established as a permanent force on the Right. In the interim, Corradini and his friends were well placed to win the struggle for control of the new association. The structure of the ANI favored their group. Between congresses, executive authority rested in a central committee of twenty-one members, each representing the different factions, but day-to-day operations were conducted by an executive junta, dominated by the imperialists, who had their base in Rome.

In March 1911, Corradini, Federzoni, Forges Davanzati, Coppola, and Maraviglia published the first issue of the *Idea Nazionale*. This paper, which began as a weekly and was transformed into a daily in 1914, became the vehicle by which the new imperialist authoritarianism spread within the association and in the country. From the beginning, the *Idea Nazionale* was the organ of the Corradini-Federzoni faction, and it remained formally independent of the ANI until 1914, when for all practical purposes the policy of the imperialists became that of the association. Collectively, Corradini, Federzoni, Forges, and Coppola were as brilliant a group of political journalists as Italy produced. If they did not know exactly what alternative regime they wanted, they felt an intense aversion to the form and direction of Italian parliamentary democracy. Like the revolutionaries on the Left, they totally rejected the political status quo; these new conservatives were willing to subvert it in order to save the economic and social structure of Italy. They embarked on a policy bred of fear and hatred, and it proved successful beyond their wildest dreams.

Two

The Great Proletarian Stirs: The Nationalists and the Libyan War, 1911–12

Irredentism, Imperialism, and the Campaign for War

In March 1911, Giovanni Giolitti returned to office, succeeding Luigi Luzzatti, who headed one of the short-lived governments which occasionally interrupted the long political reign of Giolitti. Giolitti's government, which remained in power from March 1911 to March 1914, was to be his last before World War I. Its program and composition represented the most advanced position of prewar liberal reformism. The Radical party was represented by three members, and the most important figure, after Giolitti, was Francesco Nitti, a financial expert and one of the rising stars of the center-left of the Liberal party. The program proposed by the government featured two major reforms: nationalization of private insurance companies and, more important, the introduction of universal suffrage. Both of these reforms were to act as bait for the Socialist party, which still refused Giolitti's blandishments to participate in the government. However, even this rigid adherence to Marxist orthodoxy eventually changed. The negotiations between Leonida Bissolati and Giolitti, which preceded the formation of the ministry, were especially cordial. Bissolati, who was one of the leaders of the reformist wing of the Socialist party, approved of the government's program but felt that his party was not ready to accept collaboration in a bourgeois ministry.[1]

In the end, Giolitti's optimistic visions on taking office proved vain. His attempt to enlarge the basis of the political system failed. Giolitti never adjusted to the era of mass political parties, which he himself helped create by the passage of the universal male suffrage law. Neither he nor the majority of liberals could accept the formation of an independent Catholic party, nor could they comprehend the new revolutionary dissatisfaction within the Socialist party. They continued to believe that the masses would accept the perpetual mediation of the traditional political elites. Ironically, Giolitti's suffrage bill only increased the dependence of the liberals on the clerically controlled peasant masses for support against socialism, while causing widespread fears over the future of the parliamentary system. Those fears allowed the Nationalist movement to flourish.[2]

Although the congress of Florence gave the Nationalist movement a start, the editors of the *Idea Nazionale* were determined that the association should not become just another irredentist and patriotic organization. With that end in mind, they argued for a process of ideological clarification. It was essential to find political space for the movement. Corradini emphasized that the Nationalist was a new political man, who sought to go beyond the corrupt oligarchical practice of parliamentary democracy. Radical France and Giolittian Italy were contrasted with the strength of imperial Germany. Democratic reformism meant the progressive retreat of the state before the organized masses. The Nationalists proposed the creation of a strong conservative party to oppose socialism and offered the association as the catalyst for such a new political formation.[3]

Almost from the beginning, the association took on its double role. It acted within the liberal organizations because they represented the point of contact with Italy's political and parliamentary elite class, yet the ultimate aim was to subvert and succeed liberalism. The danger was that the association might become a mere appendage of conservative liberalism. For instance, when the conservative opposition, led by Sidney Sonnino and Antonio Salandra, organized to protest Giolitti's nationalization of the life insurance companies, Federzoni adhered to the protest in the name of the *Idea Nazionale*. However, when the conservative liberals began to argue that there were no differences between nationalism and liberalism, Corradini quickly drew the line. Reminiscent of his stand as editor of the *Regno*, he stated that traditional liberalism, with its individualistic ethic, was insufficient to meet the modern challenge. Only the Nationalist stress on the collectivity could do this. Rather than a subordinate faction of the liberal system, nationalism was its true heir.[4]

Attacks on democracy and opposition to the government on the life insurance nationalization led to the first wave of protests and resignations from the association by the moderates. Even Scipio Sighele, who presided over the congress of Florence, threatened to resign unless the opinions of the *Idea Nazionale* were more clearly distinguished from those of the Nationalist Association. A deeper issue was only temporarily covered over. The moderates' vision of the association as an apolitical patriotic organization was too opposed to the position of the imperialist nationalists, whose long-range goal was to create a political party.[5]

"THE HOUR OF TRIPOLI"

At that point, the crisis within the association was interrupted by the events leading to the outbreak of the Libyan War. Tripolitania and Cyrenaica, the two Turkish provinces which composed Libya, had been at the center of Italian colonial ambitions since the beginning of the century. Gradually Italy had obtained guarantees from all the major powers for her future rights to the area. The opportunity to colonize never seemed to present itself, however, nor was there any real support in the country for an active policy in the years after the defeat at Adua. Only after the first Moroccan crisis between France and Germany, in 1905, did the problem become more immediate. The Italians feared that an 1899 accord with France for mutual support of colonial efforts in North Africa might lapse if the French managed to obtain Morocco before Italy could move in Libya. Shortly after the first Moroccan crisis, Italian economic penetration, spearheaded by the Catholic Banco di Roma, began in earnest in Libya and other Turkish territories. By 1910, partly as a reaction to the too overt Italian interest, the Turks began to obstruct Italian activity. Italy became convinced that other nations, especially Germany, wished to replace her as the leading European power in Libya. These developments persuaded influential sectors of public opinion that Italy could never acquire Tripoli by peaceful means. By late 1910, the growing Turcophobia, which had developed in political circles, found an echo in the press. While no one called for outright annexation or war, several papers, like the *Tribuna* and the *Giornale d'Italia* of Rome, called for a more assertive defense of Italian rights.[6]

Thus, Giolitti's return to office in March 1911 coincided with the beginning of the movement for war in Libya. Although it was unlikely that a colonial war was in the original governmental program, planning for a possible conflict with the Ottoman Empire continued throughout the spring and early summer under the direction of Antonio Di San Giuliano, Italy's foreign minister. Giolitti's conversion to a war policy came after the second Moroccan crisis, of July 1911, when France brought that territory under her control.[7]

Those in the government who favored action to take Libya were helped by an aggressive press campaign in 1911 on behalf of expansion in Libya. While the Nationalists did not play the decisive role in swaying public opinion, their influence was significant in focussing attention on the colonial problem. They were among the first who made Libya the central and overriding issue of Italian politics. Practically every issue of the *Idea Nazionale* from March to September had one or more articles on Tripoli and Italian rights. Moreover, through their contributions to other papers the Nationalists were able to spread their ideas beyond the confines of the association. In April, the Nationalist Giuseppe Bevione began to publish articles on Libya in the Giolittian *Stampa* of Turin. Bevione used his considerable journalistic talents to paint a desperate picture of Italian interests hampered on all sides by the hostility of the Turks and Germans. Corradini's passionate appeals backed up the regular articles of Luigi Barzini in the *Corriere della Sera*, and in July Corradini left on a tour of Tripolitania to report on the situation firsthand. Federzoni, in the *Giornale d'Italia*, Castellini, in the *Gazetta di Venezia*, and Coppola, in the *Tribuna*, rounded out the contingent of Nationalists who kept the issue before a vast sector of public opinion. Another example of

Nationalist influence came at the Congresso degli Italiani all' Estero (Congress of Italians Abroad) held in 1911, in mid-June. It was organized by a pro-Nationalist senator, Giacomo De Martino, who was also the founder and president of the Istituto Coloniale Italiano. Federzoni presented a motion to the congress calling for "energetic action on the part of the Italian government to guarantee securely our rights and interests in Tripolitania." When the Giolittian *Tribuna* protested against this effort to pressure the government, Federzoni was allowed to respond on the pages of Sonnino's *Giornale d'Italia* that the *Tribuna* could hardly reconcile its day-to-day reporting from Tripoli with the cautious, semiofficial editorial policy.[8]

This total concentration on the problem of Libya met some opposition in the association from irredentists who feared the consequences of diverting attention from the Balkans and the Adriatic Sea to the Mediterranean. Castellini, whose connections with the irredentists were good, was asked to write a book of propaganda for Libya which, according to Federzoni, would show "the inanity of the criticism made against us by some of our friends who are more irredentist than Oberdan [an Italian patriot executed by the Austrians]."[9] The imperialist faction wanted to delay the confrontation with the irredentists until the next congress, but the situation worsened when the *Grande Italia* openly attacked the attempt to substitute imperialism for irredentism as the chief goal of the Nationalist movement. Federzoni's reply was uncompromising. He proposed "the most complete suspension of every irredentist territorial claim" for the immediate future. Expansion in Libya had to take precedence over any Italian ambitions in Trieste and in the Trentino.[10]

Enrico Corradini set the tone for the imperialist propaganda chorus. In a series of articles for the *Idea Nazionale* he attempted to show that the occupation of Tripoli could only be achieved by war. Given the weakness of the Ottoman Empire, France or Germany would eventually take Libya, if Italy did not. Moreover, he thought that the colony would be an outlet both for Italian migration and investment. His interpretation of the Libyan venture, tied to his earlier use of syndicalist terminology, pitted proletarian Italy against plutocratic Europe, led by France.[11]

In a curious way, Nationalist propaganda made its way back into syndicalist writing on the war. The *Idea Nazionale* republished an article by Arturo Labriola, the noted Neapolitan syndicalist leader, which attacked plutocratic Europe in almost the same terms as Corradini. Labriola was perhaps the most prominent syndicalist who tried to show that the conquest of Libya could be in the interest of both the proletariat and the nation, but he was not the only one who accepted the Nationalist argument that the south would benefit from the war. A. O. Olivetti, the editor of the syndicalist *Pagine Libere*, justified the war as a school for revolution, and Massimo Rocca virtually saw it as a substitute for the proletarian revolution. Each of these pro-Libyan syndicalists tended to justify his stand as being in the interest of the workers, but this form of national-syndicalism benefitted only the Nationalists. Libya helped further a split within syndicalism and socialism, which became more evident at the time of Italy's entry into World War I when many of these same syndicalists joined Mussolini, a renegade from the Socialist party, in the campaign for intervention.[12]

The declaration of war on September 30, 1911, signaled a defeat for the irredentists within the association and marked their decline in importance in the Nationalist movement. The imperialists were jubilant. The Milanese nationalist leader Dino Alfieri modestly asserted that, even if the Nationalists did not singlehandedly push the country to war, they were the ones who best interpreted the national mood. The *Idea Nazionale* took complete credit for the war, and Corradini called it the triumph of the nationalist over the socialist man.[13]

To avoid being coopted and made superfluous once war had been declared, the *Idea Nazionale* moved rapidly to establish a position on Libya which would separate it at all costs from the government. The editors pressed for early annexation of the colony and for a more energetic military policy. As the war bogged down and pressure from Europe for a negotiated settlement grew, the imperialists led demands for more loyalty from Italy's allies and increased firmness on the part of the government. The Nationalists hailed the occupation of Rhodes and called for the annexation of the Dodecanese Islands as a launching pad for further expansion. Nevertheless, the extension of the war into the Mediterranean and Aegean seas gradually drew attention back to the Balkans and to the possibility of generalized war there. When the war with the Turks finally came to an end with the Treaty of Ouchy, in October 1912, it left the Italians in possession of Libya (although pacification took years) and gave them temporary occupation of the Dodecanese Islands. The war also demonstrated the impotence of the Ottoman Empire and encouraged preparations for the Balkan wars of 1912 and 1913. By then, the Nationalists had long since given up on Giolitti's war. The Treaty of Ouchy was "mediocre," and the promise to restore the Dodecanese to the Ottoman Empire was a failure of diplomacy.[14]

"ISRAEL AGAINST ITALY": COPPOLA'S ANTI-SEMITISM AND SIGHELE'S RESIGNATION FROM THE ASSOCIATION

The crisis within the Nationalist Association, delayed by the outbreak of the war, exploded during the conflict. Scipio Sighele had been privately concerned about the conservative policies of the leadership and had threatened to resign. His discontent was significant because his nationalism was a holdover from an earlier irredentist nationalism which refused to break with either liberalism or democracy. A disciple of Barrès and Taine, Sighele considered the nation to be an organism which lived and developed within a given territory. The historical process that led to the formation of nations also created certain traditions and mental structures which gradually took the form of hereditary traits. To Sighele, a nationalist was simply an Italian who was conscious of his cultural and intellectual formation.[15]

Sighele's conclusions were more democratic than his theories would lead one to expect. Influenced by his own ties to the Austro-Italian borderland, Sighele was convinced that the cultural creativity of Europe was dependent on the coexistence and interaction of many different peoples. Like Barrès, he believed that even in a single country the political organization should take into account the historic regions and local customs of the people. Sighele differed with conservative nationalism in the importance which he gave to national awareness and self-determination. Irredentism could only be based on conscious desire. The population of the Trentino and of Trieste actively wished to join Italy, but the peoples of Corsica and Nice, despite their Italian background, expressed no such desire. In the latter case, an irredentist movement was impossible. Sighele was even more critical of the antidemocratic, reactionary taint which was becoming associated with nationalism. He specifically singled out the ideology of the Action Française as offering nothing of value for the Italian situation. In Italy, nationalism had to carry on the liberal heritage of the risorgimento, or it would be an absurdity.[16]

The editors of the *Idea Nazionale* were already engaged in a debate over nationalism and democracy when Sighele launched his attack. In reply, Francesco Coppola, the most conservative editor, baldly stated that democratic nationalism did not exist and that the ideas of the Action Française were perfectly correct. He went even further by specifically accepting the anti-Semitic direction of French nationalism. In a letter to Charles Maurras, published during the Libyan War in the *Idea Nazionale,* Coppola accused "international Jewish finance" of aiding the Turks. Two prominent Jewish Nationalists Raffaele Levi and Alberto Musatti (the head of the Venetian Nationalist group) sent their resignations on the grounds that Jews could no longer belong to an overtly anti-Semitic movement. In an effort to cut off any wholesale defection, the *Idea Nazionale* denied an official policy of anti-Semitism as "repugnant to the spirit of liberty." Later Coppola, who resigned from the directorate of the ANI but not from the editorship of the *Idea Nazionale,* stated that his views were his own and not those of the other editors. Nevertheless, for Sighele, this incident was the last straw. He became convinced that there was no alternative short of resignation, which he did in a series of letters to the *Tribuna* of Rome.[17]

In fact, Sighele failed to move the association. Even an earlier resignation would not have had much effect. The congress of Florence showed no sympathy for democratic nationalism. Few, if any, of the other moderates were as open to the democratic liberal tradition as was Sighele, and no one followed him in resigning. Coppola's resignation from the leadership of the ANI silenced most of the vocal discontent, and both Levi and Musatti withdrew their resignations. By May, the *Idea Nazionale* rejoiced in its victory. Coppola trumpeted that he was a reactionary, just as Sighele said, if by reactionary one meant a person in whom "the demo-socialist, pacifist, humanitarian, and egalitarian individualism provokes the most sincere disgust." Corradini, as usual, had the final word: Sighele's departure actually strengthened the association. "By leaving, they fortify us. We need people who think, not public crybabies."[18]

THE OPENING TO THE CATHOLICS AND THE CONGRESS OF ROME: 1912

The impact of the Libyan War on Giolitti's government was devastating. The war unleashed passions which were uncontainable within the give-and-take of traditional politics. The Socialist party escaped from the control of reformists like Filippo Turati and Claudio Treves, and the new revolutionary leadership of Costantino Lazzari and Benito Mussolini, who took over the party and the editorship of the *Avanti*, was extremely bitter over the war and particularly bitter toward Giolitti. The new revolutionary attitude effectively thwarted plans for including the Socialist party in the governmental majority. Although the new suffrage reform passed the Chamber of Deputies during the war, the loosely organized Liberal party was ill equipped to deal with the large influx of new voters. A broader suffrage automatically favored the more highly organized Catholics and Socialists. In this situation, the collapse of Giolitti's support in the Socialist party led him to depend more heavily on the clericals, or politicians favoring the

Church, for his majority in the upcoming elections. That, in turn, set off a chain reaction which further weakened the government with the left-center Radicals. When clerical influence became evident after the elections of 1913, the Radicals voted to withdraw from the ministry, provoking Giolitti's resignation. The war in Libya, which Giolitti hoped would stabilize the old order, ended by eroding it further and by bringing the fall of his government.[19]

The importance of the Catholic vote did not escape the imperialist nationalists of the *Idea Nazionale* and became yet another issue in their dispute with the moderates. The Nationalists had delayed holding a congress until the Libyan War ended. Once it became clear that the war would soon be over, the moderates began to mount a campaign for control of the association. Their point of view, expressed in the *Grande Italia*, favored a popular nationalism which remained hostile to both clericalism and socialism. For their part, the editors of the *Idea Nazionale* felt just as strongly that there was no political space for a movement which set out to attack both socialism and clericalism. In short, the traditional liberal stand of separation between Church and state was inadequate for the times. Accepting as inevitable the expansion of the suffrage, the Nationalists recognized the strategic importance of the Catholic vote. No strong conservative party could, in their opinion, be created without clerical assistance.[20]

The imperialist Nationalists of the *Idea Nazionale* also wished to take advantage of the success which their wartime appeals had in Catholic circles. The Libyan War speeded the process by which many Catholics were becoming reconciled to the Italian state and began to consider more active participation in political life. The bitterness over the loss of Rome and over the anticlericalism of the first Italian governments receded with the passage of time and the rise of a Socialist threat. In the elections of 1904 and 1909, the pope had modified his ban on Catholic participation in the balloting in order to assure the defeat of Marxist candidates. During the Libyan War, enthusiasm among both clergy and laymen was strong enough to force the Vatican to intervene with a warning that it did not consider the war to be in any way a crusade against the Turk. Despite this cautionary note, clerical conservatives realized that Libya offered an occasion to further the values of nation, hierarchy, and authority against the subversives on the Left. As the Catholic bourgeoisie began to reassess its position in the light of a changing political situation, their reactions began to resemble those of the liberal national bourgeoisie, which had created the Italian state against the wishes of the Vatican. In this new perspective, nationalism seemed no longer to be equated with anticlerical excesses but rather was seen as a more forceful weapon against Freemasonry and Marxism.

Thus, when the gap between the proclerical and liberal wings of the Italian bourgeoisie began to close, the political balance in the Catholic camp altered. Those Italians who followed the political leadership of the Church were divided into roughly three camps. The old, intransigent Catholic refusal to cooperate with the Italian state, a position once dominant under Pius IX and Leo XIII, began to lose ground under the more flexible Pius X and received a death blow from Benedict XV, who moved toward de facto acceptance of the Italian state by allowing the formation of a Catholic party in 1918. A second group which shared the intransigent scorn for the risorgimental state was the modernist faction of Christian Democracy, led by the priest Romolo Murri until his excommunication by Pius X. Murri's followers aimed at the formation of a political movement based on the alliance between the Church and the people to oppose the liberal state. The remnants of the movement, led by Don Luigi Sturzo, later formed an important faction in the post-World War I Italian Popular party. The third group, perhaps the most important because of its ties to industry and finance, was made up of clerical moderates or conservatives. Led by Giovanni Grosoli, Filippo Crispolti, and Ottavio Cornaggia, they controlled a large part of the Catholic press through the Società Editrice Romana, known as the "trust," and through their influence in the Catholic Electoral Union, headed by Count Giovanni Gentiloni, they directed Catholic political power. The clerical-moderates were able to work with Giolitti, even as they later worked with Mussolini. Because they shared most of the hopes and fears of their counterparts among the liberal bourgeoisie their faction was also susceptible to influence by the Nationalists.[21]

In this perspective, the polemic which took place between the leader of the Catholic conservatives and the Nationalists gained importance. Filippo Meda was the outstanding Catholic political figure in Giolittian Italy. Moderate and prudent, he was willing to deal with Giolitti for practical reforms, while cautiously opening a dialogue with the Nationalists. The debate began with an article by Meda in the *Corriere d'Italia,* a paper controlled by the clerical-moderate trust. He predicted that as a result of the Libyan War, nationalism would emerge as a real political force. Like many conservatives he favored this development to the extent that the Nationalists were involved in the battle against socialism. Nevertheless, Meda objected to the Nationalist cult of the state and its rationalization of the use of force to settle conflicts. He admitted that national interests were superior to class goals but held that there were other values superior to both. In a carefully phrased response, the *Idea Nazionale* distinguished between the clerical and socialist positions toward the Italian state. Catholic opposition to the state, based on an obsolete historical situation, no longer menaced Italian institutions. On the other hand, socialist and Masonic internationalism was a real danger, because it arose from an important theoretical divergence. The paper concluded that Catholics and Nationalists could cooperate without difficulty.[22]

From the Nationalist point of view the important thing was not an immediate alliance. It was enough that the clericals began to accept the framework of debate offered by the association. Not all clerical politicians were as reticent as Meda. There was reason to hope that once the issue became formulated more clearly in antisocialist terms, the Nationalists would be able to approach the Catholics with far more success than would the Liberals, who were encumbered by their anticlerical past. For this reason, the debate within the association over clericalism took on importance as the congress of Rome approached. Not only were the more moderate factions closer to traditional irredentism, but they were also tied to the historical positions of anticlerical liberalism. The differences between the imperialist nationalist and moderate wings of the Nationalist Association were made clearer in a series of meetings, held shortly before the congress. The Milanese group, dominated by moderates, opted for strict economic liberalism, reaffirmed their loyalty to Italy's irredentist tradition, and called for maintaining the ANI equidistant from both clericalism and socialism.[23]

The *Idea Nazionale*'s position on the future of the association was defined in two important articles by the Roman Nationalist leader Valentino Leonardi. Leonardi wrote that the congress would have to understand the range of political options. With the Masons, Socialists, and Radicals allied in an anticlerical and reformist bloc, only two groups on the Right could be used as a counterbalance: conservative liberals and clericals. The conservative wing of liberalism was amorphous and disorganized without a leader of comparable stature to Giolitti. The Right could not do without clerical support, even if there were some danger that the Catholics might force revision of the existing balance between Church and state. Leonardi concluded that the value of the Church as an element of order and cohesion in Italian society outweighed any danger. The Roman Nationalist group made it clear that the only hope for the ANI was in a frankly conservative alliance with the clericals.[24]

As it moved toward its second congress, the Italian Nationalist Association had behind it two years of organizational activity and one notable success during the Libyan War. In a report to the membership in mid-1912, Luigi Valli noted that there were already more than twenty Nationalist groups. Youth groups had also been created in the major centers and had attained a membership of over 1,000. On the debit side, not all the growth was solid. Many of the groups existed only on paper, and the central committee was almost paralyzed by lack of funds.[25]

The congress of Rome, which opened on December 20, 1912, marked the definitive turn to the Right. The delegates accepted a motion by Corradini and Forges-Davanzati condemning outright the three evils of democracy, socialism, and internationalism. Resolutions attacking the Masons and calling for reform of the schools to achieve the civil and military education of the young were also accepted. The stand on education was particularly important because Catholics were receptive to friendly overtures on this issue. Along with denunciations of radical and pacifist professors, it was clearly implied that religious education in the schools would be acceptable as a means to national unity.[26]

Balkan problems were emphasized in Luigi Federzoni's report on foreign policy, which attacked the government for its supposed passive reliance on the Triple Alliance. The war in Libya was the subject of a speech by Corradini. Although disappointed that the war had not been conducted more boldly, he concluded that it represented a moral revolution. Italy had emerged from the period of great emigrations into her imperialistic era. Her future mission was to lead the revolt of the proletarian nations against plutocratic Europe.[27]

Critical comment on the congress, especially after the resignation of most of the moderates, was much sharper than after the meeting in Florence two years earlier. Sighele continued to predict the dissolution of the association, while another moderate, Luigi Valli, accused the Corradini faction of an unprincipled shift toward the clericals, with an eye to the upcoming elections. To the latter charge, Coppola responded that it was simply absurd to put the Catholics on the same plane as Socialists. The danger to the state came exclusively from the Left.[28]

With the congress of Rome, the Nationalists made a beginning in the elaboration of the new authoritarianism which was to be their main contribution to Italian political life. In the alliance with the Catholics they sought a mass base for the politics of reaction. The themes of order and discipline were especially designed to appeal to clerical opinion. As nationalism sought to find a place in the political struggle, Luigi Federzoni, rather than Corradini, emerged as the movement's real leader.[29]

Three

The Emergence of the New Right, 1913–14

Nationalism in Action: The Elections of 1913

The Nationalist Congress was one of the last political events of 1912, a year which had seen the passage of Giolitti's suffrage reform and the conclusion of the war in Libya. These two events changed the whole basis of the Italian political system. Both the Socialists and the Catholics took new positions with regard to Giolitti's government. The Socialists, bitterly disappointed on the issue of war, voted out the reformist leadership of Filippo Turati. On both the local and national levels cooperation between Socialists and bourgeois democrats became more difficult. The Catholics were moving in the opposite direction. After forty years of intransigence, it seemed that they were about to find a place in the liberal state. Both clericals and Socialists realized that their role would be crucial in the elections of 1913, since they were the beneficiaries of the new electoral law.

For the Nationalists, the most urgent problem was to prepare for the elections. After the congress of Rome, the movement was well on its way to becoming a homogeneous, right-wing party. Still, the exact relationship of nationalism to conservative liberalism and to clericalism remained to be settled. This process began almost immediately. A debate was arranged at the Catholic University Circle of Rome on January 15 and 16, 1913, between the editors of the *Idea Nazionale* and several Catholic leaders. Nationalist success in penetrating the Catholic movement soon became apparent during the debate. There was general agreement on social and economic policy. Under Federzoni's able leadership, the Nationalists pushed aside possible differences over imperialism and war in favor of practical accords on schools, defense of public order, and economic policy. Federzoni gambled that with the shift of the Socialist party to the left, religious differences in the middle class would become less important, and he was perfectly willing to shelve for a time the imperialist rhetoric about which Meda had earlier objected. In their discussions with the Catholics, the Nationalists were at pains to stress the obsolescence of much Catholic social doctrine, based on cooperatives and small savings banks, and the need for a theory which would adequately deal with the problems of large-scale production and distribution. This argument was not without success. Much Catholic social and economic thinking was formulated when the Catholics sought to isolate themselves from the liberal state and was ill suited to the modern economic order. The Nationalists seemed to be saying that a new economic and social system might be created outside the agnostic liberal system.[1]

The approach taken with the Catholics was part of a general shift of emphasis on the part of the Nationalists. They sensed that Giolitti's reformist coalition was increasingly vulnerable to attack from the Right. Most industrialists backed the government on the Libyan War, but they were not as certain about other aspects of Giolitti's program. In September 1911, an industrial congress called for stronger controls over unions, and Giolitti had a serious confrontation with the head of the Turin Industrial League over efforts to break the Metal Workers Union in 1913.[2] There was a growing feeling that industry was badly represented by the political leadership. This entry in the diary of Ettore Conti, the head of one of Italy's most important electrical firms, was indicative of the new mood: "We bourgeois, and I speak principally of the producers, have perhaps the failing of remaining too aloof from political life . . . I think that inevitably we must organize ourselves as a productive class and, to begin, as an industrial class."[3]

The Nationalists attempted to profit from the situation in two ways. By appealing to the clericals and by formulating policies on tariff protection and military expenditures which would draw in discontented industrialists, the association sought to avoid being shunted off to the margin of political life after the Libyan War. Moreover, the Nationalists began to plot their disengagement from the Liberal party. The most perceptive of the liberals within the association understood this plan and were determined to thwart the policy, but the *Idea Nazionale* insisted that the association had no obligation to adhere to liberal dogma on every issue and that practical problems, such as tariff protection, had to be met in the light of larger political and national issues. Corradini defined one of these broader considerations as the need to organize the bourgeoisie to meet the threat from socialism. With some exaggeration, the Nationalists offered themselves as the pivotal force for the bourgeois bloc in the elections of 1913.[4]

The Nationalist Association also announced that it would actively participate in the elections. The central committee approved Federzoni's resolution, which allowed the ANI to back selected liberal candidates or to present its own independent list. To receive the blessing of the association, prospective candidates had to declare themselves in favor of increased military spending and had to take a firm stand against the Masons. The campaign against the Masons was part of a larger electoral strategy to combat the radical-democratic electoral combinations, in which the Masons played a prominent part. During the heyday of the Giolittian system, left-wing liberals and radicals formed coalitions on both the local and national levels. These alliances or blocs often had the support of the reformist leadership of the Socialist party and served as a bridge between the bourgeois Center-Left and the moderate Socialist Left. Within the blocs, the Masons acted as catalysts. Masonic influence was strong both in the Radical party and in the reformist wing of the Socialist party. One of the most important successes of the bloc was to have conquered the city administration of Rome in 1907. Not only did the bloc take control of the city from the conservatives, but they also elected as mayor Ernesto Nathan, a former Grand Master of the Freemasonic order. Nathan was a convinced democrat and a believer in the destiny of Rome to become the capital of a lay and progressive Italy. His election was a bitter pill for Catholic opinion to swallow, especially since it was followed by further bloc victories in the national elections of 1909.[5]

Libya, however, was a turning point for the Radical blocs. The new militant leadership of the Socialist party was anti-

Masonic and no longer interested in cooperation with the bourgeois parties. Universal suffrage, while ostensibly favoring the Left, did not necessarily favor the radical Left. The Socialists under revolutionary leadership and the Catholics were the beneficiaries of the reform. Thus, the elections of 1913 offered hope to the conservatives that they might recapture lost ground from the divided Left. In this situation the enemy was not so much the revolutionary Left as the bourgeois democratic parties.

Freemasonry, in particular, symbolized all that the conservatives and Catholics opposed: anticlericalism, concessions to socialism, caution on foreign policy. In the spring of 1913, the *Idea Nazionale* began a systematic campaign against Masonic influence in the government and in the military. It was a popular cause among conservative intellectuals and, even more, among Catholics. At that time events were proceeding smoothly enough. In Rome, a conservative and clerical alliance, the Unione Elettorale fra le Associazioni Liberali Costituzionali (Electoral Union between Liberal Constitutional Associations), was formed to challenge the radical candidates in most of the city's electoral districts or colleges. The situation in the first college was particularly interesting. This seat had been held for a time by Pilade Mazza, a Republican. In 1904 Mazza was defeated, but in 1909 he returned to parliament. Shortly after his victory, he died and was succeeded by a Socialist, Antonino Camponozzi, whose activities in the postal union made him a target for conservative wrath. The radical-democratic bloc was reluctant to back a controversial Socialist and sought a safer name, who might attract broader support. The choice fell on Prince Scipione Borghese, a radical aristocrat, who had supported the Libyan War. Borghese's ties with the moderate liberals were insurance that his would not be simply a bloc candidacy. Borghese rapidly picked up the support of the mayor of Rome, Nathan, and that of Sidney Sonnino, the leader of the parliamentary Right.[6]

Plans for a single Center-Left candidate against the Socialist Antonio Camponozzi were suddenly thrown into disarray when the right-wing Unione Elettorale refused to accept Borghese and entered its own slate. The candidate chosen was Domenico Oliva, the literary critic for the *Giornale d'Italia* and president of the Nationalist group of Rome. The conservatives thus made the race a complicated struggle with the chance of Borghese's success uncertain. In addition, the conservative Unione Elettorale wanted to run the Nationalist Piero Foscari in the second college and Luigi Medici del Vascello in the fourth college. The fact that Oliva, Foscari, and Medici were Nationalists indicated the local strength of the association.[7]

Perhaps the most surprised man in Rome over the candidacy of Oliva was his employer, Sonnino. The latter's position was curious. He had been a powerful minister in both the Crispi and Pelloux governments and for most of the Giolittian era was the leader of the right-wing opposition. Nevertheless, Sonnino was a complex political leader. The failure of Pelloux's authoritarian government affected Sonnino's development. His own two brief governments were anything but reactionary, as was the support which he gave to a broadened electoral suffrage. His experience seemed to have convinced him of the need for a more dynamic conservativism. Moreover, Sonnino had strong loyalties to the risorgimental view of Church-state relations. For him, the Law of Guarantees, which regulated relations between the Vatican and Italy, was a ne plus ultra for the state in religious policy. Like many liberals, he initially viewed nationalism with some favor, but as the ANI turned toward the clerical alliance he began to take a stiffer line toward political nationalism throughout 1913. His reaction to the Oliva candidacy was particularly negative. Not only had he not been consulted, but he had also promised his support to Borghese. Alberto Bergamini, the director of Sonnino's *Giornale d'Italia,* was instructed to inform Oliva that he should withdraw. The Nationalists, who refused to accept Sonnino's strategy of a broad alliance between some elements of the Right and the Center-Left, put forward Luigi Federzoni, who also happened to work for the *Giornale d'Italia,* as the candidate to replace Oliva. This idea was even more strongly opposed by Sonnino, who considered it simply a ploy to win clerical support and sure to result in a Socialist victory. He simply could not understand the Nationalists' passion "to bind themselves hand and foot to the Catholics." Sonnino reiterated this stand to Corradini, who appealed for the backing of the

Giornale d'Italia for another electoral venture, Luigi Medici del Vascello's attempt to defeat the radical, anti-Libyan Leone Caetani in the fourth electoral college. Both Sonnino and Bergamini were far more sympathetic to Medici than to Federzoni. Faced with the choice of withdrawing his candidacy or leaving the *Giornale d'Italia,* Federzoni chose the latter. In the end, the ANI ran five candidates: Federzoni and Medici in Rome, Piero Foscari in the Veneto, Romeo Gallenga in Perugia, and Camillo Ruspoli in Lombardy.[8]

The elections of 1913 revealed the fundamental weakness of the Liberal party. Giolitti accepted clerical support for the governmental slate, the so-called Gentiloni Pact, by which candidates subscribed to a seven-point program on Catholic schools, divorce, and the rights of religious orders. Among the conservatives who opposed Giolitti very few followed Sonnino in his effort to create a progressive alternative to the government. Even Luigi Albertini, the moderate director of the Milanese *Corriere della Sera,* allowed his hostility to radicalism and to Giolitti to lead him to back clerical-conservatives like Federzoni and Medici in Rome. Although Federzoni had written to Albertini that his candidacy was in the classic liberal tradition, the specific backing which he received from the Vatican was not typical of most Liberal candidates.[9]

Federzoni's campaign led to a public rupture with the *Giornale d'Italia,* but this event was only one incident in a very bitter battle that included charges of unethical practices on both sides. Federzoni managed to squeeze out Borghese for the run-off spot against Camponozzi. In the second round the Nationalist was the favored candidate, even though the radical bloc backed the Socialist. In the fourth college Medici held a substantial lead over Caetani, and both Nationalists won election in the second round of voting.[10]

The election results were even more favorable to the Catholics. The clerical forces entered the new chamber with thirty-three seats, but more than 200 of the constitutional liberals owed their seats to Catholic support. Only the outbreak of the Great War delayed the formation of a Catholic party and the total dissolution of the old liberal system. The Nationalists were among the first to draw sweeping conclusions from the decline of the Liberal party. The *Idea Nazionale* openly proclaimed the success of its tactics of bringing the Catholics into the conservative fold.[11]

The elections also brought a significant change in the leadership of the liberal Right. Unable to adjust to the new, proclerical fashion, Sonnino tended to withdraw into solitary opposition. Antonio Salandra, his lieutenant, had, as early as 1912, prepared himself for the succession by suggesting an opening to the Catholics. Salandra's ambitions went far beyond the mere leadership of the right-wing minority. His real aim was to form an alliance with the clericals and to replace Giolitti's dissolving coalition with one of his own.[12]

There was a convergence between Salandra and the Nationalists on the need to reorganize the Right, but postelectoral analysis within the association tended to go far beyond the cautious traditionalism of Salandra. In 1914, the Nationalists moved boldly to propose an alternative to every form of liberal parliamentary rule. The elaboration of a systematic Nationalist theory of the state was the work of Alfredo Rocco, a newcomer to the ANI. Rocco, who became the legal architect of the Fascist state, was at that time professor of commercial law at the University of Padua. Before joining the Nationalist Association, he flirted briefly with socialism and radicalism and was for a time active in the local Liberal-Monarchist Association. His passion for the state and for authority drew him to the ANI. Nationalism, as he envisaged it, was to be the formative doctrine of a new technocratic and authoritarian ruling class.[13]

In an article in the *Tribuna*, shortly after the elections, Rocco delivered the first blow against liberalism. He called for a total examination of conscience on the part of the Liberals. Against socialism they offered only the personal policies of a Crispi or a Giolitti. There was no counterideology or alternative ideal. The only hope was in alliance with nationalism. A strong national-liberal party might become the vehicle by which the Catholics entered political life. As such, it would be the basis for a powerful and permanent conservative party. Rocco demanded that the Nationalists distinguish themselves more clearly from the Liberals. As long as the association was considered to be merely a faction of the Liberal party, it could not develop a clear and coherent policy. In fact, nationalism (according to Rocco) had little in common with traditional liberalism. Far from viewing liberty as a panacea for the ills of society, he believed that the general interest could only be served by the sacrifice of the individual to the higher will of the nation. He argued for the superiority of the German ethical-juridical state, in which the rights of the individual came solely from the self-limitation of the state. The state would assign and supervise the sphere of personal liberty. Rocco admitted that this approach would lead to a rupture between the Nationalists and many Liberals, but he felt that there was little hope of reforming the Liberal party from within. Reluctantly, he proposed breaking off double membership in Nationalist and Liberal Monarchist associations, except where there was a dominant Nationalist hold over the Liberal group. Corradini carried the case against the Liberals even further than did Rocco. Bourgeois Italy would have to move beyond the passive defense of its interests, which liberalism offered, in order to develop an aggressive counterprogram. Corradini stressed that such a new ideology would have to offer a direct economic appeal to the industrial and commercial classes. If nationalism was to be the successor of liberalism, it would have to be liberalism adapted to the world of modern production.[14]

Corradini and Rocco pushed Nationalist theory toward the outline of a new system. The Nationalists realized that modern society was too complex for traditional authoritarianism. Crippling the political strength of the working class demanded an alternative economic and social program. Rocco made a first approach to such a new economic policy in two articles in the *Tribuna* in mid-January 1914. He contrasted the Nationalist and the Socialist view of economics. For the Socialist, distribution of wealth was all important. Unfortunately, the Socialists failed to understand that Italy was a poor country in constant struggle against the richer nations of Europe. Distribution of poverty would gain the worker little. Nationalism was superior because it went to the heart of the problem by putting production in first place. Rocco took the Corradinian position that the solution for Italy's problems could only be found in expansion abroad. Italian emigration had to be disciplined to achieve the armed occupation of territory. Struggle abroad demanded increased unity and harmony at home so that the nation might compete more easily with other nations. To this end, nationalism aimed at a well-ordered hierarchy rather than at democratic equality. Class collaboration might be facilitated by a program of social reform, like that initiated by Bismarck in Germany, but no reforms could touch the basic structure of private property and the natural, useful hierarchy of functions within society.[15]

THE CONGRESS OF MILAN AND THE RUPTURE WITH LIBERALISM

The elections of 1913 proved fatal to Giolitti's government. Angered by the alliance with the clericals, the Radicals withdrew their support from the ministry. In March 1914, Giolitti, who made it a practice never to govern against the Left, decided to make a strategic retreat from power. After his resignation, the task of forming a new government was offered to Sonnino, who refused, and then to Salandra, whose moment finally arrived. The new prime minister set for himself two tasks: to break down the basis of Giolitti's power and to weld the liberal forces into a new formation around his own person.

With the Salandra ministry, the Nationalists had, for the first time, a friendly government. The political axis shifted to the Right, easing somewhat the isolated position which Federzoni and the other Nationalists deputies took on the extreme Right of the new chamber. In his first speech to the parliament, Federzoni proclaimed his movement to be the real heir to the classical liberal tradition. With the continuity of Giolitti's rule broken, the possibility of maneuvering the association into a position to pick up some of the pieces of the shattered Liberal party was increased. For a brief moment it seemed that the small party might even obtain a share of power, when one of the Nationalist deputies was mentioned for a minor ministerial post, but Salandra feared the reaction to such a move and the project was dropped.[16]

After the elections and the formation of the new government, the major task facing the association was to follow out the consequences of its electoral strategy. A congress was set for the spring of 1914 to solidify the organizational gains and to put the final touches on the new doctrinal position of the movement. Some notable gains had been made in the Veneto under the leadership of Alfredo Rocco. A regional federation was formed, which published its own newspaper, *Il Dovere Nazionale*. Although the network of local groups continued to grow, there are few precise figures for the actual strength of the ANI. For instance, a new branch was begun in Brescia by Castellini and Filippo Carli. According to the prefect's report, one hundred people, "among the most noted in the city," attended the first meeting. The initial interest, however, produced only twenty requests for membership.[17]

More important for the future were the ties which developed in 1914 between the *Idea Nazionale* and heavy industry, mainly steel and armaments. Early in the year the decision was made to convert the *Idea Nazionale* into a daily paper. At the beginning of April, Roberto Forges Davanzati informed his employer, Luigi Albertini, that the necessary financial backing for the new publishing company had been secured and that he would soon leave his position with the *Corriere della Sera*. Corradini handled the negotiations with the paper's financial backers: Dante Ferraris, Alberto De Rosa, Pierlorenzo Parisi, and Alberto Maria Bombrini. These men, plus Corradini, comprised the board of directors of the company. Also among the shareholders were the Machine Corporation of Milan (Società Anomina Meccaica di Milano) and several relatives of Bombrini (who was himself a director of the Cogne Mining Company). The most important of the directors was Dante Ferraris, a key figure in Turin's industrial elite, vice-president of Fiat, and president of the Lega Industriale (Industrial League). His participation in the Nationalist venture reflected a growing coolness toward certain aspects of Giolitti's reformist techniques.[18]

The relationship between the *Idea Nazionale* and heavy industry was part of an unhealthy development in Italian journalism. Giant steel, mining, and manufacturing conglomerates, like Ilva and Ansaldo, desperately needed government subsidies in the form of tariffs and commissions. Naturally this dependence made them turn to the most obvious means of influencing parliament and public opinion. No major papers were free from this control unless they had very strong directors. Luigi Albertini's *Corriere della Sera,* which enjoyed a large measure of independence from the Crespi family textile interests, and Alfredo Frassati's *La Stampa,* which had a similar relationship with the Agnelli family and Fiat, were among the rare papers so favored. In this case, the protectionist stand of the *Idea Nazionale* was consistent with the basic principles of Nationalist ideology. Rather than a shady financial deal, there was a convergence of interests between the Nationalists, who wished to increase their influence, and the industrialists, who could hardly be blamed for supporting a paper which so carefully reflected their views.[19]

The immediate problems facing the association were more ideological than economic. The upcoming congress offered the orthodox liberals a last chance to mount a counterattack against the authoritarian and protectionist leadership of the movement. To emphasize their will to do battle with the *Idea Nazionale,* the liberals initiated a publication of their own, *L'Azione,* in May 1914. Its directors, Paolo Arcari and Alberto Caroncini, set for themselves a task which the official Nationalists ignored: the search for middle ground between conservative authoritarianism and democracy, between militant antisocialism and social concern, and between the political use of patriotism and certain antinational currents in the country. Unfortunately, by dealing only in generalities, their effort had little chance for success. Alberto Caroncini's theories of liberal individualism clearly lacked the power of Rocco's authoritarianism. Caroncini offered neither security for the bourgeoisie nor promise of future gain for the workers or peasants. Giovanni Amendola could attack the "provisional order of Giovanni Giolitti," but he proposed nothing in its place except a return to virtue. The tragedy of the liberal-nationalist movement was that, despite its good intentions, it revealed how few options were left for traditional liberalism. In practice, on issues like Giolitti's system, socialism, intervention in World War I, the *Azione* was forced to take the same positions as the *Idea Nazionale*.[20]

The liberal-nationalist critique did serve to underline the domination of the Milan congress by the *Idea Nazionale* group. The congress, which opened on May 16, 1914, was almost monolithic in approach. The major reports were given by authoritarians, and objections from the liberal opposition were systematically rejected. Federzoni and Maraviglia presented the political report. Their analysis pointed to only one conclusion: the necessity for an independent Nationalist party. Membership in other political formations would, in most cases, be incompatible with belonging to the association. The report, studded with favorable references to the Catholics, proposed for the Nationalists the leading role as guardians of the forces of order.[21]

The substantive work of the congress came in the reports on economic and social policy. The first report, "The Fundamental Principles of Economic Nationalism," presented by Alfredo Rocco and Filippo Carli, was the most important theoretical statement of prewar nationalism. The authors argued that nationalism could not be considered simply a political doctrine. The new nationalism offered a total or integral view of the state as a radical alternative to both socialism and liberalism. The latter ideologies were, for all practical purposes, lumped together under the heading of anarchic individualism. According to the authors, both ideologies shared a common origin in the ideas of Adam Smith and David Ricardo and in the various contractual theories of the state. Because they considered the individual to be the raison d'être of social organization, the renunciation of liberty had to be kept within the strict limits of necessity. The goal of liberal economic policy became the maximization of pleasure with minimal effort. Socialism shared this hedonistic premise of liberal economics. Individualistic utilitarianism was simply transformed into materialistic utilitarianism. The class struggle and the socialization of the means of production attempted to reach essential individualistic ends. Furthermore, the whole idea of social class was to Rocco and Carli a fiction designed to conceal the basically atomized view which socialism took of society and of the state. In fact, class was not an organic but a formal unity. Within each class many gradations existed and often had conflicting aims.[22]

In sum, socialism and liberalism had to be rejected because the principles upon which they rested were false. The individual was not the end of social activity, nor did the state exist as a means to individual self-realization. Society raised man from the animal level. It was the custodian of higher values and thus had interests which continued for centuries, far surpassing the life of a single person and the duration of his particular interests. When individuals, who were nothing but the instruments of society, attempted to set themselves above it, civilization inevitably declined. It was no less false to view society as extending beyond the boundaries of a single state. Humanity was too nebulous to have much meaning. The nation, the highest form of human solidarity, organized people living within a determined territory. This unity was maintained by the consciousness of a common origin, language, traditions and culture, but above all "the individual lives in the nation of which he is an infinitesimal and transitory element and of whose finality he must consider himself the organ and instrument." There is in this theory no hint of blood and soil, merely a fixation on the nation and its embodiment in the state as the highest of all values.[23]

Moving more specifically to economic problems, the authors tried to show how the principles of liberalism would be disastrous for a poor country. Growth was not governed by fixed economic laws but was an act of will on the part of the nation. The development of Germany was cited as the finest example of economic growth in violation of the principles of pure liberalism. Liberalism's great defect was that it was a doctrine of nonsolidarity, of individual competition between producers in the same branch of industry, between primary and secondary producers, and between producers and consumers. These beliefs conflicted with the economic realities of the day. Only by forming industrial cartels could the disadvantages of liberal economics be overcome. The English example of natural selection through competition was a wasteful, blind struggle, whereas disciplined production would be less costly and technically more perfect. Both the workers and the consumers would profit from the abandonment of free competition because only industries capable of large-scale planning and production would be able to insure high wages and lower prices. As competition tended to diminish within the state, it would be transferred to the struggle between nations for a larger share of the world market. Cartels in each branch of industry would be unified into a national association of industrial syndicates which would provide overall supervision of trade and industrial growth.[24]

In their efforts to emphasize domestic production and international trade, Rocco and Carli did not neglect the social aspects of their doctrine. In theory, they argued that the working class could use any economic means to improve its position, but this concession was immediately retracted. The proletariat's demands could not be allowed to hamper production by disturbing the social peace or by absorbing an excessive part of the resources of the state. Nationalist social policy was based on a "natural law of inequality." It aimed only to coordinate better the existing differences in a way which would not interfere with social hierarchy. The state would be strictly limited in its ability to intervene in the economic system to correct social disequilibria, nor could the state meddle in production. The entrepreneurial class was considered to be an instrument of the national interest. Private initiative would be subject to control only when it failed to fulfil its larger obligations. The main duties of the state were to provide the structure of power and authority within which the productive classes might organize.[25]

The full weight of the Nationalist authoritarianism fell on the proletariat. The workers would be confronted by a system of industrial cartels which would control every aspect of a given branch of industry. No longer could worker's unions be free to pressure the employers for improved conditions. The Socialist party as an instrument of political action would be eliminated. The workers were to be integrated into a powerful system, whose primary goal was increased production, and into a political structure based on the perpetuation of a rigidly stratified society. The Rocco-Carli report was an innovation with regard to traditional forms of authoritarianism because it accepted the existence of large-scale proletarian organizations and a certain degree of politicization. The Nationalists understood that once political control of these organizations was transferred from the Socialist party to the state, worker unions were an excellent means of social control.[26]

The congress concluded with what amounted to a declaration of independence from the Liberal party, although its immediate impact was lessened by the political weakness of the ANI. The most serious consequence was the loss of some support in heretofore friendly conservative circles, who were shocked to realize that the movement which they had favored as a slightly more exuberant liberalism had become a political force in its own right. Speaking for the liberal nationalists, many of whom had worked with Corradini during the *Regno* period, Giovanni Amendola sadly noted that nationalism had finally broken with the idealistic hopes of the generation of the *Leonardo* and the *Regno*, which had envisaged opposing social democracy with a revived liberalism in the risorgimental tradition.[27]

The new relationship with the Liberal party was apparent in the two Nationalist candidacies in the June by-elections. Giuseppe Bevione of *La Stampa* and Enrico Corradini attempted to enter parliament. The most significant race was in Turin, where Bevione contested the seat of the recently deceased Socialist deputy, Pilade Gay. The industrialists Dante Ferraris, Pietro Diatto, and Pietro Ceriana (all important in the Turin Nationalist group) felt that they had found in Bevione the ideal candidate to recapture the seat from the Left. Bevione's candidacy forged the kind of coalition which the Nationalists sought to produce more often on the national level. Not only was Bevione able and articulate, but he also won much public acclaim for his articles on Libya. Money for his campaign was raised outside of the Liberal association, and there was a strong appeal for Catholic support. Even the pro-Giolittian *La Stampa* backed the campaign, which was aimed at the fear of socialism on the part of small businessmen and merchants.[28]

Much weaker was the position of Enrico Corradini, who ran in the Catholic Veneto. Hampered by his past as an amoral pagan and by increasing assertions of Catholic independence,

Corradini was in trouble from the start. Although he went out of his way to appeal to clerical opinion, he was defeated. These first electoral ventures of the ANI revealed the potential strength of the conservative, industrial, clerical coalitions, provided that the right candidate carried the Nationalist standard. Federzoni, Medici, and Bevione ran their successful campaigns independently of the local liberal organizations.[29]

Nationalism in Action: The Red Week of June 1914

The general strike of June 1914, known as the "Red Week," during which the Nationalists had a small but important role in promoting the reaction, foreshadowed both the revolutionary fervor of the postwar period and provided one of the first examples of the paralysis of the Socialist party in the face of a truly revolutionary event. To understand the week of June 7–14, 1914, it is necessary to recall the polarization which marked Italian political life after the Libyan War. Within the ranks of syndicalism and socialism, radicalization took the form of increased antimilitarism. The Red Week began as one of the many Sunday protests against the military, in the Adriatic town of Ancona. This time a number of factors combined to make the occasion exceptional. It took place on a patriotic holiday to point out the contrast between the interests of the proletariat and the established order of crown and army. The city, like the rest of the Romagna and the Marches, was a stronghold of revolutionary socialism and had earlier in the year been the scene of the maximalist victory at the national congress of the Socialist party. The presence of strong anarchist, syndicalist, and republican currents, coupled with the general desire for a showdown with the rightist Salandra government, made the situation extremely explosive.

The spark came when the demonstration was curtailed by the soldiers, who fired on the crowd. The response of the revolutionaries was almost inevitable. Carried along by the wave of protest which developed in the Romagna, even the moderate leaders of the General Confederation of Labor (CGL) surrendered to the more militant directorate of the Socialist party and proclaimed a general strike. For a time, the strike succeeded, but the Socialist party was unable to provide a revolutionary outlet for the energies released. The lack of preparation on the part of the maximalist leadership and the fears of the reformists allowed events to outrun the actions of both the party and the CGL.

The strike gained force on June 8 and reached a high point on the following day. On June 10, a new situation began to emerge. A strong reaction set in among liberal and Nationalist groups who sensed that the worst was over and that they could act against the politically motivated strike. This reaction, which had its origins in the patriotism generated by the Libyan War, finally led to open violence. The bourgeois counterattack, like the later Fascist assault, began only after the high tide of revolutionary action had been reached. By June 10, when Renato Rigola, the leader of the CGL, terminated the strike, it was clear that the troops could control the revolutionary contagion outside of the Romagna. On the same day, the Nationalists and their allies took to the streets. In Milan, where on the previous day strikers had imposed a suspension of business, the Nationalists helped organize a counter-demonstration in the center of the city. On June 11, the Socialists were forced to ask for police protection for their newspaper. Other major northern cities saw a similar pattern of violence. Large numbers of people gathered to parade in favor of the king and army. Fights broke out, forcing the police to intervene to restore order. The Nationalists staged their most successful antisocialist action in Rome. On June 10, during a five-hour demonstration, 4,000 marchers gathered at the Collegio Romano, circled the center of the city, and ended in a meeting outside the parliament building. The events in Rome provided a disagreeable preview of the interventionist riots of May 1915, but an additional fact of some importance was the Nationalist and patriotic strength in the south. A police report mentioned "a very impressive nationalist parade in Naples," and in Palermo the president of the Nationalist group organized a protest involving several thousand participants, including the mayor.[30]

The *Idea Nazionale* enthusiastically reported the signs of reaction: "For the first time since socialism had exercised its dismal and bloody tyranny over the town squares and over the people. . . , an Italian city found the necessary force and concord to rebel against this tyranny." The strikers' tactics justified the measures of self-defense taken by the bourgeoisie. The paper was quick to blame Giolitti, whose excessive concessions to the workers allowed state authority to become a parody of law and order. Alfredo Rocco offered another variation on the theme of total collapse. Giolitti's legislation on universal suffrage, the life insurance monopoly, toleration shown to peasant leagues and railway unions, all worked to undermine the state: "the revolution does not have to be made, for it has been accomplished already."[31] To Rocco, the strike meant much more. The power shown by the workers called the whole parliamentary system into question. The Nationalists had the task of seeing that the evolution to a new order was along lines compatible with the internal unity and authority of the state. With his usual clarity Rocco set the future course for the ANI. The parliamentary system, incapable of meeting the attack of the popular forces, would have to go.[32]

Four

The Nationalists and Intervention in World War I

The Nationalists from the Triple Alliance to the Entente

In retrospect, the Salandra government, the Red Week, and the polarization of Italian politics which developed after the Libyan War marked a turning point in the life of the country. What had promised to be a slow transition to a broad-based liberal democracy never took place. As the framework of Giolittian politics disintegrated, the various forces which it tried to encompass began to press for more rapid and drastic change. In this context, World War I came as an almost providential event. Between August 1914 and May 1915, the crucial question for Italy revolved around intervention in the war, but, more than that, the war took on the character of a revolt against Giolitti which aimed at the creation of a new political system. The crisis over intervention and the long war that followed became a struggle over succession to the dying Liberal regime. In those chaotic days, the synthesis between extreme Right and Left, which lay at the basis of fascism, began to form. During the campaign for intervention, both the Nationalists and Benito Mussolini embarked on the course which united them in power eight years later. It was in September 1914, that Mussolini, pushed by ambition and impatience with what he saw as the passivity of the Socialist party, broke with the official neutralist policy of his party on the war and urged intervention by Italy on the side of the Entente. Unable to shake more than a handful of Socialists from the party's traditional opposition to war, Mussolini was forced to resign from the editorship of the *Avanti*, a post which he had held since the party congress of 1912. A few weeks later, he began to publish his own independent socialist paper, *Il Popolo d'Italia,* and the rift which was to carry him further and further from his old comrades became permanent.

Intervention offered the Nationalist Association a chance to change the course of both domestic and foreign policy, and the Nationalists moved with almost unseemly haste to seize the moment. They have often been accused of opportunism in 1914, when they rapidly changed from a pro-Triple Alliance position to one urging war against Germany and Austria. Although there was a turnabout in Nationalist sympathies in the first weeks of August 1914, this change is less striking when seen against the background of a long history of ambiguity over the alliance with Austria. The association began as a coalition of anti-Austria irredentists and imperialists who had vaster dreams of expansion. The victory of the imperialist faction did not mean that the association was henceforth wedded to the Triple Alliance. The renewed crisis in the Balkans after 1912 forced the irredentist question to the fore. It also symbolized the basic opportunism of Nationalist foreign policy. They were open to any and all possibilities for territorial gain. The Nationalists held firmly to no alliance. The more confused the international situation, the more they tended to keep their options open. Thus, the *Idea Nazionale* could simultaneously criticize the early ratification of the Triple Alliance during the Libyan War and bitterly attack France. During the Balkan wars, they discussed potential alternatives to dependence on Austria. Gualtiero Castellini cautiously advanced the possibility of an Albania divided between Greece and Serbia as less dangerous to Italy than an independent Albania, susceptible to Austrian domination. Despite their strong anti-Slav feelings, the Nationalists viewed Austria and, to a lesser extent, Greece, as more serious rivals.[1]

While it is true that Maffeo Pantaleoni, the prominent economist, and Alfredo Rocco declared themselves in favor of the Triple Alliance in late July 1914, there is equally good evidence to show another side to Nationalist policy. Roberto Forges Davanzati, Giuseppe Bevione, and Luigi Federzoni were somewhat more cautious in their enthusiasm for Italy's allies. Two further things might be added to put the Nationalists' reaction to the outbreak of the war in better perspective. First, neither Rocco nor Panteleoni was an exceptional case among Italian conservatives in their instinctive reaction to side with much-admired Germany. However, far more important was the clear implication from earlier criticism of the pro-Austrian policies of their government that the Nationalists expected to use the opportunity afforded by the war to exact major concessions from the alliance partners. Keeping this in mind, it is clear that any desire to fight on the side of Germany and Austria would be short lived because the Austrians had no intention of paying Italy's price at that time.[2]

Once the government publicly declared its neutrality, on August 2, 1914, other factors became operative for the Nationalists. Despite his contempt for sentimental irredentism, an imperialist like Corradini was drawn to the obvious opportunity for expansion in the Adriatic area. This growing ambition put the Nationalists on a collision course with any pro-Triple Alliance policy. Reinforcing the desire for territorial gain was the feeling that Italy could not remain extraneous to the war and protect her position as a great power.[3]

Although most Italians, including the Nationalists, supported the declaration of neutrality, conservatives faced a delicate problem. Against the background of the Red Week and the hostility of the Left to the Triple Alliance, Italian neutrality could be interpreted as a victory for the Left with somewhat subversive overtones. The same thing might be said of the first requests to join the war on the side of the Entente, which came from the Republican, Radical, and Social Democratic parties. These center-left groups split from the Socialist party over the war and became the earliest proponents of intervention on the side of France and Belgium. Because the pro-Entente position seemed to reflect democratic sympathies, many conservatives, who favored the Triple Alliance but were aware of the difficulties involved in bringing Italy into the war on the side of the Central Powers, settled on the idea of a semipermanent neutrality. Most Catholics followed the Vatican into rigid neutrality in this war between Catholic Austria and France. Leading politicians, notably Giolitti, were against the war when it became clear that Italy could not fight beside her long-time allies. Moreover, Giolitti was skeptical of Italy's ability to face the strain of a long war. It was precisely the reaction of so many members of the large center-right liberal bloc in favor of neutrality which made the position of the *Idea Nazionale* and that of the ANI so significant. Unlike the liberal editor of the *Corriere della Sera*, Luigi Albertini, who shared common ground with the moderate democratic interventionists, the Nationalists forged new ideological and practical weapons for the power struggle which they felt was bound to come in an Italy polarized by the campaign for war. In calling for war, the Nationalists even broke temporarily with the clerical interests, which they had courted so assiduously before the August crisis. Their conviction that the liberal state was disintegrating justified even the most hazardous tactics in the overall strategy to substitute their new authoritarianism for the old liberal ideology.[4]

Throughout 1914 and the early months of 1915, the Nationalists hammered their arguments for war at often reluctant conservatives. Appeals to material interests were mixed with patriotic, diplomatic, and military considerations. Much of the Nationalists' pro-war propaganda reflected the close alliance which had developed between the *Idea Nazionale* and certain sectors of heavy industry. Solidly for war on the side of the Entente was Dante Ferraris, whose extensive financial holdings in defense industries made him a key transmission point between Turin's heavy industry and the pro-war politicians. Industrial support for the Nationalist position broadened as time went on. In January 1915, a preparedness committee was formed in Turin by important industrialists and Nationalists. During this same period, the *Idea Nazionale* completed its transformation into a daily newspaper. Financial backers of the paper included Carlo Esterle of the Edison firm, Luigi Parodi, who held extensive shipping interests, and Emilio Bruzzone of the sugar trust. The success of the Nationalists' campaign in business circles made a mockery of Giolitti's hopes for neutrality based on the self-interest of the industrial class. The editors of the *Idea Nazionale* sought rather to demonstrate how war could aid industrial growth once Italy sided with the Entente and could receive financial support from Britain and France.[5]

Strategic considerations were also brought forward to justify war. Very much like Salandra, the *Idea Nazionale* argued that Italy could not remain neutral while other nations of Europe participated in the "great adventure" of the war. The old balance of power in Europe had been shattered beyond repair. It was up to Italy, as Alfredo Rocco pointed out, to create a more favorable order in which both Austrian and French predominance might be avoided. The new center of gravity for Italy's foreign policy was the Adriatic Sea, but, although the Nationalist program shared common ground with the government's program, which was later embodied in the London Pact, the Nationalists saw Trieste and the Adriatic as part of a vast imperial design. It was their open-ended imperialism which made them reject German-Austrian offers of gains limited to areas in which the population was largely Italian. Commercial and naval considerations drew the Nationalists beyond Trieste to demand the whole of Istria, including Fiume, Dalmatia, and the islands of the Adriatic. The reasons given for the annexation of Fiume were typical of the expansive view of international relations taken by the *Idea Nazionale*. The city had to be Italian, not so much because the population of the town was Italian (which it was), but because it was a rival port of Trieste and had to be kept from either the Austrians or the Slavs. Unlike Sonnino, Italy's foreign minister throughout the war, who left Fiume to the Austro-Hungarian Empire, the Nationalists quite easily envisaged the total destruction of Austria. Nor was there much of a place for Slavic aspirations in the Nationalist plan. A deep-rooted contempt for Slavic culture blinded the *Idea Nazionale*'s editors to the fact that the South Slavs could have demands which would conflict with those of Italy. It was simply taken for granted that the claims of the Italian urban minority in Dalmatia far outweighed the rights of the Slavic peasant majority.[6]

The Nationalists continued to press Italian demands in other directions as well. Francesco Coppola argued that simply by her neutrality, Italy had made an extremely valuable contribution to French resistance in the crisis period of August–September 1914. Thus, in joining the Entente, Italy should receive precise and generous guarantees for her future growth: control of Albania, an equal share in the Ottoman Empire, a voice in the Dardanelles Straits question, and colonial concessions in Africa. The economist and irredentist Mario Alberti advanced the extraordinary argument that because Trieste, which Italy would have at the end of the war (provided, of course, she joined the Entente and won), was a great port for Middle East trade, Italy should have the largest and richest zone of Asia Minor to correspond to her predominant economic interests. In an Alice-in-Wonderland way it was argued that Italy should obtain rewards for things which she did not even possess. That such reasoning could come to be accepted by a large part of Italian public opinion explains why Italy found herself so isolated at the peace conference and so bitter when her demands were not met. As time went on, the debate was not between the realistic program of the moderate democrats, Leonida Bissolati and Gaetano Salvemini, and the various extreme programs but between the government's version of *sacro egoismo* (sacred egoism) and the even more extravagant claims advanced by the Nationalists.[7]

Domestic Consequences of Intervention

Within Italy, intervention took on revolutionary overtones. War was seen by conservatives and radicals alike as a clear and decisive break with the hated past. For Mussolini and his friends, formerly of the revolutionary Left, the war represented both vindication and an opportunity to attack the whole system by means of a "revolutionary war." Democratic interventionists, like Salvemini and Bissolati, hoped that the crisis would destroy the Giolittian system, which they saw as an obstacle to modern political development. Yet many conservatives wished just as strongly to break with the past. Salandra wanted to manage intervention to restore the predominance of conservative liberalism under his direction. For the Nationalists, the war marked the end of an era in domestic political life. Like the revolutionary interventionists of the far Left, they believed that the war would bring enormous changes in its wake and that violence in the war would only be a prelude to further violence at home. Unlike the democratic idealists, the Nationalists sensed that it would be possible to divert the political ferment unleashed by the European conflict to their own ends. Corradini stressed that the Salandra government had the power to undo the gains of the democratic reformers if it could seize the opportunity provided by the war. In short, the Nationalists were convinced that they could deepen the political divisions in the country because the war would force the kind of social collaboration which would serve their purpose by making old-style politics meaningless. The *Idea Nazionale* waged a double war against the Giolittian and Socialist neutralist opposition and against the idea of a war for democracy. Above all else, the Nationalists worked for the destruction of the Giolittian parliamentary system. Giolitti and his followers were not simply mistaken in their opposition to the war; they were traitors, incapable of seeing beyond their own financial and political interests.[8]

Because Giolitti had for so long dominated parliament and had accumulated enemies across the political spectrum, opposition to his political machine tended to make strange bedfellows. Left and Right, the supporters of a revolutionary war and the conservative government, were locked in a de facto alliance. This confusion worked to the advantage of the Nationalists, who knew what they wanted and were willing to use any means to achieve it. Thus, at times they urged support for Salandra and at other times supported the direct tactics which were normally the property of the Left. In one of the most important articles of the interventionist campaign, Alfredo Rocco defended the new politics of violent demonstrations. During the Red Week, he argued, the Nationalists used violence in defense of public order. Now they had taken to the streets for an even higher cause, "the future and perhaps the very existence of the nation." Rocco conceded that these tactics were shocking, "but if the piazza is an instrument of government . . . then it is necessary that the Nationalists use and direct it to the urgent needs of the nation rather than abandon it, as do the other constitutional parties, to the adversaries of the state and of the nation."[9]

One of the most obvious tactics of the Nationalists was to widen the gap between the government and parliament. During the cabinet crisis of October 1914, which followed on the death of Antonio Di San Giuliano, the foreign minister, the *Idea Nazionale* called for the formation of a government of national emergency which would be above parties and free from parliamentary interference. When the government was reorganized in November to include Sidney Sonnino at the foreign ministry, the Nationalists tried to press for a cabinet less tied to parliament. They also launched a bitter press attack on Sonnino and intervened privately against him with Ferdinando Martini, the colonial minister. Corradini constantly exhorted Salandra's new government to break with the corrupt and decadent Chamber of Deputies. The decision for war, he noted prophetically, would have to be made against parliament, which was incapable of carrying out the national will. Even the king did not escape Corradini's menaces. The monarchy was acceptable as long as it fulfilled a national function, which to Corradini meant thwarting the will of parliament. Should the king fail to opt for war, the Nationalists hinted that their loyalty to the throne was not limitless.[10]

Hostility to parliament and suspicion of the government's weakness took concrete form with the arrival of Prince Bernhard von Bülow, who as German ambassador extraordinary had the difficult task of reconciling Austrian and Italian territorial claims. Bülow's arrival in December 1914 provoked a long crisis which lasted throughout the early months of 1915. The appearance of the new German ambassador, coinciding as it did with the opening of parliament, seemed to presage a neutralist offensive against the government. The Nationalists responded with sharp attacks on both Bulow and

Giolitti. Francesco Coppola belittled the "crumb" which Bülow was prepared to offer in the Trentino. But Ruggero Fauro, an anti-Slav imperialist, touched on the essential reason for the Nationalist refusal of German mediation. To accept would have meant the abandonment of all hopes for further expansion in the Adriatic and in the Mediterranean. Even total German concessions were insufficient if after the war Italy found herself exposed to the threat of increased German power in the Adriatic and in the Balkans.[11]

The possibility that neutralist pressure might push the government to accept Bülow's mediation drove the Nationalists to despair. The editors of the *Idea Nazionale* understood that a defeat for Giolitti was a defeat for the neutralist parliamentary majority which might have accepted Germany's terms. Their worst fears seemed to have been realized when Giolitti wrote a letter to a parliamentary colleague, Camillo Peano, which was subsequently published in the *Tribuna* on February 2, 1915. Giolitti argued that Italy might obtain most of her territorial aspirations through negotiations with Austria. In response, the Nationalists retorted that the bourgeoisie could never retain its supremacy within the state without a victorious war. By following Giolitti, the middle class would doom itself.[12]

The Nationalists feared that Giolitti might blackmail Salandra into negotiations in exchange for continued support. An even worse possibility loomed. The growing economic and political crisis might make it more advisable for Giolitti himself to take over the prime ministership. To Forges Davanzati, this was an outcome which had to be avoided at all costs. No change of government would be tolerated by the interventionists unless it meant war. The Nationalists reasserted their conviction that the only real solution to the crisis could be extraparliamentary. If the parliamentary route were tried, Corradini threatened recourse to the streets. He told Ferdinando Martini that, should the Salandra government fail, there would be 15,000 youths ready to take to the streets and that the ANI would not hesitate to ally with Mussolini and even with the Republicans. Once it became clear that the government would not fall, the *Idea Nazionale* returned to a much more conservative stance. Luigi Federzoni called for confidence in Salandra and denounced further demonstrations as counterproductive.[13]

Corradini's threat of an alliance with the extreme Left hinted at the Fascist synthesis, which was only in its formative stage in 1915. The Nationalists did participate in meetings with the revolutionary and democratic interventionists (much to the embarrassment of the latter). In so doing, they stressed the common denominator of patriotism and urged that social and economic aspirations be set aside for a future date. Contacts with the Left came mainly through common membership in irredentist organizations (a good example of the ambiguity of patriotism, on which the Nationalists constantly played). Members of the ANI, like Castellini and Livio Marchetti, had ties with Cesare Battisti, the Socialist leader from the Trentino, and Salvatore Barzilai, a moderate Republican deputy from Rome. The Trento-Trieste Society, headed by the pro-Nationalist Giovanni Giuriati, sponsored many of Battisti's meetings in Italy and had Nationalists as important officers in Milan, Genoa, and Venice.[14]

There were several indications that the democratic interventionists feared Nationalist encroachment on their movement. The Republicans tried unsuccessfully to exclude the Nationalists from a meeting of the Trento-Trieste Society in Bologna. In October 1914, a plan to have the Nationalist deputy Federzoni speak at a meeting which would also have featured Battisti brought a strong protest from Gaetano Salvemini, who felt that the presence of the Nationalists would alienate those democrats and socialists, still hesitant about intervention in the war.[15]

Sporadic contacts with the democratic interventionists did not preclude a continuing attack on the ideology of the democratic war. Coppola's article "For Democracy and Not for Italy" set forth an argument which was used to good effect throughout the war. The war was not a crusade against German autocracy and imperialism, but rather a struggle for the realization of Italy's own imperialist ambitions. It was the great patriotic war, which offered a last chance to complete the territorial conquests of the risorgimento. Corradini elaborated on a theme which he had begun to develop in the *Regno*. War involved a revolution, but not the one envisaged by Socialist interventionists. It was rather a revolt against the ideas and values which guided Europe during the nineteenth century. Viewed in this light, the German invasion of Belgium was not an immoral violation of a treaty, but a truly revolutionary action, which was designed to protect the interests of the German nation. Nations were not bound by moral laws but by national interest, the only true measure of state conduct.[16]

The role of the Nationalist Association during the crucial days of May 1915 was limited, yet significant. In the massive demonstrations, which began on May 14, the Nationalists saw the vindication of their position that the solution for the crisis could only come in an extraparliamentary way. From the very beginning of the crisis, the *Idea Nazionale* denounced Giolitti's return to Rome and insisted that the government was perfectly representative of all constitutional forces. Between May 10 and 14, when the neutralists pushed hardest against the government and the London Pact, which was to bring Italy in the war on the side of the Entente, the tone of the *Idea Nazionale*'s editorials became truly desperate. Giolitti was branded "an enemy of Italy" and his political allies were "a band a delinquents," who had to be treated as such in order to purge "once and for all this small and vile cancer from the political and moral body of Italy." Perhaps the most extreme point of this campaign was reached by Maffeo Pantaleoni, who wrote that a fortunate accident freed France from Jean Jaurès (the leader of the French Socialist party, who was murdered in 1914 by a nationalist fanatic), and the fury of the people eliminated Joseph Caillaux (a Radical politician with a reputation of favoring reconciliation with Germany, who was involved in a scandal shortly before the war). Similar remedies, he concluded, "will save our country."[17]

True to their earlier position that the crisis could only be resolved outside parliament, the Nationalists appealed to the king. The destiny of Italy could not be a matter for discussion in parliament but touched on the royal prerogative. In a distorted argument, the Nationalists insisted that Giolitti's use of parliament to undo the London Pact was a violation of the constitution, which reserved such decisions to the throne.[18]

As far as possible, the Nationalists were active in the pro-war demonstrations of May. They joined the other interventionists parties in appeals to support the government. During their entire campaign, which culminated on May 14 and 15, the Nationalists became the most outspoken advocates of unlimited territorial expansion. In addition, they used the war to further the synthesis between conservative ends and revolutionary direct action, which later appeared as a hallmark of fascism. By linking Giolitti with parliament, intervention in the war became more than the defeat of a political leader but that of the very idea of parliamentary government. After years of preparation, the Nationalists finally won their point that only by transforming revolutionary impulses into external aggression could domestic unity be enforced. On May 16, the lead editorial of the *Idea Nazionale* proclaimed: "Placed before the dilemma, war or revolution, we say loudly and clearly . . . that the outbreak of revolution must be avoided. It is necessary to make war." Five days later, they had their war. The campaign for intervention was over; the death agony of the liberal state began.

Five

The Great Patriotic War, 1915–18

The Interventionist Coalition and the Conduct of the War

Unprepared both psychologically and morally and led by a weak government, Italy declared war on May 24, 1915. Of all the great powers, hers was the most difficult position domestically. The war evoked no great stirring of popular emotion. Rather than actively willing the war, the majority of Italians passively submitted to it. The neutralism of the Socialists and of the Catholics was no match for the passionate fervor of the interventionists, but the pro-war forces were a small minority in the country. They were largely outsiders, isolated from the masses and from the government. Salandra, whose whole conception of governing precluded broadening his ministry to take in the extraparliamentary forces of both Left and Right, was firmly committed to the Liberal ministry which brought Italy into the war.

Even militarily, Italy worked under several disadvantages. The declaration of war was directed only against Austria. From the start, there was a feeling among the allies that the Italian theater was a secondary front, and this feeling persisted even after Italy declared war against Germany in 1916. Moreover, the Austrians were exceedingly well placed to defend the mountain terrain with a minimum of men. To overcome these disadvantages Italy had to mobilize her resources and coordinate policy and tactics with the major Western Allies and with the minor Balkan powers. Unfortunately, relations with Serbia remained marred throughout the conflict by the shadow of the London Pact. General Luigi Cadorna, the Italian military commander, was able enough, but neither he nor the government conceived of a war which demanded the total mobilization of the material and moral resources of the nation. The interventionist forces, from the extreme Left to the nationalist Right, were far more sensitive to the need to bridge the gap between the government and the people.[1]

From May 1915 to June 1916, when Salandra's ministry fell, a complicated struggle took place between those who had urged war from the streets and the government over restructuring the ministry to include the whole gamut of interventionist parties. Confusing the issue were two other political battles. The first was between the interventionists and the neutralists in parliament, the Socialists, and the Catholics. The second battle took place between the interventionists of Left and Right. In this struggle, the Nationalists worked to strip the war of any radical social and economic character.

Viewing the war from the perspective of the ANI, these points become clearer. There was no relaxation of the association's political and ideological campaign. The themes of the interventionist period were enlarged and explored on several levels. Giolittian and Socialist neutralism remained a prime target, and the fact that those forces still had their strength in parliament made more urgent the call for a government above parties and independent of the Chamber of Deputies. Ever conscious of the interventionists' minority position, the Nationalists stressed unity of the pro-war forces around the theme of victory. They urged the democratic parties to put aside projects for basic reforms until the end of the war and demanded that the government turn to the industrialists, merchants, and financiers for counsel on how to organize production for the war effort.[2] Finally, the Nationalists continued to insist that Italy's war be defended "against the unconscionable falsifications of the democratic-humanitarian interventionists, against Francophile logic, and against irredentist limitations."[3] The war was confirmation of the Nationalist thesis that conflict abroad could strengthen Italy internally and internationally. It was the completion of the risorgimento and the door to vaster dreams of a new, imperial Italy.[4]

The declaration of war only increased the Nationalists' hostility to the Socialist party. Immediately after the outbreak of hostilities, the *Idea Nazionale* demanded the suppression of the *Avanti* and dissolution of the Socialist party. In fact, however, the Nationalists were quite content with the antiwar position of the revolutionary socialists, for it allowed the *Idea Nazionale* to picture the Italian Socialist party (PSI) as a willing tool of German policy. More importantly, if only indirectly, the antiwar stand of the Socialists favored the Nationalists by weakening the democratic interventionist forces. One pro-war socialist bitterly noted that conservative control over the war effort and the definition of war aims remained unshaken. He understood that the conservative attack on the Socialist party was really an assault on all forms of socialism.[5]

Closely connected with their antisocialist campaign was the Nationalists' persistent criticism of parliament and of Giolitti. In general, they had little success in their direct attacks on Giolitti, who was too shrewd to expose himself to charges of disloyalty during wartime. The Nationalists did, however, watch closely for any signs of a political comeback by the former prime minister. They rejected the appeals to modify their hostility in the interest of national unity. Nothing could make them forget the 300 calling cards left by various deputies at Giolitti's home during the May 1915 crisis, when it seemed that he could topple Salandra. Political power could never rest with the Giolittian majority in the chamber but had to be sought in the confidence of the king and of the nation. Yet the Nationalists were aware that Salandra remained incapable of giving energy and direction to the conservative cause. Their ideal was an emergency executive which would suspend parliamentary prerogatives for the duration of the war.[6]

Toward the other large neutralist group the Nationalists were much more cautious. They hoped that the war would continue to heal the rift between the Catholics and the state. Coppola agreed that the pope had to remain formally neutral, but Italian Catholics could be free to choose the patriotic cause. After all, he argued, Italy, France, and Belgium were fighting for Latin Christianity. Even Benedict XV's denunciation of the war as a "useless slaughter" met only the mild comment that it was designed to help Austrian and German Catholics.[7]

More interesting than the polemics which continued prewar battles was the effort by the Nationalists and the other interventionists to circumvent parliament and the Giolittian majority. In Italy, as in the other belligerent powers with parliamentary systems, the war produced notable tension between the military, the civilian government, and the parliament. On the one hand, there were pressures from the military to limit parliamentary control of war policy. On the other hand, parliament itself was increasingly frustrated in its efforts to cope with the economic, social, and administrative problems of the war. Power slipped from elected assemblies to select war cabinets and to the bureaucracies which administered economic mobilization. In Italy, the situation was further complicated by the strong neutralist sentiment in parliament. Even those democrats who might normally be expected to defend parliamentary rights joined the Nationalists in attacking the "gap" between the Chamber of Deputies and the real country, which supposedly backed the war effort.[8]

Political realism made it impossible for any government to ignore parliament. The followers of Giolitti numbered too many able politicians to be excluded completely. Thus, while the interventionists demanded that each successive government break totally with the neutralist opposition, no prime minister dared take such a step. Antonio Salandra initially had a favored position. In the first rush of enthusiasm for war, criticism was muted on all sides. The political truce lasted into early 1916, when the failure of the Italian offensives to reach Trento and Trieste, the symbolic goals of the war, led to a double pressure against the military leadership of General Cadorna and against Salandra. The Nationalists were staunch defenders of Cadorna and initially of Salandra. Yet they wanted the impossible from Salandra, whose failure to grasp the nature of total war and preoccupation with his parliamentary base made him the last man to break with the system and install a wartime dictatorship. His successor, the feeble Paolo Boselli, whose government of national unity lasted from June 1916 to October 1917, went somewhat further toward compromising with parliament by bringing together Leonida Bissolati, a pro-war reformist socialist; Sidney Sonnino; and V. E. Orlando, a politician with friendly relations with the Giolittian opposition. When Boselli's government collapsed in 1917, Orlando passed from the interior ministry to the presidency of the council of ministers and continued the policy of juggling parliamentary forces until the end of the war. Each of these governments felt obliged to come to terms with the former neutralists. Rather than suppress the *Avanti* and launch a frontal attack on the Socialist party, the government accepted the "neither adhere, nor sabotage" formula proposed by the Socialists and used censorship and sporadic police represson to keep dissent in line.[9]

The relationship between the Nationalists and the government must be viewed against this background. Fundamentally, the *Idea Nazionale* demanded three things: a more aggressive internal policy toward the Socialists; closer ties between the goverment and the interventionists, both inside and out of parliament; and a more vigorous prosecution of the war. The basic disagreement between Salandra and the Nationalists was over the kind of war to be fought. Although Salandra's hostility to socialism led him to discourage the Socialists from changing their position on the war, so as not to weaken the claim of the Liberals to the fruits of victory, he did not go beyond traditional means of dealing with the Socialist party.[10] Nor did Salandra use to good effect the mandate which he was supposed to have received from the *piazza*, in May 1915. The Nationalists felt that he deliberately ignored the interventionists, while moving exclusively in the orbit of the Liberal party. Salandra's rare moves outside the traditional leadership elite, such as the appointment of the patriotic republican Salvatore Barzilai to a government post, met with Nationalist approval but, in general, Salandra's government did not fare well under Nationalist scrutiny. One of the chief targets was Sidney Sonnino. The campaign against Sonnino developed during the spring and summer of 1916, when the *Idea Nazionale* seemed to be working for his substitution by Tittoni, Italy's ambassador to France. Sonnino's supposed lack of a broad Mediterranean vision justified asking him to step down during the June 1916 crisis of Salandra's government. Later, in 1917, there was evidence that the Nationalists worked with officials in the foreign ministry to force their definition of war aims on Sonnino. He was never a favorite of the *Idea Nazionale,* although as time went on he became the symbol of the minimum Nationalist program against the "renunciatory" programs of the democrats.[11]

The development of the crisis of Salandra's government between March and June 1916 illuminated the basic differences between the Nationalists' dynamic conservativism and the static politics of Salandra. The beginning of the crisis came after the prime minister's speech to the Unione Monarchica (Monarchical Union) of Turin, in which he called for consensus behind the leadership of the Liberal party. Salandra specifically rejected requests to enlarge his government, pledging himself to maintain the hegemony of the "party of Cavour." Needless to say, this speech was not well received by the Nationalists. In a letter to Luigi Albertini, written during March 1916 when Salandra almost fell from office, Forges Davanzati revealed the complicated line which the ANI attempted to follow. He defended the association's opposition to the government, not only because of Salandra's weak policies, but also because of the key role which the Nationalists wished to play in the interventionist coalition. By backing the Left against Salandra, the Nationalists attempted to prevent the antiministerial challenge from coming solely from the democratic interventionists: "I have no need to tell you of the danger which one has before one's eyes: the further weakening of an already weak government, the preparation of an alibi for the postwar by the parties of the extreme Left, who will be able to defend themselves by saying that they wanted the war, not the errors." The Nationalists' demand for a broad national government was designed to involve the Left in the responsibility for the war. Forges complained that neither the government nor the *Corriere della Sera* understood this policy: "I am more persuaded of the burden which we have taken on our shoulders and, often in the most difficult moments, even the friends on whom we count let fall on us the greater weight of their absence." In an article for the *Idea Nazionale,* Forges developed still another reason for the involvement of the Left in the government. He thought that it would mark a definitive break with the Socialist party and that it would make even more difficult the resumption of any independent political activity by the democratic interventionists.[12]

The actual crisis of the government developed into a game of cat and mouse between the Nationalists and their democratic allies, who were well aware of the dangers of entrapment. When parliament opened in March 1916, the democrats decided to make a major effort to broaden the government or to replace it with a more popular alternative. On March 10, there was a meeting of all interventionists under Bissolati's leadership. Both Federzoni and Foscari attended. This group appealed to Salandra, who rejected their criticisms and threatened to appeal to the crown for support. The *Idea Nazionale* denounced Salandra's efforts to thwart parliamentary pressure and instead supported a request made by Giuseppe Canepa in the *Messaggero* that the Social Democrats enter the government. When the vote on Salandra finally came, Bissolati maneuvered to force the Nationalists to reject a common declaration of principle agreed upon by the other interventionist parties. The Nationalists, however, did vote against the government, along with the Left and against the majority of Liberals.[13]

Salandra managed to survive the March crisis, but the ministry's days were numbered. On June 6, the Nationalists signed a motion, critical of Salandra, which called for the creation of a parliamentary committee to assure better cooperation between government and parliament in the conduct of the war. As support for the ministry dwindled during the debates over war policy, Salandra resigned, opening the way for the involvement of all groups in the war effort. The *Idea Nazionale* noted that, while Salandra never understood that war was more than the administration of war, the next government had to draw maximum advantage from the fact that war unified parties over a broad spectrum, both inside and out of parliament.[14]

The new government, formed under the leadership of the seventy-eight-year-old Paolo Boselli, was essentially a coalition of conservatives from the old government, a few interventionists, and men like Orlando who had ties to the

Giolittians. Even Piero Foscari joined the government as undersecretary at the Colonial Ministry. Except for Orlando's presence, the Nationalists initially seemed pleased with Boselli's government. Friendly relations were short lived, however. The Nationalists could not accept Orlando's refusal to crack down on the Socialists. Substantially the same criticisms came from the leftist interventionist press, Mussolini's *Popolo d'Italia* and the somewhat republican *Fronte Interno* of Rome. The campaign had some impact. Orlando, who as minister of interior had responsibility for public order, considered imposing martial law to counter charges that his policies were too weak.[15]

The real problem was not the supposed defeatism of the former neutralists, but rather the aims of those forces who wished to use the war to modify the country's political structure. Most guilty of this political use of the war was the ANI, although it was probably true that the Nationalists could never determine what kind of wartime dictatorship they wanted. There is no real proof that they thought in terms of a military coup. An infinite distance separated the political minds of the Nationalists from the traditional military attitudes of a Cadorna. In fact, both Corradini and Federzoni were rebuffed by Cadorna in their efforts to propagandize the troops. Rule by the general staff was clearly not the solution they desired.[16]

The wartime crisis brought the association into continuous contact with the other interventionist forces. The Nationalists used a three-part approach to deal with their pro-war allies: emphasizing the national ideal, combatting any democratic or social content in the war effort, and involving the Left in responsibility for the war (as was done during the crisis of Salandra's government). Nationalist influence spread in a number of ways but mainly through fellow-traveling papers and their participation in the *fasci* (groups) for national defense. These *fasci* spread throughout Italy during the war. They had multiple aims but served primarily to link the small parties which had supported entry into the war. For instance, the Roman *fascio* brought together Liberals, Republicans, Social Democrats, Radicals, and Nationalists. The weakness of these interventionists was their lack of a solid base in the country. The *fasci* offered a possibility to create such a base. Especially after Italy's defeat at Caporetto in 1917, they served as local vigilance committees to maintain morale and to intimidate supposed defeatists. Within the context of interventionist unity, it was hard for the more leftist groups to exclude the Nationalists, who fully realized the potential of interclass and interparty cooperation.[17]

Although the Nationalists had little influence in the *fasci* of Milan and elsewhere in the revolutionized north, they became one of the predominant influences in Rome. At the beginning of the war the interventionist parties began to meet regularly in Rome. A committee for internal defense was formed on the evening of May 23, 1915, by Nationalists, Radicals, Republicans, and Social Democrats. The aim was to pressure the government on war policy, but the Nationalists used the committee to press their program of political unity and a declaration of war on Germany. The Nationalists managed to participate on both the parliamentary and local levels. As noted, they took part in the organization of pro-war parties during the crisis of Salandra's government. The Nationalists consistently followed out the policy of blocking independent action on the part of the democrats. In July 1917, when Alceste De Ambris, a syndicalist, persisted in presenting a motion to the Roman *fascio* which seemed to stress the democratic ideology, the Nationalist representative threatened to withdraw. On this occasion, the group split, with the more conservative faction going to the Nationalist headquarters and the others to the offices of the *Popolo d'Italia*. However, despite these differences, the interventionist left and right were bound in uneasy partnership by a common hostility to the neutralists and to Orlando's moderate policies.[18]

Another important source of Nationalist influence on the Roman scene was through the *Fronte Interno*, the paper of the local interventionist *fascio*. According to a report of the Interior Ministry, Tommaso Monicelli of the *Idea Nazionale* promised to raise the funds for the *fascio*'s paper from the same group which financed the *Idea Nazionale*. Whatever Monicelli's role, the money for the venture did come from the Perrone-Ansaldo interest which controlled the *Messaggero* of Rome, the *Secolo XIX* of Genoa, and the *Mezzogiorno* of Naples. Although the *Fronte Interno* was nominally leftist (P. Pirolini and Francesco Guerrazzi, the directors, were both republicans), the prominent Nationalist Maffeo Pantaleoni and his friend Giovanni Preziosi, a former priest and editor of the *Vita Italiana*, took an important part in the affairs of both the Roman *fascio* and the *Fronte Interno*. The paper, which was printed on the presses of the *Idea Nazionale* until almost the end of the war, followed the main lines of Nationalist policy.[19]

The Crisis of Caporetto

The Italian military defeat at Caporetto, which began on October 24, 1917 and ended on the Piave River on November 9, coincided with the crisis of the Boselli government and the formation of the new Orlando ministry. Both events marked a radicalization of the political struggle in Italy. As the future of Boselli's government became doubtful in September 1917, there were renewed efforts on the part of the interventionists to eliminate Orlando from the succession and countermoves by the Giolittians to prevent any radical change in the parliamentary situation. In October, forty-seven Giolittians formed the basis of what became the *Unione Parlamentare* (Parliamentary Union), a group of over one-hundred former neutralists and pro-Giolittian deputies.[20]

The opposing interventionist organization was the Fascio Parlamentare di Difesa Nazionale (Parliamentary Fascio of National Defense), formed after Caporetto to give the pro-war parties a greater voice. Federzoni participated in the Fascio Parlamentare from its beginning in early November 1917. He was listed with Piero Foscari as belonging to the hard-core membersip when the Fascio formally came into being in December. As was the case with the local Roman *fascio*, the Right dominated the Fascio Parlamentare, giving it a strong anti-Orlando coloring. The first meetings were even held in the offices of the pro-Nationalist *Vita Italiana* of Giovanni Preziosi. From the outset, Federzoni attempted to make anti-socialism one of the major themes of *fascio* propaganda. On December 16, he attacked Orlando for the government's weakness toward internal subversion and in the secret session of December 22 on the causes for the rout at Caporetto, he blamed the Socialists for the defeat. Throughout 1918, the Nationalists steered both the parliamentary and local *fasci* toward their domestic and foreign policies, but differences over the latter made it impossible to succeed. When unity finally proved too difficult, the Nationalists led a split in the Roman *fascio* and even refused to allow the *Fronte Interno* to use the presses of the *Idea Nazionale*.[21]

The immediate cause of political tension at the beginning of 1918 was Caporetto, which seemed to the interventionists the ultimate brush with doom. Immediately after the defeat, Bissolati wrote:

> It is finished for us. We must disappear. We have been the ones who have created the dream of a greater Italy. We wanted to create a military Italy. We erred. We built on a void. The Italians were not prepared. We created illusions. We have brought Italy to this point. Therefore we must pay and disappear.[22]

Even Luigi Albertini was prepared to accept the participation of the Giolittians and some Socialists in his shock at the enormity of the defeat, and the moderate Socialists Filippo Turati and Claudio Treves urged the proletariat to rally to the national cause.[23]

The real significance of Caporetto was not the initial solidarity, but the increased polarization once the shock passed. The Nationalists went from horror and disbelief to a more calculating judgment rather rapidly. Even the obligatory call for national unity was conditioned in the pages of the *Idea Nazionale* by the demand for penal sanctions against those who betrayed Italy. Unlike the other interventionists, the Nationalists were also firm against accepting overtures from the Giolittians. Still, lurking behind the bravado was a hint of fear and doubt which must have been nearly overwhelming.

Alfredo Rocco could not forget that time: "The mind shrinks in horror at the thought of what would have happened if the last act of our war were our defeat."[24]

Luigi Federzoni was quick to draw practical consequences from Caporetto. In a series of articles he argued that renewed social content had to be given to the war. Even though he proposed only a limited series of reforms in favor of the peasants, it was an important gesture for it involved the creation of a new myth. Federzoni was careful to distinguish between the heroic peasant soldier and the industrial worker who stayed at home. Like Mussolini, who was to make the aristocracy of the trenches one of the pillars of his new politics, Federzoni pointed out that the workers did well from the war and that it was really the peasant who bore the brunt of the fighting and suffering.[25]

Alfredo Rocco drew quite another moral from the defeat. The responsibility for the collapse was laid at the door of the democratic system. Only by a new concept of the state and of authority could the government realize its historic mission in the war. The state had to conquer all resistance to its will by psychological and moral coercion and, if necessary, by force: "The state has the duty to be inflexible with those who persist in remaining outside of national life." More ominously, Rocco noted that the state had at its disposition a powerful apparatus of force, which reached down into the smallest village through the person of the mayor or teacher. All means were legitimate because the ruling classes, as Rocco saw it, had no choice but to win the war.[26]

The Nationalists and the New Productivist Theories

The real measure of Nationalist politics was not the artificial alliance between the ANI and the Left, but the association's function in developing a conservative ideology and its success in establishing solid ties with the economic establishment. Important industrial groups, represented by Dante Ferraris and the Bombrini family, had given the Nationalists vital assistance before the war. World War I brought a major shift in backing for the *Idea Nazionale.* At the beginning of the conflict, the Nationalists engaged in a bitter campaign against the Banca Commerciale and its director, Joël, for being instruments of German economic domination of Italy. In the past, the Commerciale had come under attack from the Nationalists for its ties to Giolitti and because it was one of the largest financial institutions with German backing during the period of neutrality, but the new campaign had surprising results. Giovanni Preziosi's *Vita Italiana* led off and was quickly seconded by the *Idea Nazionale.* These attacks eventually involved the Ferraris family, which represented the German AEG (United Electric Society) interests in Italy, and resulted in Dante Ferraris's resignation from the board of the L'Italiana publishing house (the parent company of the *Idea Nazionale*).[27]

After the rupture between Ferraris and the Nationalists, the Perrone-Ansaldo interests with the Banca Italiana di Sconto (Italian Discount Bank), provided desperately needed funding for the *Idea Nazionale,* which ran a million-lire deficit in 1917 and lost 15 percent of its circulation in 1918. As a result, the *Idea Nazionale* became a sort of advertising agency for the Perrone family and Ansaldo. Even the continuing attacks on the Banca Commerciale were part of an effort by the Perrones to take control of the bank.[28]

The *Idea Nazionale* openly admitted its links with heavy industry and the fact that the industrialists gave money to "a paper which defended their interest."[29] The Nationalist paper supported efforts by industrialists to further unity among themselves and cooperation with agrarian interests. It attempted to prove that the fears of southern agriculture toward northern business had to be overcome for the common good of both. When the Associazione fra le Società Italiane per Azioni (Association among Italian Joint Stock Companies), met with a number of agricultural producers, Pasquale Nonno of the *Idea Nazionale* participated in the meeting and hailed the creation of a committee to study common policies on tariffs and other questions. G. L. Franchi argued that the tariff issue was overrated and that there was a substantial community of interest on questions of transportation, banking, commercial organization, and the formation of accords to regulate production. The *Idea Nazionale* also gave much publicity to the Associazione per la Difesa dell'Agricoltura (Association for the Defense of Agriculture). Its paper, *Terra,* was extensively cited by the Nationalists to support arguments against collectivization and state intervention in agriculture and to urge cooperation with industrial groups.[30]

Almost daily, the Nationalists urged that government policy favor the needs of industry both for the war effort and for postwar reconstruction. Specifically, they called for a national munitions committee with broad powers to aid the changeover to war production. The universal remedy for the ailments afflicting the Italian economy during the war was to centralize controls in the hands of practical businessmen rather than politicians. The Nationalists were quite frank in their belief that it was the moment to push for reforms which could never be achieved in a peacetime parliamentary situation, such as comprehensive protection for heavy industry, with special favors for engineering and shipbuilding (Ansaldo). Finally, they urged caution on proposed taxes on wartime surplus profits. This economic program was the vital other dimension of the antiparliamentary stance of the *Idea Nazionale*.[31]

The various fragmentary analyses were worked into a broad theory by Corradini. The war represented a massive liberation of the productive forces of society. In a real sense, Corradini argued, the war was imperialist by its incessant conquest of new sources of production and wealth. It was also a social fact which overwhelmed single individuals and revealed the power of the nation-state. The new imperialism, or "the march of the producers," was the central idea to emerge from the conflict. No nation could win the war by its military power alone. The strength of a nation was in its industrial organization: "Today the director of a plant must *produce* the victory as much as an army general." The core of this new productive elite was to be found in the bourgeoisie. The "productive bourgeoisie" represented the whole nation, whereas the "political bourgeoisie" betrayed the true interests of the producers.

Corradini contended that classical democracy, with its fragmentation of society and subordination of interests to electoral needs, was the greatest obstacle to the achievement of power by the productive bourgeoisie. He urged the producers to use their position in the state to seize the mechanism of universal suffrage in the interests of a new elitist conception of democracy. The industrialists had to organize for the collective defense of their interests against a parliament which remained unresponsive and against a bureaucracy which stifled energies.[32]

In his wartime writings, the Nationalist leader elaborated a myth of a defenseless and neglected industrial class, totally at the mercy of a highly organized proletariat. His program was designed, as he put it, to counteract the harmful effects of the class struggle, which aimed exclusively at distribution within the state and negated the vital struggle between nations. If the war proved anything, Corradini felt, it was that the class struggle had been superceded by the necessity for association within the nation. Corradini's new conception of democracy demanded the participation of all classes, with the understanding that "rule is always aristocratic."[33] Speaking before an audience of Nationalist workers in Naples, he described a system in which the worker would take his place in a hierarchical national community. Although Corradini denied that he opposed collective worker self-defense, he was extremely critical of strikes and urged the industrialists to organize against them. In his state there were minor producers, the workers, and major producers, the industrialists. Harmony merely demanded recognition of this fact on the part of the proletariat: "We must have the courage to be antipopular out of love for the people."[34]

Just how far the ideas of Corradini influenced Mussolini is difficult to determine. After the latter's break with the Socialist party, the logic of patriotic socialism, even in a pseudo-revolutionary guise, demanded acceptance on Mussolini's part of a high degree of class collaboration. The productivist ideology, as Corradini and others defined it, was ideally suited for Mussolini's *iter* from revolutionary to "national" Left. The crucial similarity between the Nationalist and the Mussolinian positions was in the definition of the producers. For Mussolini, "the producers are not necessarily all bourgeois, not necessarily all proletarians. The engineer who designed the machine is a producer. There are hierarchies of producers, and these hierarchies must be respected as the fruit of experience, study, and responsibility. Between producers there exists no disagreement." As he saw it, the essential problem was to produce more, and that demanded collaboration among all categories of labor. Thus, it was never a question of attacking social hierarchies or of discipline because there would always be a hierarchy of ability. In the long run, it was a matter of organizing the state for the well-being of the greatest number: Mussolini's residual socialism. For the short term, "the workers have not yet either the muscles or the brains sufficient for this great task."[35]

Mussolini's renunciation of the class struggle, his acceptance of hierarchy which transcended the process of technical production to invade the social system, and his de facto acceptance of a reformist short-term strategy within the capitalist system led him to a political stance which was not significantly different from that of Corradini. There were, however, differences in emphasis. Mussolini still hinted at a transformation of capitalism in the direction of socialism. He also stressed the role of the soldier-proletarian more than Corradini, but the slogan implied the acceptance of the corporate and hierarchical structure of the army as a unity of production. Such an idea had real appeal for Corradini, as did the change which Mussolini inserted on the masthead of his *Popolo d'Italia* from "socialist" to "*combattenti* (soldiers) and producers," with the term "soldiers" extending "from Diaz [the commander-in-chief] to the last infantryman." Like the Nationalists, Mussolini began to argue that the old concepts of socialism, democracy, and radicalism had no meaning. In a muddleheaded way, he sought a "national socialism," which in the Italian context was bound to be no socialism at all. When he called his former socialist comrades parasites and disrupters of national unity, he was carrying more than just a drop of water to the Nationalists' mill.[36]

FOREIGN POLICY AND THE BREAKUP OF THE INTERVENTIONIST COALITION

If the pressures of domestic political conflict drew the interventionists together in a way which favored the aims of the Nationalists, foreign policy tended to disrupt the pro-war bloc as a viable force. Even this split was not totally to the disadvantage of the Nationalists, for they had always worked to weaken the democratic interventionists and to separate their position from that of the pro-war Left. In fact, the definition of Nationalist war aims was done without any thought of their allies. This scorn was apparent in the Nationalists' call, justified on the grounds of Italian imperialism, to extend the war to Germany. The leaders of the ANI emphatically rejected any idea of a limited, irredentist war. Moreover, the small Balkan states were relegated to the role of pawns between Germany and the Entente. The Nationalists were determined, the nationality principle notwithstanding, to minimize the contribution of the Balkan nations so as not to create any sense of obligation for a future peace.[37]

The necessity of maintaining Italy on a par with the other major powers was a constant preoccupation. Federzoni felt that the war represented a tremendous expansion of French and English power, and he wondered if Italy would be the only state to take the ideology of the democratic war seriously. Forges made it clear that cooperation was for the realization of each country's single aims. The concern that Italy was being neglected by Britain and France colored much Nationalist writing on the war.[38]

The sensation that Italy was being ignored affected domestic politics. The question of war aims was the crucial test on which relations between the Nationalists and all other interventionist parties hinged. Although the pro-war parties more or less agreed on the destruction of Austria-Hungary, there was strong disagreement on the extent of Italy's claims to the pieces. Differences also arose over the kind of war Italy was fighting and over the personification of that war in the persons of Sidney Sonnino and Leonida Bissolati, the foreign minister and the leading democrat in the cabinet. For the Nationalists, the war was simply an exercise in power. Forges felt that the Entente was trapped in its own principles, seeking an elaborate justification for the liberation of peoples who neither desired to be liberated nor were capable of self-government. It was absurd to fear the charge of imperialism. He was sure that the doctrine of self-determination would please the British and the French no more than the Italians if it were to be applied to the Ottoman Empire.[39]

With their vision of the war as an imperialist struggle, the Nationalists generally did not respond to the importance of the Russian Revolution. They had never been overly bothered by having Imperial Russia as an ally. Their reaction to the first Russian revolution was technical and military. The fall of the Romanovs meant the disappearance of the last vestiges of German influence. Still, by May 1917, the *Idea Nazionale* was increasingly preoccupied with the discipline and cohesion of the Russian army and the liberty allowed to Bolshevik subversion. High-minded declarations of liberty made by the provisional government were dismissed as typical democratic nonsense.[40]

Prophetically, Corradini saw the revolutionary process at work in Russia as marking a shift in the war from a struggle against Germany to a war of ideas, but neither he nor the other Nationalists drew many conclusions from this insight. The more conservative Federzoni blamed Germany for the new menace to European society. Alfredo Rocco put the case against even the moderate first revolution in dramatic terms: "The Russian Revolution had destroyed the state, annihilated every civilized organization, had made a valorous army into an unwarlike mass of fleeing men and, to compensate, had created the soviet, that is the permanent meeting open to all the spies and all the traitors." Thus, even before the Bolsheviks came to power, the judgment of the Nationalists on the revolution was totally negative. On this point, however, they differed sharply with Mussolini, who felt that the first revolution confirmed his thesis of the revolutionary war. Revolution was not the dissolution or defeat of the state, as the Nationalists contended, nor were the difficulties of the Russian army to be blamed solely on the revolution.[41]

By the time the Bolsheviks took power, the Nationalists could hardly contain their hostility. To a certain extent, they welcomed the radicalized revolution as a clarification of the situation. There was no longer any doubt: the enemy was in power. The Bolshevik revolution was part of a German plot to weaken the Entente. From Zimmerwald to the Finland Station, it had been the Germans giving aid to the revolutionaries. To Corradini, the revolution was the final proof that democracy and socialism were but perversions of the state. All the false doctrines of the West had been applied with disastrous effect in Russia. Lenin became the symbol of spiritual collapse: "Lenin is all the spiritual illnesses which affect men and peoples." Russian socialism was the antithesis of the new civilization which Corradini saw emerging out of the war.[42]

Between Mussolini and the Nationalists there was total agreement on the Bolshevik revolution. Mussolini argued that the Italians had been betrayed when his conception of the revolutionary war backfired. By mid-1918, the *Popolo d'Italia* welcomed intervention in Russia by the Czech Legion and by Japan. Needless to say, the *Idea Nazionale* also encouraged intervention of any sort to bring down the Bolsheviks. No one, least of all the Nationalists, paid heed to the words of Arturo Labriola, who pointed out that the West was partly to blame for Kerensky's fall by pushing him constantly into new offensives. He felt that it would be a great mistake to think that Lenin and Trotsky would disappear. The only possible policy for the Entente was to try to limit German influence on the new Russia.[43]

The same underestimation of the changed nature of the war appeared in the Nationalists' reception of Wilson's Fourteen Points. Forges insisted that each power had the right to define its own war aims and that Italy would expect what she had been promised. Underlying the Nationalists' harsh reaction was the feeling that Wilson might strengthen the Italian democrats in the ongoing debate over war policy. Although the *Idea Nazionale* could not yet envisage an American challenge to Italian war aims, a growing uneasiness led the paper to urge Orlando to speak out on Italy's war program as did Wilson and Lloyd George.[44]

On specific war aims, the *Idea Nazionale* held to the minimum program outlined in the Treaty of London, with the addition of Fiume and a series of colonial territories. There was no question that Albania should fall into the Italian sphere and that Italy should receive the southern part of Asia Minor. Strangely enough, in the light of later disagreement over foreign policy, the *Idea Nazionale*'s program was well received by Luigi Albertini, who appreciated the Nationalists' efforts to examine the broader ramifications of foreign policy.[45]

One of the weaknesses of the Italian Wilsonians became immediately apparent as the war drew to a close. Unable to move Sonnino away from the strict application of the London Pact of 1915, the democrats were forced to use indirect means, such as appeals to public opinion. A meeting of oppressed nationalities was scheduled for the spring of 1918 in Rome. The congress was to be a major step in the indirect pressure which the democratic forces attempted to put on Sonnino. To further impress the government, the organizers attempted to involve the Italian Right in the planning for the congress. In this way, the entire spectrum of pro-war opinion would be on record in favor of a peace of reconciliation between the various nationalities of the Hapsburg Empire. Unfortunately for the democrats, in a contest to win public approval the Nationalists were more than prepared to do battle. Up to 1918, they had consistently ignored the democratic program, while openly manifesting their contempt for Slavic culture and rights. No friends of the movement for southern Slav unity, they urged Sonnino to oppose the merger of the Serbs and Croats into a single state. The Nationalists also sought to work within the interventionist front to channel it along the same lines. In this campaign they were seconded by the *Fronte Interno*, which very early took a hard line on Italian rights in the Adriatic and Dalmatia. Within the *fascio*, the

Nationalists and their allies fought efforts to redefine war aims to recognize Yugoslav rights in Istria, Dalmatia, or the Adriatic islands. Paradoxically, the Nationalists also put forward Italy's claim to be the patron of the smaller Balkan nations.[46]

The Nationalists willingly participated in the planning for the Congress of Oppressed Nationalities. The executive committee included Forges Davanzati, Federzoni, and Pantaleoni, as well as supporters of reconciliation like Luigi Albertini, Gaetano Salvemini, and G. A. Borghese. The resulting lack of political coherence favored the Nationalists, who wanted a vague and meaningless document. In fact, only the influence of Wickhan Steed and R. W. Seton Watson, the two British experts, saved the pact from completely losing its democratic and innovative qualities.[47]

The *Idea Nazionale* expressed satisfaction over the results of the congress, which really did little to clarify Italo-Yugoslav relations. The Nationalists continued to encourage the illusion that Italy would have no difficulties at the peace conference and successfully resisted efforts to discuss the basic issues. It took until mid-1918 for the latent dispute to break out into full debate, and even then the Nationalists tried to minimize the problem. A good example of this tactic came when Albertini's *Corriere della Sera* attempted to initiate a full-scale debate in August. Italy, the *Corriere* pointed out, had two foreign policies: one, developed by Sonnino at the beginning of the war, was derived from the London Pact; the other, based on the new diplomacy, had been set forth in the Pact of Rome at the end of the Congress of Oppressed Nationalities. Sonnino, however, seemed totally unaware of the challenge to Italian policy posed by the United States and by the nationality principle. Defending Italian rights as rigidly set out in the 1915 treaty was "insufficient." The *Corriere* called for a major revison of policy to meet the changed circumstances of the war.[48]

Reaction to Albertini's gambit was discouraging. Few democratic interventionists had the courage openly to abandon the concrete benefits of the London Pact. The moderately democratic *Messaggero* expressed the hope that Italo-Yugoslav differences could be composed peacefully. The more conservative *Tribuna* dismissed the arguments against the London Pact. Sonnino even emerged from the debate with increased support from the Fascio Parlamentare. The Nationalists were content to play on the ostrichlike attitudes of their countrymen. They contended that both the London Pact and the Pact of Rome aimed at the same thing, the destruction of the Austrian Empire. By distorting the meaning of both documents, they were made out to be compatible. Cleverly rejecting the *Giornale d'Italia*'s contention that the nationality principle had to take second place, the *Idea Nazionale* emphasized that "Italy cannot delude herself about fobbing off a narrowly nationalistic policy under the democratic mask of the nationalities policy. She must, if she wishes to succeed, be capable of conducting a policy of true and healthy democratic nationalism." Although this statement had a progressive ring to it, it was essentially ambiguous and was negated by the criticisms directed at the *Corriere* for doing a disservice to Sonnino by hinting that the United States might not support Italian demands. According to the *Idea Nazionale*, everyone agreed (except perhaps for a few extremists like Salvemini) on the wisdom of Italian policy and on the possibility of conciliating the various parts of that policy with the nationalities principle. The Pact of Rome was merely a means of realizing the London Pact.[49]

During the last year of the war Mussolini's position on foreign policy drew closer to that of the Nationalists. In July 1917, he set forth a policy of expansion which called for the annexation of Trieste, Istria, Fiume, and Dalmatia. The Adriatic Sea would become commercially Italo-Yugoslav, while remaining militarily Italian. Although he differed from the Nationalists in not caring overly about colonial questions, he took an increasingly strong stand toward Yugoslav demands. With reservations on Italian rights in Fiume, Mussolini considered the London Pact to have been fair to all sides. Thus, during the debate over foreign policy in August 1918, Mussolini criticized Sonnino only because he was not anti-Austrian enough, but he dismissed Albertini's arguments on a real peace of reconciliation.[50]

As the war drew to a close, the weakness of the interventionist forces, lacking a popular base and isolated from the Socialist party and the proletariat, could not be overcome. Threatened in the existing parliament, menaced by extinction in the future chamber, and condemned by the logic of political alliances based merely on national solidarity, the democratic interventionists prepared for their Caporetto after November 1918. Salvemini's bitter comment accurately summed up the situation: "Nothing is more desirable for *man* than the alliance between man and the horse; during four years the Nationalists and the conservatives have been man, and the democrats have been the horse."[51]

Six

The Nationalist Association in the Red Years, 1919–20

Reorganizing the Movement for Postwar Battles

The postwar era in Italy was marked by a series of irrepressible economic and social conflicts which overwhelmed the liberal democratic system. Two separate problems converged at the end of the war. The expansion of Italian industry during the conflict could not be sustained once the war had ended. The industrialists were determined to proceed with a systematic retrenchment at the same moment when the proletariat, faced with declining real wages, was determined to push for higher salaries and job security. The second series of problems arose from the Russian Revolution and the political aspirations of the working class and the peasantry. Immediately after Caporetto, promises of land reform were made to the soldier-peasants. Behind the lines, the Socialist party and a large part of the proletariat were caught up in the vision of a Soviet-style revolution. In their exclusive preoccupation with domestic politics, Socialists left foreign policy issues to the government and the bourgeois parties. However, the Russian Revolution and the Socialist agitation also created a Nationalist backlash. Democratic interventionists were swept away in this tide. Their cause had been reform through victory, but reform was preempted by those who called for radical change and cared little about the victory. Men who had backed the war with enthusiasm were carried forward by the logic of their position to seek justification in a maximum peace program, as a way both of relieving economic pressures and of reinforcing the social situation in the country.[1]

The political-economic pincer movement caught the weak Orlando government unprepared. Beginning in the last months of 1918 and continuing throughout the next year and a half, there was constant agitation in industry and on the land. The politics of Italy changed in the process. The Liberal party, based on a network of local clienteles and of liberal-monarchist associations, dissolved both electorally and politically into a hopeless series of subfactions that had little hope of recovery. Its parliamentary forces were drastically diminished in the elections of November 1919. These same elections marked the emergence of the Socialist and Catholic parties as the largest parliamentary forces. The Catholic Popular party (PPI), created in 1918, theoretically provided the best possibility to bolster the flagging liberal system, but the Catholics were not yet ready to take on the task of saving the state which they had opposed for so many years.[2]

The period of crisis lasted from the end of the war until the failure of the factory occupations in September 1920 and the decline of peasant agitation in the fall of the same year. The administrative elections of 1920, which saw a slow revival of the conservatives, and the rise of agrarian violence in the form of attacks by Fascist squads against socialist peasant organizations marked a turning point away from revolutionary change toward the triumph of fascism.

Although the period of the war was successful from the Nationalist point of view in carrying forward the ideals of the ANI, the four years saw a decline in organizational support. When at the end of 1919 the *Idea Nazionale* attempted to assess the association's position, the paper noted that many groups had practically ceased to exist after the members volunteered for the war. The Roman group lost 12 percent of its membership in that way. In early 1919, Umberto Guglielmotti was appointed administrative secretary to supervise the reorganization of the movement. After a year of activity, ninety-four groups had been reconstituted, although many still had very few members. While the strongest section was in Rome, groups in Bari, Venice, and Milan had been reorganized, and special emphasis was given to the youth groups and the recruitment of veterans. In Bologna, the first of the Nationalist squads were organized even before the formal constitution of Mussolini's *fascio* in March 1919. These Sempre Pronti per la

Patria e per il re (Minutemen for the Fatherland and the King) were formed in February by Dino Zanetti, and on March 16, 1919, they had the first of many fights with the Socialists.[3]

The financial condition of the Nationalist press was still delicate. Shortly before the end of the war, the *Idea Nazionale* lost 15 percent of its readership when the price of paper increased. In 1919, the newspaper had a deficit of 2,613,000 lire. The following year, the paper's parent society was reorganized, with ties to the Perrone family becoming even closer. P. L. Parisi, a brother-in-law of Pio Perrone, represented the family interests on the board of directors of the Società Editrice dell'*Idea Nazionale* (Editorial Society of the *Idea Nazionale*). The Parisi bank participated in the reorganization of the company, and Alfredo Rocco, rather than Corradini, became the dominant figure. Rocco also became a shareholder in the Ansaldo financial empire. Thus, by June 1920, the Perrone group had almost complete financial control of the *Idea Nazionale*. The background to the reorganization can be reconstructed from a report to Giovanni Giolitti. In February 1920, the old society, which had been organized by Corradini in 1914, collapsed under the huge deficit. The next month Alfredo Rocco acquired the stock of the bankrupt company with a loan from the Perrones and formed a new company. Stock in the venture was divided as follows: 300 shares to Rocco, 1,500 to the Nationalist deputy F. S. D'Alaya, 600 to Avv. Giorgio Ghigi of Bologna (a lawyer involved with large agricultural interests in the Emilia), 600 to Domenico Vannisanti of Rome. Vannisanti, an official of the Parisi banking interests, represented Parisi and Perrone. The interpenetration between the Nationalists and the Parisi-Perrone interests went even further. Vannisanti also represented the Parisi interest in the Uranio Chemical company, which had Luigi Federzoni as a member of the directing council. Rocco, in possession of 100 shares of Ansaldo, was able to nominate one of the members of the administrative council at the annual stockholders' meeting. In addition, the Perrone loan came through E. V. Parodi and the Parisi bank. Parodi, closely connected with the Perrones, was secretary of the National Federation of Ligurian

Shipbuilders and was involved in several banks, including the Credito Italiano and the Banca Italiana di Sconto (with the Perrones). He had been one of the early backers of the Nationalists.[4]

Apart from the reorganization of the *Idea Nazionale,* several other Nationalist newspapers began publication. In 1919, regional papers appeared in Turin (*La Riscossa Nazionale*), Milan (*Dovere Nazionale*), Genoa (*La Polemica*), Naples (*Volere d'Italia*), Bari (*L'Adriatico*), Palermo (*Fiamma Nazionale*), Fiume (*La Vedetta d'Italia*), and Perugia (*La Voce dell'Umbria*). Perhaps the most important of these ventures was the publication of *Politica* by Alfredo Rocco and Francesco Coppola, which remained for more than twenty years the chief theoretical journal of the Nationalist movement.[5]

Organizational and ideological problems merged in April 1919 at the second congress of Rome, called to reorganize the party after the war and to work out a new program for the postwar period. Shortly before the congress, Alfredo Rocco and Francesco Coppola set the main themes of the association's program in a "Manifesto," published in the *Politica*. The great issue of the day was the restoration of the state and bourgeois society. Only the government could maintain the necessary discipline, hierarchy, and order to make the general interest prevail, but the liberal state was unable to deal with man's anarchic nature by using its vast power to regulate the relationships between persons and social classes. Three things were necessary for the state to regain its authority over the citizens. First, the tremendous fear which reigned in bourgeois Italy had to be overcome. Second, the state had to regain control over its own bureaucracy by ending the strikes by government workers. The moral conviction of being part of the state had to be instilled in the bureaucracy. In his report to the congress of Rome, Corradini stated the third task: the need to strengthen the industrial class in order to balance the power of the socialist unions. Only in this way could class collaboration become a reality.[6]

The Nationalists were convinced that force was the only answer, and they sought to convince the bourgeoisie. For all their idolatry of the state, neither Rocco nor Corradini really believed that the state could, in the short run, recover its authority. They were aware that mass participation had changed the structure of politics. Rocco stressed that there were only three forces capable of organizing the electorate: Socialists, Catholics, or the government itself. Elections were simply questions of technique, but the government seemed incapable of meeting the challenge: "The liberal state is absolutely unprepared to be the coordinating and propelling organ of the vital forces of production."[7]

The Nationalist congress of Rome and Rocco's writings of early 1919 set forth the basis for an alternative regime. Corradini's speech to the congress enunciated the outlines of the problem. He demanded that the class struggle be resolved in a unitary and organic system of class collaboration in order to move ahead with the vital task of increasing production. In place of the unions, he called for a series of syndical organizations, totally free from the Socialist party, to represent the true interests of the economic categories. The end result would be direct representation of industrialists and workers through a system of councils and parliaments which would take the place of the old Chamber of Deputies.[8]

Rocco further refined this concept of "national syndicalism." Only by unity could Italy conquer the resources which she lacked. A poor nation could not afford to disperse its energies in internal struggle. Modern technology demanded an organic system whose highest expression was the professional syndicate: "This is the era of syndicates. The isolated individual, the amorphous and inorganic masses of individuals, which still dominate our political life, are nothing." The Nationalists had to encourage the creation of these syndical organizations as substitutes for proletarian unions. The evolution of the system would be toward a complete corporative structure, called integral syndicalism, in which the professional organizations of workers and owners would meet. The new system would do away with both the existing chamber and Senate in favor of bodies representing professions, communes, and various other regional and functional groups. Rocco defended the broad application of the corporative principle as the basis for a hierarchical and socially disciplined state. He pointed out that the system could give more representation in the state to industry and agriculture. His crucial change, however, would make the unions and professional syndicates instruments of the state through legal recognition and supervision. These bodies would be given the right to make legally binding contracts, a right which they had never received from the liberal state.[9] As he put it in an article in *Politica,* industrial concentration and large-scale unionization were the wave of the future. Only in a corporative state could these changes be controlled and disciplined by the state. Under the liberal regime the unions had gotten out of hand, but Rocco understood that the solution was far more complicated than mere suppression of worker organizations: "It is necessary . . . to proclaim obligatory membership and . . . to place them resolutely under the control of the state, defining with precision their functions."[10]

The Nationalist Association set for itself the goal of encouraging militant employer organizations to combat the proletariat. The *Idea Nazionale* gave ample coverage to organizational activity on the part of industrialists. The paper reported with approval Dante Ferraris's proposal at the meeting of the Associazione fra le Società Italiane per Azioni for a cohesive organization of producers. Mario Lombardi of the ANI was among the promoters of a series of meetings between industrialists in Bergamo, Milan, and Genoa in early 1919. These meetings, held to counteract the socialist offensive, allowed Lombardi to press for a national organization of the industrial class which would create a new framework for relations between workers and management. This proposal, like that urging the landowners to form a single national organization, was enthusiastically welcomed by the *Idea Nazionale*.[11]

Furthermore, the *Idea Nazionale* called on the citizens to defend themselves against strikes. If the state was incapable of protecting their interests, the people were justified in taking matters into their own hands. Just as during the Red Week of 1914, the Nationalists were among the first to act. Even before the formal organization of Mussolini's Fascists in Milan in March 1919, the Nationalists formed their own squads in February 1919 and clashed with the socialists of

Bologna in March. In Rome, on April 10, 1919, veterans, influenced by the Nationalists, organized a protest against a general strike. The event unfolded in a way which was tragically repeated throughout Italy in the following years. The socialists proclaimed a demonstration of solidarity with Soviet Russia and revolutionary Berlin. When the police banned it, the socialists called for a general strike. The government then prohibited all demonstrations and moved in troops. On the day of the strike, the police broke up a socialist demonstration, but the Nationalists, who had urged defiance of the strike, managed to stage a parade which ended in a rally and a speech by Federzoni. In this small way, the futility of the socialist tactics and the ability of the rightists to defy the law revealed a Left which did not know how to use its power and a Right which could retaliate under the guise of legality.[12]

Much more serious than the events in Rome was the destruction of the *Avanti*'s presses in Milan on April 15, 1919, by Mussolini's followers and the veterans. This action won the wholehearted support of the *Idea Nazionale*, which argued the distinction between "patriotic" and "revolutionary" illegality. It attacked the government for threatening to punish those guilty of sacking the Socialist paper.[13]

Although in 1919 the Nationalists were solidly on the Right and Mussolini was still nominally a man of the Left, common hatreds brought them together. The first meeting of the *fascio di combattimento*, in Milan on March 23, 1919, was covered for the *Idea Nazionale* by Orazio Pedrazzi. Pedrazzi reserved judgment on the radical and republican tinge to the Fascist movement, but he was quite sure that it would be important in the anti-Bolshevik struggle because of its mission "to channel the revolutionary forces economically and politically into the national camp." Shortly after the formation of the first *fascio*, the young Nationalists of Bologna invited Mussolini to speak before their group. The Neapolitan *fascio* had its first meeting in the local headquarters of the Nationalist Association, and the Nationalists tried unsuccessfully to turn the Fascist movement in Naples into an exclusively anti-Bolshevik front for the ANI. Despite these early attempts at cooption, fascism and nationalism developed separately until late 1920, when it became clear to the Nationalists that fascism was their only alternative on the Right.[14]

In 1919, the Nationalists placed more stock in their ties to the veterans and the *arditi* (former members of special combat forces) than in the still obscure and poorly organized Fascist movement. When the *Avanti* was sacked, the *Idea Nazionale* singled out the *arditi* for special mention as the avant-garde which broke the myth of Socialist invincibility. After an assault on the labor chamber of Bologna on June 15, 1919, the Nationalist Sempre Pronti joined the *arditi,* and the *Idea Nazionale* openly defended this sort of violence: "We do not at all deplore these incidents because we do not share the opinion of old-style liberalism that passive neutrality of the citizens before the assault of the subversives on the state is the best one can do—or not do— . . . We believe . . . that it is the duty of the citizens to react." Although they acted to support the violence of the *arditi* and veterans' organizations in 1919 and 1920, neither the large veterans' associations nor the *arditi* movement became the mass base which the Nationalists sought for their reactionary politics.[15]

THE NATIONALISTS AS MYTH MAKERS: THE MUTILATED VICTORY

In early 1919 the major preoccupations of the Nationalists involved the Versailles Conference and the Italian peace proposals. The "London Pact plus Fiume" became a sort of dogma which could in no way be modified by the use of the nationality principle in favor of Yugoslavia. The Nationalists dismissed the wartime Pact of Rome as merely a means to pressure the Italian government into a more active policy on the future status of the Austro-Hungarian Empire. The specific territorial demands advanced by the Nationalists conflicted with ethnic rights of Germans and Slavs on several points: the northern border of Italy to the Brenner pass; the annexation of Fiume and Dalmatia; total military and commercial domination of the Adriatic Sea, with provision for some commercial outlets for the Yugoslavs; and a more active policy of occupation of strategic points in the Austrian Empire as bargaining counters. The association urged the annexation of part of Asia Minor and an equal share in Germany's rail concessions in the Middle East. In Africa, the Nationalists called for border rectifications in favor of Libya on the part of Egypt, expansion in the Red Sea area, and a series of commercial and economic advantages, such as easier access to raw materials and outlets for Italian goods. This program was no more unreasonable than the nationalist programs of the other countries. Its essential weaknesses were the attempt to keep up with stronger imperialist powers without regard for diplomatic realities and its total neglect, even for cosmetic purposes, of the nationality principle and of alternative possibilities for gain based on cooperation with the Slavs. As a corollary to their rejection of any rights for the Slavic majority in Istria and Dalmatia, the *Idea Nazionale*'s editors rejected the right of the great powers to interfere by arbitration or in any other way with Italy's territorial demands. If necessary, they felt that Italy would have to find a government prepared to act alone to annex the territories in question. This position of total intransigence worked for the creation of two myths: that of the "mutilated victory" and that of the renunciation of the fruits of victory by successive weak governments.[16]

Given these positions, there was inevitably going to be a conflict with Wilson. During the last year of the war, the Nationalists were lavish in their praise of the American president. The rupture came first with Leonida Bissolati, Italy's leading advocate of a peace of reconciliation. Bissolati's growing disagreement with Sonnino and his failure to draw Orlando clearly to his peace program led the democratic leader to resign from the government at the end of December 1918. Although critical of Bissolati, the Nationalists tried to continue their policy of minimizing differences by declaring it a personal affair and noting that Ivanoe Bonomi, another Social Democrat, entered the cabinet. Nevertheless, this dispute could not be ignored. The wartime Fascio Parlamentare of democrats and conservatives was too hetereogeneous to survive once the war ended. The Nationalists, who had hoped to use the various *fasci* which had sprung up during the war, were forced to adjust their plans. Bissolati's very critical interview in the London *Morning Post* made it impossible for the Fascio Parlamentare to be represented at his major address at La Scala in Milan in January 1919. When Mussolini disrupted the speech, the *Idea Nazionale* headlined the event: "Milan Stops Bissolati from Speaking against the Sacred Rights of Italy."[17]

By the time the peace conference opened, the lines were sharply drawn between those who favored and those who opposed a peace of reconciliation with the Slavs. With the prominent Wilsonians out of the government, the Nationalist attack shifted to the program of the American president. They adamantly rejected Wilson's idea of equality of states in any future security organization. A new international order of collective security without Germany and Russia was absurd. As neither of those two powers could be included, the only solution was a coalition of the victorious Great Powers. In the Nationalist view, the real agenda of the Paris conference had to deal with the practical aspects of political and economic cooperation among the victors.[18]

During the April crisis, when Wilson foolishly appealed to Italian public opinion over the heads of the government, the Nationalists fully exploited the withdrawal of the Italian delegation. The *Idea Nazionale* called for independent action on the part of Italy: "The truth is this: Italy has been alone in war and is alone in peace. Alone she conquered, alone she will win her peace." In article after article the myth of a "mutilated victory" was fashioned, along with its corollary that a strong government could act alone in defiance of the allies. When Orlando and Sonnino returned from Paris, the *Idea Nazionale* was vocal in its support. The Roman group of the ANI called on its members to meet the train to welcome the delegation back. On April 28, the paper reported on a meeting at the Augusteo Theater in Rome to whip up support. Representatives of the Nationalist Association, the Naval League, the Dante Alighieri Society, the *arditi*, the futurists, and various Tyrolian and Dalmatian organizations attended, and Corradini gave the major address. The Roman group of the ANI then passed a motion supporting annexation of the Brenner frontier, all of Venezia Giulia, Fiume, and Dalmatia.[19]

After the withdrawal of the Italian delegation, the Nationalists demanded further resolute action from the government, something spectacular like the unilateral annexation of Fiume, but Orlando had no plans for any such rupture with the allies. Gradually the weakness of the Italian position began to dawn on all concerned. It became apparent that Italy had been isolated. The *Idea Nazionale* charged that Italy was formally excluded from the camp of the victors: "Our isolation thus formalizes our position of the conquered among the victors."[20] The thesis of the "mutilated victory" was totally vindicated: "After the prostration of Germany it seems that the conference had no other aim than to annul Italy's victory. The Italian victory politically no longer exists. . . . It had already been transformed into a defeat."[21] The humiliating return of the Italian delegation to Paris allowed the other Nationalist myth to operate. The ineptitude of the government had played into the hands of Wilson. Corradini argued that no government which half accepted the democratic ideology could hope to stand up for Italian rights at the conference. The only consolation was that Italy might win in the long run what she had failed to gain at the conference. The *Idea Nazionale* pointed out that Wilson and Lloyd George would soon turn away from the problem. If Italy would be patient, she could outlast her opponents. Above all, nothing should be done to compromise future rights. As for Orlando's government, it was already a dead issue. It lost its mandate when it returned to Paris empty-handed. On June 12, the *Idea Nazionale* called for Orlando's resignation, and in the Fascio Parlamentare Federzoni moved that the group withdraw its support from the government.[22]

D'Annunzio, the Nationalists, and the Seizure of Fiume

The fall of Orlando's ministry in June 1919 brought Francesco Saverio Nitti to power. Nitti, a progressive liberal with a reputation for financial expertise, seemed the perfect candidate to deal with the social and economic problems of postwar demobilization. Although the Nationalists suspected his ties to Giolitti, their judgment on his work as treasury minister during the war was substantially favorable. Unfortunately for Nitti, he inherited more than the difficult financial situation. The stalemate over the Adriatic question and the city of Fiume diverted a large part of the government's energy from its domestic mission. Even more than Orlando, Nitti suffered from the myth that only a strong government was needed to resolve the crisis with Yugoslavia.[23]

The situation in the two key border cities, Trieste and Fiume, was explosive. It was certain that Trieste would go to Italy, but the city was cut off from the Austro-Hungarian market which it had served. Moreover, the Yugoslavs made it as difficult as possible for the city in order to pressure the Italians for concessions on other issues. Trieste's industrial and commercial middle class was dissatisfied with the Italian government's failure to resolve the Dalmatian and Fiumian questions in favor of Italy. Shipping concerns feared that their city, which had been a central port under Austria, might no longer be a major factor in the Adriatic. In the hands of a hostile power, Fiume might become a serious rival. A strong coalition of political and economic forces existed to support a unilateral Italian settlement of the border issue. In fact, shipping interests, headed by Oscar Sinigaglia and the Cosulich family, provided financial backing for much of the plotting which centered on seizing Fiume for Italy.[24]

The situation in Fiume was extremely tense. Originally, under the terms of the London Pact the city had been left to Austria-Hungary. However, the collapse of the empire left the city in limbo. The Yugoslavs claimed it as their future major outlet on the Adriatic Sea. The Italians, who had earlier rejected the nationality principle, shifted ground and claimed Fiume because the city proper was largely Italian. Wilson, basing his stand on the overwhelming Slavic character of the surrounding countryside, refused to budge on Yugoslavia's right to Fiume. Its status remained deadlocked throughout the months of the peace conference. Failure to resolve the problem only increased the economic difficulties. A confused political atmosphere, weak governmental authority, and the delicate position of the British and French occupying forces vis-à-vis the Italians provided the context for the explosion.[25]

The Nationalists joined a number of patriotic organizations to force the government's hand over Fiume. The Trento-Trieste Society, whose president, the former Nationalist Giovanni Giuriati, was involved in the plotting for Fiume, allowed the society's branches in Venezia Giulia, Istria, and Dalmatia to cooperate with the Italian military and to recruit volunteers. The veterans' leader Giovanni Host Venturi organized the Fiumian Legion, and on May 21, 1919, an accord to use the Trento-Trieste Society to recruit a force to act in Fiume was formally worked out. With these plots as background and with the bitter disillusionment of those in Trieste and Fiume, who felt abandoned by the Italian government, Nationalist propaganda found fertile ground.[26]

Events moved rapidly after April 1919, when the Italian delegation left the peace conference. The Nationalists organized demonstrations in favor of unilateral annexation. Meetings were held, press and propaganda campaigns waged. Gradually the issue caught fire. Much of the credit for the success was due to Gabriele D'Annunzio, who was then closely connected with the *Idea Nazionale*. In late December 1918, he wrote Corradini about the gravity of the situation in Fiume and spoke of a violent solution to the crisis. D'Annunzio's collaboration with Albertini's *Corriere della Sera*, which had lasted throughout the war, was increasingly strained by disagreements over foreign policy.[27] Some time in early 1919, Corradini offered to open the *Idea Nazionale* to D'Annunzio, if he wished to collaborate. On February 15, the poet wrote: "I am very happy to have seen you and to have been able to speak frankly with you. I believe that nothing can separate us." In the same letter he mentioned a letter which was to be sent to Pio Perrone.[28] It should be remembered that the *Idea Nazionale* was in serious financial difficulties at the beginning of 1919 and that Corradini as the president of the old publishing company was struggling to resolve them. The addition of the war hero and poet D'Annunzio to the list of writers for the *Idea Nazionale* would have been a real coup.

Not only that, but it also promised to ease the financial problems of the paper by attracting more money from Pio Perrone and Ansaldo. By March, the relationship between D'Annunzio and the Nationalists had proceeded to the point where the poet was willing to act as intermediary between Perrone and Corradini: "I had a long talk with P. P. I don't believe one can count solidly on him for a violent action, but over our economic tragedy he gave me precious information. Moreover, he assured me that he will do all he can to consolidate the *Idea Nazionale* according to your desires. He alluded also to my collaboration as an element of greater success."[29] From March onward, the Nationalists worked closely with D'Annunzio. With other patriotic societies, they sponsored a series of lectures, ostensibly to support the Italian delegation's stand in Paris, but working more to create the image of a weak government. The *Idea Nazionale* continued to publish the poet's speeches and articles.[30]

The months of June and July were full of rumors of a possible coup d'état. The present state of documentation makes it hard to judge how far these plans went. Collaboration between the Nationalists, patriotic groups, and the military had been going on in the disputed territories since the beginning of the year. In the army there existed a group of officers who were receptive to the idea of political intervention to assure a solid military frontier. Generals Giardino and Pecori Giraldi, Admiral Thaon di Revel, and the Duca D'Aosta were most often mentioned. Aosta was a member of the ruling house of Savoy and head of the Third Army, which was strategically stationed in the Adriatic region. He was also frequently mentioned as a rightist alternative to the king, although he was seriously handicapped by political ineptitude. On the Nationalist side, the names of Federzoni and Oscar Sinigaglia cropped up. Sinigaglia had been involved in the wartime munitions committee and devoted his postwar efforts to almost full-time plotting. The aim of the coup was the establishment of a separate state under the Duca D'Aosta in Venezia Giulia, Fiume, and Dalmatia, the so-called Tre Venezie. It seems unlikely that a realist like Federzoni would seriously consider those plans since most of the important military commanders like Diaz and Badoglio were loyal to the king.[31] D'Annunzio, who was supposed to be involved in many of those plots, mentioned the rumors in a letter to Corradini, but it is hard to say whether he denied involvement or simply was annoyed that word got out: "I am hearing a story of a military plot of which I am supposed to be the head! A newspaper of Florence has, it seems, published the invention with the most extraordinary particulars. From here I cannot see clearly. Here is the protest that I have sent to Florence this morning, requested by *La Nazione*!"[32]

Despite the Nationalists' denials, too many references to a plot exist to dismiss them out-of-hand. Moreover, there is evidence that the Nationalists sought to neutralize the army in case of right-wing demonstrations. An interior ministry report stated that several meetings, which many officers attended, had been held in the offices of the *Idea Nazionale*. Special propaganda was designed for the troops so that, in case of demonstrations on the part of officers in uniform, troops charged with maintaining order would not stop those officers from passing through the lines. The rumor was also spread among the troops that Nitti's government might delay demobilization to use the army for police duty. At a heavily Nationalist demonstration on June 29, with Corradini, Host Venturi, and Sinigaglia in attendance, Sinigaglia called on the *arditi* present to march on Nitti's hotel. Only the presence of troops prevented what might have been the beginning of a coup.[33]

Preparation for direct action in Fiume continued throughout the summer months, although D'Annunzio seemed to have been unsure of his own plans until almost the last minute. In two letters to Corradini, written on August 18 and 19, he expressed discouragement at the removal of Admiral Umberto Cagni from Pola and the dissolution of Aosta's Third Army. There was even some talk of making a spectacular trip by air to Tokyo. However D'Annunzio felt, Giuriati and Host Venturi continued to enroll volunteers, and Sinigaglia moved ahead with the collection of arms and supplies.[34]

Finally, on September 12, the infection burst. D'Annunzio decided to lead the expedition which seized Fiume. The foreign troops offered little resistance. England and France looked to Italy to solve the problem. Nitti looked to his army, hesitated, and did nothing. It was almost inevitable that in a land blinded by rhetoric, the one-eyed poet D'Annunzio would become king.[35]

The Nationalist role in the financing and organization of the "March on Fiume" was important. Money for the venture came from men close to the ANI like Sinigaglia. It also seems certain that the real Nationalist aim was not Fiume but the fall of Nitti's government. Filippo Turati mentioned a strange offer by Sinigaglia to withdraw from Fiume in return for a Socialist vote against the government. However, Nitti, after the first shock, maneuvered ably to contain the damage. His foreign minister Tittoni met with Giolitti, Salandra, Turati, and Orlando on ways to reorganize the government, but only Salandra accepted the idea of giving way to force. By means of a crown council on September 24, Nitti managed to bind all parties, including the ANI, to his policy of continued negotiations with the allies, rather than outright annexation.[36]

From September to December 1919, when their influence began to wane, the Nationalists sought to obtain maximum benefit from the Fiume expedition and gave D'Annunzio their wholehearted support. The *Idea Nazionale* organized meetings and fund-raising efforts on the poet's behalf. The paper also published a list of prominent Nationalists who were actively involved with D'Annunzio: Massimo Rava of Turin; Orazio Pedrazzi, a journalist for the *Gazzatta del Popolo* of Turin; Captain Umberto Gaglione of La Spezia; and Dino Zanetti of Bologna, who was singled out by the prefects of Bologna, Ancona, and Trieste as an extremely active recruiter. In their activities, the Nationalists made no secret of their desire to use D'Annunzio's expedition to Fiume as a lever to pry concessions from the allies and to topple Nitti. They argued that Nitti's failure to use the Fiume occupation in his discussions with the allies proved his ineptitude. The pro-Nationalist Fiumian paper, *La Vedetta d'Italia,* took the position that no negotiations were possible as long as Nitti held office.[37]

The month of October was filled with renewed rumors of a coup. There were reports from the prefects of an invasion along the Adriatic coast and disruptions during the electoral campaign of November 1919. It is certain that the Nationalists were deeply implicated. They approached D'Annunzio's second-in-command, Giuriati, with the idea of a march on Rome. On October 9, 1919, Corradini and Piero Foscari arrived in Fiume with a proposal to extend the venture to Venezia Giulia and then to Rome. They told Giuriati that they came in the name of other, unnamed, friends, who felt that the time was right, that an entire brigade of infantry would come to the aid of the revolt, and that the carabinieri would also side against Nitti. Giuriati remained unimpressed by the evidence. In his view, public opinion was unprepared, the logistics of the march on Rome would give Nitti too much time to prepare countermeasures, and no overall plan existed should the coup succeed. Shortly after this visit, Alfredo Rocco and Francesco Coppola arrived in Fiume to urge D'Annunzio to move on Trieste in order to forestall general elections. They argued vainly that by moving on that nearby city the situation in Rome would crumble.[38]

The failure of attempts to spread the insurrection led the Nationalists to use their remaining influence to liquidate the venture on terms favorable to the Right. Foscari, for one, feared the negative effects on the Dalmatian cause if Fiume dragged on too long. Moreover, D'Annunzio was too unstable and ideologically unreliable for the Nationalists' taste. Throughout November and December, they sought a conservative solution for the crisis by direct negotiations with the hated Nitti. One of the earliest intermediaries between the poet and the government was the Nationalist journalist Orazio Pedrazzi, who was also press officer for the Fiumian command. On October 29, Pedrazzi returned from a trip to Paris to announce that he had discussed with Tittoni a proposal involving Italian rejection of the American-drawn frontier with Yugoslavia, adherence to the London Pact for Dalmatia, and no pressure to force D'Annunzio out of Fiume. What seemed to be the basis for the beginning of negotiations broke down under D'Annunzio's stubbornness, but increasing Nationalist impatience was apparent in Pedrazzi's article in the *Vedetta d'Italia* asking D'Annunzio to find a way out for the Italian delegation in Paris.[39]

The next effort at a peaceful settlement was more important. Oscar Sinigaglia made contact with Carlo Sforza of the Foreign Ministry on November 13 to propose that the government declare that it would indefinitely hold to the armistice line between Italy and Yugoslavia in lieu of an acceptable final frontier. On November 21, Sinigaglia, with Giovanni Giuriati and Giovanni Preziosi, left Fiume for Rome, where they met with Sforza and another official, Francesco Salata. In these negotiations, which lasted from November 22 to 24, the sticking point was the government's insistence that D'Annunzio abandon Fiume. Then on November 26, Sinigaglia reduced his terms. He wrote that, given the gravity of the situation, he and his friends would leave aside all considerations of internal politics in order to offer a sort of spontaneous collaboration to the government. The terms which he proposed included official recognition of Fiume's desire to be annexed by Italy, a promise by the government to maintain the status quo in Fiume and Dalmatia, and financial aid for the city, whose final fate would await negotiations with the allies in Paris. Discussions continued in early December. Finally, on December 6, Sinigaglia and Preziosi were again in Rome for a meeting with Sforza, and an accord was reached two days later.[40]

At this point, Badoglio, commander of the military region around the frontier, took over for the government. Between December 13 and 18, it seemed likely that a settlement would be reached. The pro-Nationalist *Vedetta d'Italia*, reflecting the economic concerns of the isolated city, urged acceptance of the compromise. However, D'Annunzio was unable or unwilling to control the extremists in Fiume. The referendum on the proposals was stopped by force on December 18. Foscari made a last-minute effort to save the situation. Although the Nationalist deputy had been defeated in the November elections, his connections in both Fiume and Rome were good. He acted as an intermediary between General Caviglia, who succeeded Badoglio, and the forces of D'Annunzio but had no more success than earlier negotiators. To their discredit, none of the Nationalists involved in these negotiations dared destroy the myth surrounding D'Annunzio. For political reasons they refused to recognize the government's willingness to seek a peaceful solution. Nitti was and remained the scapegoat.[41]

The Elections of November 1919

Among the factors which forced the Nationalists to reconsider their position of total support for D'Annunzio was the national election of November 1919. Elections in Italy were overdue for a parliament whose membership had not been renewed since 1913. Conservative Italy was on the defensive and lived in constant fear of revolution. The Nationalists looked on the elections with pessimism, the more so since it was Nitti who controlled the electoral machinery. The ANI's leadership did hope to pick up a percentage of the declining liberal vote, however. As the elections drew near, the Nationalist strategy was to work for conservative alliances against the socialists. Almost everywhere this was an uphill struggle. Not only did the wartime division between interventionists and neutralists continue, but also the interventionist front itself had split on the peace issue. Further complicating matters was the electoral influence of Nitti's government, which the Nationalists opposed, but which commanded the loyalties of many centrist liberals. Thus, in Milan, the old interventionist front split into a right and left grouping. In Rome, a large liberal coalition could only be constructed at the expense of neutrality toward the government. Federzoni refused to pay this price, and the anti-Nitti conservatives fielded an independent list. In most cases, the executive junta simply forbade electoral alliances with former neutralists. The ANI presented candidates in Rome, Turin, Milan, Genoa, Ferrara, Venice, Ravenna, Ancona, Naples, Terano, Palermo, and Catania. Significantly, no agreement was reached for a whole list of important cities including Alessandria, Novara,

Brescia, Como, Bergamo, Cremona, Treviso, Verona, Florence, Pisa, Parma, Siena, Perugia, Aquila, Siracusa, Trapani, and Sassari. The failure to form unified bourgeois blocs was disastrous. The only consolation was that Federzoni, still popular in Rome, headed the National Alliance list and was elected. Elsewhere most of the Nationalists were defeated. The *Idea Nazionale* bitterly attacked the liberal parliamentary leaders for abandoning their position before the socialist onslaught.[42]

The new Chamber of Deputies, in which the Socialists and Catholics together formed a majority, turned a page in the political history of Italy. The *Idea Nazionale*'s lead editorial, "The Forty Percent Chamber," argued that the elections were a victory for organization over the old electoral methods. Putting matters in the best light, the paper expressed confidence that the Socialists would lose some of their strength because of divided leadership and that the Catholics might join the forces of order, if only the conservatives could rally their troops. In the postelectoral climate of 1919, that seemed like mere whistling in the dark.[43]

Seven

Italian Nationalism and Giolitti: The Failure of Liberal Restoration

Giolitti's Return: From Honeymoon to Divorce

Nitti's fall in June 1920 brought Giovanni Giolitti back to power after an absence of almost seven years. Initially, his return symbolized the end of the wartime divisions between neutralists and interventionists. More important, under Giolitti the Socialist surge lost momentum and the Fascists achieved their first electoral successes. In all, the period of Giolitti's government from June 1920 to June 1921 marked a watershed between the postwar era and the Fascist march to power. Certain problems from the war, such as Fiume, were liquidated. Old divisions were replaced by new ones as the powerful coalition behind fascism began to form. The conservatives, who were on the defensive when Giolitti came to power, recovered the initiative by the end of 1920. Curiously enough, Giolitti, the shrewdest and most forceful politician of liberal Italy, allowed the mechanism of the state to slip from his grasp.

Looking back, perhaps the surprising thing about the Piedmontese statesman's return to power was the great consensus behind it. There was an almost universal longing on the part of the bourgeoisie for firm government. Alberto Bergamini, whose *Giornale d'Italia* reflected the views of Giolitti's rival, Salandra, promised to support the government if it would work for the integral application of the London Pact. Luigi Albertini of the *Corriere della Sera*, the most prominent supporter of reconciliation with Yugoslavia, was equally well disposed toward a government which he hoped would carry on negotiations with the allies and bring internal peace. His only reservation was that the government counter the Nationalist threat. Yet the same Nationalists, whose propaganda the government was supposed to fight, also jumped on the bandwagon. They had taken an extreme anti-Giolittian position for most of their history, especially during the war. After 1918, the Nationalists had damned Nitti simply by lumping him with the archenemy Giolitti. As late as March 1920, the Nationalists still called Giolitti the man of a second-rate foreign policy and the great corrupter of domestic political life.[1]

This attitude began to change when it became apparent that there was no better choice in the offing than Giolitti. After canvassing the leadership of the Popular party and the Social Reformist Bonomi, the *Idea Nazionale* reluctantly began to reconcile itself to the inevitable. The first signs of a shift came in June, during the formation of the new government. Not only was the usual hostility missing, but there was also a note of optimism. The paper set forth a positive program on which it would back the government: restoration of order in public services, with limitations on the right to strike; renegotiation of the border question; and a policy of industrial reconstruction: "The government can and must demand from the productive bourgeoisie all the cooperation which it can give for the salvation of the state, but the government must offer the means for the bourgeoisie to carry out its function in economic development and expansion. The government must know how to fulfill the first of its duties: to insure order."[2]

The change in attitude was so striking that the *Idea Nazionale* was forced to respond to charges of inconsistency from the *Corriere della Sera*. The Nationalists answered that after Nitti any change would be for the better. Giolitti's government had to be given a chance to find an Italian solution to the Adriatic problem. The paper emphatically denied rumors of disagreements in the ANI over the new line, although it was precisely at that moment that Corradini left the paper and the new publishing company was formed. The *Idea Nazionale* pointed out, however, that Corradini attended the meeting of the central committee which unanimously approved the new policy toward the government.[3]

The new cordiality between the association and its old antagonist went to strange lengths. There was even a curious word of praise for Giolitti's honesty in refusing to court the interventionists. Yet most of all, the new mood reflected the Nationalists' confidence that Giolitti could restore the solidity of the constitutional bloc in a way that Nitti never could. The Nationalists also hoped that Giolitti would begin to renegotiate the whole Adriatic settlement. Perhaps the earlier contacts between Sinigaglia, Giuriati, and Carlo Sforza, Giolitti's foreign minister, encouraged such hopes. At any rate, Corrado Zoli, a reporter on the *Idea Nazionale* and an undersecretary of state in the Fiume government, presented a memorandum to that effect to Luigi Ambrosini, who later was press officer in Giolitti's government. Zoli urged that Giolitti begin negotiations with Fiume for a modus vivendi. With goodwill on both sides, he considered it likely that a settlement could be reached.[4]

By the middle of the summer, however, the honeymoon on foreign policy was over. The Nationalists had wanted Giolitti to act decisively to reverse Italian concessions to Greece in Albania and Asia Minor, which Nitti and Tittoni had made earlier by sharing influence in Albania and by leaving Smyrna to Greece. Attilio Tamaro, a frequent contributor to *Politica* on foreign policy questions, demanded a reappraisal of existing policies and even argued for a frankly anti-Versailles policy which would isolate Yugoslavia by a series of accords with Austria, Hungary, Bulgaria, and Rumania. It soon became clear that neither Giolitti nor Sforza would do any such thing. Coppola, Tamaro, and Rocco began to attack what they saw as new government concessions to Greeks and Slavs.[5]

The complete rupture came over Fiume. Sforza worked for a negotiated settlement with the Yugoslavs based on the division of the disputed territory around Fiume and the creation of a free state for the city itself. In Dalmatia, he was prepared to renounce the balance of the coast in exchange for Zara and some offshore islands. It was a reasonable settlement, which ended the abnormal situation for all concerned. This policy, formalized in the Rapallo Treaty on November 12, 1920, was violently criticized by the Nationalists, who rejected any negotiations which implied giving up any part of Fiume or Dalmatia. As their campaign against Sforza gained in intensity, discussions for a coup were held in the headquarters of the ANI during the month of October. Forges Davanzati acted as a link between the plotters in Rome and in Fiume, where Corrado Zoli was the Nationalist agent. According to Rocco's later statement, these plans were relatively far advanced when the Rapallo accords were signed and the whole scheme collapsed. Although the Nationalists denied the existence of a plot, they were widely suspected of being involved. In a letter to Albertini, Giovanni Amendola noted that Giolitti was quite confident that he could handle a revolt by simply dissolving any regiments or even a whole army, if necessary. When challenged on this drastic measure, which ran the risk of opening the door to revolution, Giolitti answered that the Nationalists might consider that danger as well.[6]

The Rapallo accords had an interesting effect on relations between the Nationalists and the Fascists. Giolitti had initially put together a broad coalition supporting his government. The Nationalists dropped out fairly rapidly, but Mussolini and Giolitti remained bound in a de facto alliance. Giolitti hoped to disarm part of the vocal opposition to a settlement in Fiume, while Mussolini saw an enormous advantage in eliminating D'Annunzio as potential leader of the antiregime forces. Consequently, Mussolini argued that opposition to Rapallo was tied to the outdated positions of 1918 and 1919. He favored the treaty as an intelligent response to new conditions. (He later followed the same liberal policy in working out an accord with the Yugoslavs.) No such practical or theoretical advantages existed for the Nationalists. They preferred D'Annunzio in Fiume to a settlement which "renounced" any part of the victory. Their arguments against Rapallo reverted to the old thesis that negotiations by a weak, incompetent government lost the fruits of the victory. In the chamber, Federzoni contended that Yugoslavia had already been isolated diplomatically and that Italy might have had a settlement on her own terms had she not lost patience. He felt that Rapallo would have a negative effect on any anti-Versailles alliance system which Italy might construct in eastern Europe. Singling out Mussolini's support for Giolitti, the *Idea Nazionale* noted that such actions only underscored the consistency of the Nationalist program. It pointedly remarked that there were many in the Fascist movement who did not support the *Popolo d'Italia* on that question, a tactic used later with great effect.[7]

After the signing of the Rapallo accords, the Nationalists devoted their energies to sabotaging the execution of the pact. Forges Davanzati urged D'Annunzio to resist any solution which would create a neutral state in Fiume. Federzoni took part in a parliamentary mission to Fiume on December 5, and on his return to Italy he urged that the government not act against the city. These efforts were in vain, however, for on December 24 Giolitti ordered the army to drive D'Annunzio from Fiume. The poet's great drama came to an inglorious close.[8]

The Red and the Black: The Beginning of the Fascist Reaction

The rupture over foreign policy was only one of the things which destroyed the consensus behind Giolitti's last government. Throughout the first half of 1920, tension had been increasing in the factories and in rural Italy. In September 1920, the Metalworkers Union (Fiom) capped a period of agitation for recognition of its factory commissions by calling a strike. The proposed strike was really more of a defensive action, prompted by fear of a lockout. The workers decided on an unusual tactic. Rather than walk out, which might have been welcomed by the owners, the workers occupied the factories. Although he was under great pressure from the conservatives, Giolitti refused to bring in troops. Negotiations were resumed under government direction, and the settlement granted the workers a limited victory. In normal times

Giolitti might have been hailed as a wise leader, but those were far from normal times. Polarization had gone so far that there was simply very little middle ground. If a few of the more enlightened industrialists understood Giolitti's policy, a substantial part of the bourgeoisie was deeply offended by his failure to defend the rights of property.[9]

The Nationalists responded to the growing impatience of propertied Italy. Talk of restructuring industrial relations through national syndicalism, which had been so prominent in the first congress of the ANI, disappeared in the second, held in April 1920. Government controls on the right to strike, especially in public services, became a major demand of the Nationalists. Support for Giolitti's ministry had been predicated on the hope that the government would move decisively in that area. Needless to say, Giolitti's position during the factory occupation disappointed the Nationalists. The "old Giolitti" had returned to subvert the state: "the intervention of Giolitti is the confession of a real abdication of the state and of an incapacity to govern. . . . Thus, does the generation of Adua attempt to strangle the victory."[10]

The verbal violence involved in the reaction to the strike wave was frightening. Hysterically, the *Idea Nazionale* headlined its appeal to the nation: "Italy in the throes of Anarchist Violence." An editorial of the day hailed a Fascist attack on the Socialist paper of Trieste, *Il Lavoratore*: "The veterans must voluntarily, *on their own initiative,* deal with the new enemy which stabs the nation in the back. . . . The example of the veterans of Trieste must be immediately copied in the whole country."[11] By autumn 1920, Italy teetered on the brink of civil war. The spark which set off the conflagration came after the municipal elections of November 1920. During the electoral campaign the Nationalists drew the lines as sharply as possible. Not to stand with the Right was to side with the socialists. Wherever possible, they urged the formation of antisocialist coalitions, such as that in Rome, where the "National Concentration" list extended from the Radical to the Nationalist party and had the support of democratic papers like *Epoca, Il Messaggero,* and *Il Tempo,* as well as the conservative *Tribuna, Il Giornale d'Italia,* and the *Idea Nazionale.*

On balance, the local elections marked a slight resurgence of the Right. Conservative coalitions emerged victorious in Naples, Rome, Bari, Palermo, Florence, Turin, Pisa, and Genoa and almost succeeded in Milan. The Right did not crack the "Red Belt" of the Emilia Romagna, nor did the elections slow the Socialist and Catholic advance at the expense of liberal Italy. Of 8,327 communes, the Socialists took 2,166 and the Catholics 1,650.[12]

It was perhaps logical that the spark which set off the agrarian reaction to the Socialist advance should have taken place in Bologna. The city was at the center of the network of peasant leagues and cooperatives, which had been built up throughout the Po Valley since the end of the previous century. After the war, the peasant leagues made a concerted effort to gain a monopoly over the labor supply. A particularly bitter strike had ended with the victory of the peasants on October 25. A successive victory in the local elections of November made the inaugural ceremony of the Socialist city administration a symbol of the new order in Bologna and in the rest of Italy. This situation was precisely what the Nationalists, the Fascists, and their allies the veterans could not accept. They let it be known that they would not tolerate the red flag to be flown from the city hall. When the challenge was taken up, the resulting violence left many hurt on both sides and a right-wing assemblyman dead. The murder of the conservative became a symbol to bourgeois Italy. Succeeding days were marked by fights between the Nationalists and Fascists and their Socialist opponents. In the Chamber of Deputies, Federzoni declared that the government's refusal to restore order in Bologna forced private citizens to do it. Merely flying the red flag justified the response from the Right.[13]

The incident in Bologna was the symbolic beginning of the rural reaction to socialism. After mid-1920, the Fascist movement, the main beneficiary of the reaction, began to grow rapidly, passing from 88 *fasci*, with 20,000 members at the end of the year, to 834 *fasci*, with almost 250,000 members at the end of 1921. During this period, Fascist squads seized de facto control of much of the Po Valley, Tuscany, and Umbria. The

Nationalists were unable to match this orgy of violence, but wherever they could, they joined in. In Bologna and the surrounding area, under Zanetti's leadership, the Sempre Pronti were especially active in attacking socialist organizations.[14]

The Nationalists realized that the Socialists were not prepared for the reaction and that the tide had actually turned. Gleefully, the *Idea Nazionale* noted that the Socialists invoked the protection of the much-scorned bourgeois state: "Thus, victorious Italy in its guise of fascism and nationalism . . . broke the revolutionary menace, rendering a great service to the country." This favorable reference to fascism marked a first tentative approach to the new movement. The Nationalists still regarded fascism as merely a violent instrument, but one of increasing importance. D'Annunzio's stock was rapidly declining as he surrounded himself with radical advisers in Fiume. Both Corradini and Maraviglia expressed serious reservations over the poet's activities. Yet fascism was still something of an unknown quantity. Its radical origins and revolutionary slogans made it suspect in Nationalist circles. As a precaution, the ANI continued to develop its own Sempre Pronti, both to support and to balance the Fascist Blackshirts. Gradually, however, the Nationalists stressed the similar spiritual origins of nationalism and fascism. The *Idea Nazionale* promoted fascism to the place formerly held by the veterans' movement: "The new forces of Italy, Fascist and Nationalist, are directed against all the antinational elements which infest Italian life, against the anti-Italy wherever it is found."[15]

THE ELECTIONS OF 1921

During the election campaign of 1921, the real importance of the Fascist movement became completely apparent to the leadership of the ANI. The realization that the Fascists had ambitions beyond mere violence came as a mixed blessing, however. Mussolini became both an ally and a competitor in the struggle to seize control of the state. The election also marked the general resurgence of the Right after the defeat of 1919. Instead of entering the electoral campaign divided, the rightist parties formed solid electoral alliances, which allowed both the Nationalist Association and the Fascist movement to establish themselves as serious parliamentary forces.

Preparations for the elections took place against the background of Fascist brutality, which Giolitti dismissed as "fireworks" that would quickly burn out. Both Giolitti and the Nationalists were eager to include the Fascists in the bourgeois bloc. The *Idea Nazionale* hailed Mussolini's statement that there was no objection to the various *fasci* joining those alliances. The program of the ANI was phrased in the most general terms so as not to conflict with the residual republicanism of the Fascist platform. It was limited to a simple appeal to restore state authority by controlling Socialist excesses and ending strikes in public services.[16]

The situation in Rome was especially interesting because it was in the capital that the Nationalists exerted the maximum influence on the Fascists. Nationalist participation in the Roman *fascio* dated from its origins, a fact which bothered many members of what was still seen in 1919 as a revolutionary movement. During the electoral campaign of that year, Fascists like Enrico Rocca and Giuseppe Bottai, who had ties to the *arditi* and the futurist movements, rejected the conservative alliance and tried to bring the issue before the general assembly of the *fascio*. Even after an independent line, more in tune with national Fascist policy, prevailed in early 1920, Nationalist influence was never entirely eliminated from the Roman *fascio*, nor was that seen by Mussolini as a totally desirable result. Umberto Pasella of the Fascist central committee rejected a policy of excluding the Nationalists or any other party from the movement. Singling out the Nationalists, Pasella noted that "the Fascists are, in general, closer to the Nationalists on various parts of the program than to other parties."[17]

Despite Pasella's reassurances, tension between the ANI and the Fascists remained. Part of the problem stemmed from the fact that in Rome the Nationalists were relatively strong and the Fascists were weak and debt ridden. The most obvious sign of the local weakness of the *fascio* was that its headquarters were in space given by the ANI. At the end of 1920, the Nationalists demanded that the Fascists vacate the premises, a move which caught their tenants by surprise. However, during the electoral campaign of 1921, cooperation between Nationalists and Fascists made more progress. The "National Union" list was made up of Fascists, Nationalists, Liberals, Constitutional Democrats, a Radical, and one Liberal-Fascist. Luigi Federzoni, Alfredo Rocco, and Gelasio Caetani were the Nationalist candidates; Giuseppe Bottai and Alessandro Dudan represented the Fascists in an alliance which the *Idea Nazionale* felt revealed the spiritual affinity between the two movements.[18]

Similar alliances were made outside of Rome between the Fascists, the ANI, and the bourgeois constitutional parties in Turin, Padua, Trieste, Genoa, Bologna, the Marches, the Abruzzi, Florence, Livorno, Perugia, Palermo, Catania, Campobasso, Catanzaro, Caserta, and Siena. In Trieste, the Nationalist Fulvio Suvich ran with Francesco Giunta, the leader of the local *fascio*. In Naples, the Nationalist Raffaele Paolucci, a famous war hero and surgeon, was drafted by the Fascists for their autonomist list. He also ran as a government-backed candidate in the Abruzzi. Difficulties arose in the Nationalist camp in Milan, where the central committee of the ANI attempted to force Corradini on the local group. Dino Alfieri wanted the place for himself. In the end, neither Corradini (who also lost a chance to run in Florence) nor Alfieri ran.[19]

In the balloting the ANI had a discreet, but solid, success. Federzoni, Rocco, and Caetani were elected in Rome, D'Ayala in Catania, Suvich in Trieste, Luigi Luiggi in Genoa, Paolucci in both Naples and the Abruzzi, Mazzolini in Ancona, and Paolo Greco in Caserta. Several members of the ANI were elected as Fascists or veterans: E. M. Gray in Novara, Giuseppe Caradonna in Bari, and Giovanni Chiggiato in Venice. In Rome, where only one Fascist (Bottai) was elected, the Nationalists clearly benefited from the alliance with Mussolini's movement. The *Popolo d'Italia*, after backing Bottai and Dudan, who were the official Fascist candidates, was forced to limit its other preferences so as not to offend Federzoni. As Cesare Rossi, Mussolini's trusted lieutenant, put it, " . . . in such delicate questions, Federzoni also being a member of the *fascio*, precedents are lacking . . . "[20]

The Origins of the National Right

The elections opened the political crisis. Giolitti's calculations proved totally mistaken. He had hoped to use the Fascists to "teach" the Socialists a lesson and to make them more reasonable. In fact, the Socialists and Communists together emerged almost as strong as before and less willing to deal with Giolitti. The Catholics felt that Giolitti had been exploiting their movement, and the thirty-five supposedly docile Fascists joined the Nationalists and Salandrans on the extreme antigovernmental Right. The immediate aim of the ANI was to fuse the Right into a coherent opposition force. With some pride, the *Idea Nazionale* announced that, henceforth, the Nationalists would be numerous enough to form their own parliamentary group and called for an alliance with the Fascists and Salandra Liberals.[21]

The Nationalist proposals raised the question of the relationship between the Fascist movement and the other parties. Several of the Fascist deputies were members of the ANI. They included Gray, Luigi Siciliani, Paolucci, and Massimo Rocca. Mussolini understood the dangers of a suffocating embrace by the established conservatives. Immediately after the elections, he made his famous statement to the *Giornale d'Italia* about the republican orientation of fascism. Nothing was more calculated to infuriate the Right and to keep alive Mussolini's options on the Center-Left. Mussolini knew that fascism would lose some of its leverage if it identified totally with the extreme Right. The Nationalists, supported by the conservatives in the Fascist movement, sought just such an identification. The *Idea Nazionale* pointed out that many members of the *fasci* did not share Mussolini's equivocation on the institutional question, and the ANI's executive junta called on Nationalists in the Fascist movement to work for a monarchical policy. The fact that the Nationalists could make such a threat must have strengthened Mussolini's determination to eliminate extraneous elements from his movement. The declaration on republicanism was designed to force the Nationalists into the open. Both Paolucci and Gray opted for the ANI's parliamentary group, and Paolucci put his considerable talents to work organizing the Nationalist militia, the Sempre Pronti, as an effective paramilitary force.[22]

Only in Naples was the Nationalist overture to fascism totally rejected. Aurelio Padovani, a veteran whose radical and republican version of fascism tended to avoid contamination with the established clienteles, was opposed to Nationalist influence. Although his success in purging the *fascio* allowed Padovai two more years as head of the Neapolitan Fascist movement, it proved his undoing in the long run. The monarchists and conservatives passed over to the ANI and backed its squads in nearby Caserta. They built up a formidable rival to fascism in the towns around Naples. The Nationalist Sempre Pronti, organized by Franz Turchi, were integrated into Paolucci's militia, and the political arm of the ANI was given new life by Paolo Greco, the newly elected Nationalist deputy, who, as representative of the most brutal reaction, challenged Padovani's base in Naples from his own fief in Caserta.[23]

Despite the furor over Mussolini's republican statements, the Nationalists, Salandrans, and Fascists cooperated during the crisis of Giolitti's government in June 1921. On June 18, the *Idea Nazionale* announced the formation of an alliance between the various groups on the Right. After Giolitti's resignation on June 27, Federzoni proposed a common foreign and domestic program to increase the leverage of the Right during the crisis. On July 2, the leaders of the conservative groups met: Mussolini, Celesia, Bottai, Acerbo, and Giunta for the Fascists; Federzoni, Rocco, and Siciliani for the Nationalists; and Salandra, Ricci, Alfredo Codacci-Pisanelli, and Alfredo Petrillo for the liberal Right. The meeting resulted in agreement on policy along the lines suggested by Federzoni: revision of the Rapallo Treaty, no repression for the "national" reaction, discipline in public services, Italianization of the newly annexed regions, benefits for veterans, and aid to industrial development.[24]

The Nationalists seemed on the verge of becoming the controlling elite in the right-wing coalition. A few days after this meeting, Luigi Albertini wrote that the true leader of the Right was no longer Salandra, but rather Federzoni, who dominated even the Fascist party. Although he felt that the Right was responsible for pushing the new Bonomi government over to the Left by refusing to take part, the Nationalists were quite content with the weak, politically colorless government which succeeded Giolitti's and which was incapable of controlling the conservative and Fascist resurgence.[25]

Federzoni's optimistic calculations were rapidly upset. The bombshell came in the form of an announcement that a "Pacification Pact" had been signed between the Fascists, the Socialist party, and the General Confederation of Labor. The accord of August 2, 1921, worked out by the government and the president of the Chamber of Deputies, called for the cessation of attacks by and on all signatories. Mussolini's tactic of separating himself from the Right was greeted by howls of disapproval from both the conservatives and syndical elements within fascism, who feared that the enemy might recover once the pressure was off. The more radical Fascists rejected an attempt to come to terms with the Socialist union organization which they hoped to replace with one of their own. The reaction of the Nationalists was equally negative. The *Idea Nazionale* argued that by putting patriotic and socialist violence on the same level, the Fascists did themselves a disservice. The Nationalists then used the technique which they had threatened earlier. They offered space in the *Idea Nazionale* to the dissidents in the Fascist movement. By reducing the options of the larger Fascist movement, the Nationalists showed their determination to remain the brains of the Right coalition, while the Fascists continued to provide the brawn: "Fascism is essentially a movement of action;

nationalism is a movement, richer in experience and in political content, slower, but more secure, in its development."[26]

In mid-August, Mussolini was driven temporarily to resign as leader of the Fascist movement. The *Popolo d'Italia*'s annoyance at its conservative critics was evident from several articles in which the *Idea Nazionale* was specifically attacked for playing on the divisions in fascism. The same charge was levelled against the conservative *Giornale d'Italia*. Both the Nationalists and the Salandrans had much to gain, Mussolini noted, if the Fascist movement broke into its component parts. In the end, the outcome of the "Pacification Pact" was much less dramatic, although still favorable to the conservatives. At a meeting of the Fascist National Council on August 26–27, Mussolini was forced to abandon the pact, and a decision was made to call a congress of the movement to ratify its transformation into a political party and to draft a new program. After August there was a decided lessening of tension. In a letter to the executive commission of the Fascist movement, Mussolini admitted that of all the Roman papers only the *Idea Nazionale* and the *Giornale d'Italia* were consistently favorable to fascism. For their part, Mussolini's critics agreed that the Fascist party had to avoid the elitism of the ANI in order to form the mass base which the Nationalists lacked.[27]

The *Idea Nazionale* expressed satisfaction with the results of the Fascist congress, held in Rome on November 7, 1921. Special attention was paid to Giacomo Acerbo's report, which called for a continued alliance with the Right. Not even the transformation of fascism into a party bothered the Nationalists. At a special meeting of the association, just before the opening of the Fascist congress, Forges Davanzati minimized the impact of the decison on those who held dual membersip in both parties. In fact, the Fascists' decision to eliminate dual membership, as Massimo Rocca pointed out, had little impact on his personal position, as he resigned neither from the National Fascist party (PNF), nor from the ANI. Rocca guessed that Cesare Maria De Vecchi would not resign from the Liberal Association and that E. M. Gray would remain in the ANI, while both men continued as active fascists.[28]

The Fascist congress of Rome was another step in the movement's shift to the Right. The conservative economic and political program of the new National Fascist party closed the gap between reality and doctrine. The formal movement to the Right also led to efforts to define the relationship between fascism and nationalism. The most important overture came from a conservative Fascist, Cesare Maria De Vecchi, in an interview given to the *Idea Nazionale* on November 16, 1921. After noting his personal loyalty to the dynasty and his admiration for the Nationalists, he continued: "I cannot conceive of the relationship between fascism and nationalism in terms other than those of unity." De Vecchi was immediately answered by Federzoni, who suggested closer cooperation rather than fusion. He reversed the terms offered by De Vecchi. Rather than the Fascists absorbing nationalism, the PNF, as its program was better defined, would come closer to the ANI.[29]

As the debate continued in the *Idea Nazionale* and the *Popolo d'Italia,* it became clear that talk of fusion had been premature. Apart from De Vecchi and a dissident Fascist, Piero Marsich, no one on the Fascist side was interested in a merger. Typical in this regard was the intelligent and independent minded Giuseppe Bottai, who argued that the process of clarification going on inside of both movements made it too early to think of anything but cooperation. However, Bottai strongly criticized the idea that fascism should serve merely as the army for the Nationalist elite. Mussolini, who distrusted these pro-Nationalists, spoke only of an accord between the PNF and the other parties of the Right. This idea suited the *Idea Nazionale,* which hailed the decision of the Fascist parliamentary group to work with the Right as a victory in the creation of a solid conservative alliance. Less to the Nationalists' liking was the article by Dino Grandi, the young Fascist leader from Bologna, who argued that it was up to the Nationalists to accept the leadership of the PNF. The Nationalists were like generals without an army, who had little real possibility to change the structure of the state without the help of fascism, while the Fascists, Grandi felt, could get along very well without the Nationalists.[30]

Many of the Nationalists were no less cool to the idea of fusion at that time. They assumed that fascism was simply an outgrowth of the Nationalist movement. As Francesco Ercole, a professor at the University of Padua, put it, better to maintain independence and attempt to influence the Fascists from the outside than to subject the older Nationalist movement to the upstart Fascists.[31]

THE NATIONAL RIGHT AND FASCISM

The final months of 1921 saw the Nationalists continue their tactic of drawing the Fascists into an alliance with the traditional Right. The debate which took place between the *Idea Nazionale* and the *Popolo d'Italia,* while it showed no overwhelming enthusiasm for fusion, at least revealed that a substantial portion of both movements thought in terms of closer cooperation. Political developments continued to favor the conservative drift of the Fascist party. Bonomi's government failed either to bring about pacification by negotiation with the Fascists or to exploit the crisis within fascism which the pact provoked. Instead, the government stumbled throughout 1921. Bonomi almost fell in December, but the conservatives hesitated to topple his government while there was still hope that it might intervene to save the large Perrone-controlled Banca Italiana di Sconto. When it became clear in January 1922 that the government's action would be ineffectual, the Right, joined by both the Fascists and the Socialists, voted against the ministry.[32]

After Bonomi's resignation on February 2, 1922, the Right prepared to exact the maximum benefit from the crisis. The Fascists agreed to cooperate with the other parties on the Right to develop a common policy. The *Idea Nazionale* responded positively and urged "extreme vigilance" to see that the outcome of the crisis would be favorable. On February 4, Mussolini, Federzoni, and Riccio (Salandra's deputy) began to coordinate their efforts. In Salandra's absence, Federzoni appeared as the figure with the most parliamentary experience and prestige. The outcome of the crisis was far from certain, however. Much depended on negotiations which were held between the parties of the Center and Left. If they failed to reach an accord, the Right could no longer be ignored. As it turned out, the two major parties of the Left and Center were never even close to agreement. Internal resistance in the Catholic and Socialist parties was too great. In addition, Giolitti's return to power was vetoed by Luigi Sturzo of the Catholic party, who distrusted Giolitti personally and politically. Less serious as a left-center alternative was the emergence of Nitti as a mediator among the parties. Giolitti successfully blocked his rival in the vain hope that Sturzo's veto would be lifted on his own candidacy. When Orlando and Enrico De Nicola, the president of the Chamber of Deputies, also failed to form a government, one of Giolitti's lieutenants, Luigi Facta, took over negotiations in an effort to circumvent Catholic opposition and to hold the government for the return of his leader. Facta sought his parliamentary support on the Center-Right. Although there was some talk of a rightist government of national concentration, with the participation of both Fascists and Nationalists, Mussolini, for one, rejected any premature bid for power. Nor did the Nationalists feel the need to push for that result. It was enough to wield significant influence.[33]

Cooperation between the three right-wing parties which formed the Destra Nazionale, or National Right, continued throughout the crisis. Federzoni spoke for the three parties in rejecting Bonomi's abortive bid to form another government. Meetings were held regularly until after the formation of Facta's new ministry. On February 25, after discussions between Facta, Federzoni, De Vecchi, and Riccio, the National Right announced that it would support the new government. A sign of increased conservative influence was the successful veto of Giovanni Amendola's appointment to the War Ministry. The position went instead to Pietro Lanza di Scalea, a conservative, with close ties to the ANI. Vincenzo Riccio, at the Ministry of Public Works, was the semiofficial representative of the Destra Nazionale in the government. Although neither the Nationalists nor the Fascists participated, Federzoni was elected to the vice-presidency of the chamber, and Acerbo became one of two secretaries.[34]

The outcome of the crisis could not have been more satisfactory. Not only did the important political figures continue to neutralize one another, but also the paralysis of the Center-Left greatly increased the leverage of the Right, which was numerically smaller. Soon after the elections, an attempt was made by the conservatives to perpetuate and formalize their alliance. Salandra drafted a project for an accord between his liberal group, the Fascists, and the Nationalists. The project called for meetings between the leaders and coordination of press and propaganda campaigns. Again the conservatives pressed too hard. Although Mussolini recognized the drift to the Right, he was not willing to abandon freedom of movement for the PNF by accepting the terms of Federzoni and Salandra.[35]

Salandra himself noted the increasing strains in the Destra Nazionale after the February ministerial crisis. Disputes were common between Fascists and Nationalists, who were beginning to compete for the same electorate in the center and south of Italy. There were also signs that the Nationalist militia structure was another complicating factor. The ANI continued to build its base, often in direct competition with the Fascist squads. On November 6, 1921, Forges Davanzati proposed strengthening the national organization of the Sempre Pronti, which formally became the military arm of the ANI. Members of the local Nationalist groups were required to take part in the militia. Its aims were to provide support for the monarchy and to further the military spirit in the young. In practice, the Nationalist squads were to serve to break Socialist resistance and to man public services during strikes. At the Congress of Bologna in April 1922, Raffaele Paolucci was appointed inspector-general of the Sempre Pronti and proceeded to expand further the organizational structure. Because the Nationalist militia was completely dedicated to the monarchy and the Fascists still carried over some of their old republicanism, there was always a chance of conflict between the two groups. Paolucci recalled in his memoirs how, even in his case, the Fascists were not above using direct intimidation. At a meeting in Marina di Massa, Fascist squads, led by Renato Ricci, surrounded the hall in which Paolucci was speaking and forced him to make a speech much more favorable to the Fascists.[36]

Some of the difficulties between Fascists and Nationalists were tactical. The ANI represented only one option for Mussolini because he was convinced that the alliance with the traditionalist Right would not be enough to open the door to power. His contacts with Giolitti and other political leaders, who were increasingly vying for his participation in their governments, offered more promise. This did not mean that Mussolini was unwilling to seize an important opportunity when it arose. For instance, in June, even as he was engaging in sniping at the ANI, he made contact with Enrico Corradini. Corradini, in turn, approached the Duca D'Aosta on the possibility of engineering the king's abdication in favor of his son, with the duke as regent. Although these soundings did not produce concrete results, they might have had some influence on Victor Emmanuel in October 1922.[37]

Throughout the spring of 1922, Mussolini continued publicly to draw back from the Destra Nazionale alliance. In a speech to the National Council of the PNF on April 4, he bluntly attacked the ANI: "I am beginning strongly to distrust the professions of sympathy from the Nationalists. I do not want them to become the 'sharks' of fascism, exploiting and enriching themselves at our expense." On April 16, Mussolini again raised the question of the monarchy. The Nationalists responded by stressing that the Fascists accepted the monarchy de facto and that Mussolini seemed to be seeking argument for its own sake. The *Idea Nazionale* noted that, apart from minor questions, the Fascists were "natural allies" whose "actions coincided perfectly with ours."[38]

During this period foreign policy presented few problems. The great diplomatic event was Lloyd George's attempt to create a framework for European economic reconstruction at the Genoa conference. In his comments on the conference, Mussolini was more optimistic and constructive toward the English effort, but the Nationalists opted for a pro-French hard line. When the news of the Rapallo pact between the

Soviet Union and Germany broke on the unsuspecting delegates, differences between the Nationalists and Mussolini vanished. Both were extremely critical of Germany. Yet even more than the Fascists, the Nationalists were pursuing contradictory foreign policy aims: defense of the victory but anti-Versailles revisionism, anti-Slav policies but expansion of Italian influence in the Balkans, revision of the Mediterranean balance of power but no clear option to dependence on Britain and France. As a consequence, they tended to simplify diplomatic difficulties, only to become more disappointed at the slowness of complex negotiations.[39]

Only over Fiume was there an apparent carry over of earlier disagreements between the ANI and the PNF. The collapse of D'Annunzio's adventure and the signing of the Rapallo pact between Yugoslavia and Italy led to the establishment of an autonomous municipality under Riccardo Zanella. Although the Fascists and Nationalists attempted to disrupt the elections of 1921 in Fiume, Giolitti refused to be intimidated and insured Zanella's accession to power. Thereafter Zanella became the object of a running right-wing attack. Weak backing from Rome after Giolitti's fall undermined the Autonomist party's control and gave renewed hope to the Right that it might be able to bring Zanella down. The opportune moment came under Facta's conservative government. On March 3, the squads drove Zanella from Fiume. A machine-gun unit of the Sempre Pronti was in the vanguard of the assault. The Nationalist deputy Suvich, who immediately appeared on the scene, pressed for the appointment of a special commissioner from Rome. In his diary, Italo Balbo complained that the Nationalists seemed to want to push the Fascists aside by treating them as mere foot soldiers: "It is true, rather, that the Fascists know how to act with blind personal sacrifice and with absolute discipline, which one cannot say of the Nationalists, each of whom believes himself inspired by the Holy Spirit."[40]

Eight

The March on Rome

From Facta . . . to Facta, April–August 1922

Relations with the Fascists were very much on the minds of the delegates to the Nationalist congress in Bologna, on April 24–26, 1922. The party completed its retreat from the relatively innovative syndicalist program of 1919. Again, there was little mention of programs for massive restructuring of industry into a national syndicalist system; instead, the official reports attacked future nationalizations, state intervention in private industry, strikes in public services, political activities on the part of unions and cooperatives, and government attempts at taxation and financial reform, such as Giolitti's law for publication of stock ownership. The association pressed for the formation of a broad political alliance, extending from the Fascists to the conservative liberals and Catholics, within which the Nationalists would play a directing role. Even though it was clear that Mussolini was not willing to lend himself to this tactic, the Nationalists felt that they could not abandon it without giving up all pretense to a major political role.[1]

The Nationalists were not alone in facing serious problems in their relationship with the Fascist movement. The dilemma of how to tame the tiger was just as acute for other political factions. The constitutional liberals of the pre-World War I variety could no longer win elections against the Socialists and Catholics and so were drawn to the tactic of winning fascism's mass base. They embarked on the dangerous game of using the Fascists to save the constitutional structure. In any such competition the Nationalists had an enormous advantage over the liberal politicians because they had no stake in the existing constitutional order. The ANI sought only to maintain the social-economic structure of Italy, which the Fascists really did not menace. Thus, the Nationalists were spared the embarrassment of using Fascist illegality to preserve the legal order.[2]

To bolster their position in dealing with the Fascists, the Nationalists attempted to strengthen their ties to the industrialists and agrarians. During the spring and summer of 1922 the ANI sponsored a series of meetings among various chambers of commerce and the Confindustria (Italian Confederation of Industry). On the parliamentary level, the Nationalists gave their support to an alliance of industrial and agrarian deputies, the Alleanza Parlamentare Economica (Parliamentary Economic Alliance), which had Gino Olivetti, the secretary of the Confindustria, as its president. Gray, Luiggi (connected with Genovese shipping interests), and Arturo Marescalchi were the Nationalist participants. The positions taken by the *Idea Nazionale* were also designed to appeal to the most militant section of the bourgeoisie. The agrarian Nationalist Giorgio Ghigi of Bologna set forth a basic program for the National Right, which included a refusal to take on labor from socialist peasant leagues and an end to the privileged position of Socialist organizations in public works programs.[3]

Shortly after the formation of the Alleanza Parlamentare Economica, the Facta government fell. The ministry had been a temporary expedient from the start. When the Popular (Catholic) party decided to withdraw its support, the game was up. Sturzo judged the government a failure in its economic policy and in its efforts to pacify the country. By provoking a crisis, the Catholic leader hoped to separate the Fascists from the rest of the extreme Right, which favored the continuation of the government. Unfortunately, Sturzo failed to draw maximum benefit from the tactic by accepting responsibility for the next government. Initially, the maneuver had some success. The Nationalists and Salandra, fearing a shift to the Left in the next ministry, voted for Facta. Mussolini, who saw a perfect occasion to break with the confining alliance of the Destra Nazionale, instructed his group to support the Catholic party's no confidence measure. To eliminate any doubts over Fascist policy, Michele Bianchi, the secretary-general of the PNF, gave an interview to the *Resto del Carlino* in which he scornfully referred to the relationship between the Fascists and the Right as increasingly artificial. On July 23, the *Idea Nazionale* replied that the Destra Nazionale was the natural expression of the mood of the country. It also pointed out that fascism found success only when it moved to the Right and accepted the program of the ANI. However forceful the Nationalist response, the fact remained that the Fascists were increasingly unwilling to treat with the smaller parties of the Right as equals. Italo Balbo wrote that the Nationalists remained leaders without an army. It was especially galling to have to tolerate their intellectual arrogance.[4]

The crisis of the Facta government presented serious problems for the Right. Federzoni could do little to counter Sturzo's efforts to exclude the Destra Nazionale from any new government. Luckily for the Nationalists, there was no majority to take the place of the Facta government. The Vatican's hostility toward cooperation with the reformist Socialists and the Popular party's veto of Giolitti made a stalemate inevitable. Facta reemerged as the most inoffensive choice. His new government was, however, slightly less oriented to the Right. Massimo Soleri, an anti-Fascist Liberal, became minister of war. Giovanni Amendola, a strong opponent of fascism, continued as colonial minister, and a tough, former prefect, Paolino Taddei, took over the Interior Ministry. The Right was weakened by the split between the Fascists and the rest of the Destra Nazionale, but it continued to be represented in the government by Vincenzo Riccio, Salandra's lieutenant. It was this hybrid and fragile ministry which faced the final crisis of the liberal state.[5]

Preparations for the March on Rome

During the weeks between the beginning of August and the March on Rome at the end of October, the Nationalists worked to push both the PNF and the Facta government toward a solution which would be satisfactory to the Right.

To an extent, they could count on the sympathy of many Fascists who were little more than conservative monarchists. At the same time, the Right used its influence on Facta. Salandra advised the government that there was no choice but to come to terms with the Fascist party.[6]

At the beginning of August, the leaders of the General Confederation of Labor and of the Socialist party made a serious error. They attempted to call a strike against Fascist violence, the so-called legalitarian strike. The use of a strike to win over bourgeois opinion to the antifascist cause was ill chosen. The Fascists immediately declared that they would allow no interruption of services, and the Nationalists, sensing a chance to close ranks, rushed to support this threat. The strike, which was begun on August 1, collapsed by August 3. In Milan, Fascist squads, backed by a contingent of Sempre Pronti, stormed the city hall and attacked strikers. The *Avanti* was sacked yet another time, and Socialist resistance was swept aside in the Lombard capital. In Rome, the Nationalists attempted to persuade shopkeepers to defy the strike. With the aid of Sempre Pronti and the Nationalist worker organization, the ANI manned the city transportation system and the postal and telegraph services. In Livorno and Ancona, the same pattern repeated itself: small contingents of Nationalists joined the Fascists to force a resumption of public services. In parliament, Alfredo Rocco defended these punitive actions by arguing that the right-wing violence had the moral quality of leading the masses away from socialist demagoguery and further represented the legitimate desire of the middle class to protect its property.[7]

With the exception of Rome, the Nationalists were clearly the junior partners in the antistrike activities. They did, however, profit from the rightward shift in the country. Just by glancing at the *Idea Nazionale* at the end of August and the beginning of September, one can see that the ANI was growing rapidly. Even allowing for exaggeration, Franco Gaeta calculated that 250 new sections were founded between August and October 1922. Of these, 124 were in the center-north and 126 in the south. Paolucci estimated that the

Sempre Pronti had reached 80,000 members by 1922, with most of the strength coming from the Marches, Lazio, Piedmont, and the areas south of Rome.[8]

The growth of the ANI resulted from many factors. In some cases, the Nationalists took in members in areas where the Fascists had been weak, such as the south and the Marches. In the south, where politics had been traditionally marked by personal or family rivalries, one faction might go Fascist, while their opponents went over to the ANI. In such a situation, the association offered a refuge for conservatives, opportunists, and even socialists, who, for one reason or another, could not join the PNF. This kind of growth was bound to increase the misunderstandings between the two parties. In the south it occasionally led to violence. A good example was the situation in Taranto, where politics were somewhat murky anyway. Opposing clienteles joined the ANI and PNF. The resulting political conflict led to the death of the Nationalist secretary on September 17. When the Nationalist deputy Alfredo Misuri was sent to Taranto to work out an accord between Fascists and Nationalists, he too was attacked. Given Misuri's recent break with the Fascists and his passage over to the ANI, he was perhaps not the best emissary. Although the pro-Fascist *Giornale di Roma* blamed Misuri for provoking the incident, the *Idea Nazionale* tended to minimize it. Mussolini referred to the incident during a speech at Udine on September 20, in which he requested that the Fascists refrain from violence against allies in the national struggle. The *Idea Nazionale* pointed to the speech as a sign that fascism was abandoning its republican past.[9]

Mussolini, however, had no desire to embrace the strategy of the Destra Nazionale once more. He rejected Salandra's idea of a ministry dominated by the three leaders of the National Right. Far more interested in Giolitti's plans than in any purely conservative projects, Mussolini knew that obstacles to his seizure of power could come only from the Center and Center-Right, not from the extreme Right. There were schemes to bring Giolitti back, with or without Fascist support, and Nitti was attempting to draw D'Annunzio and

Mussolini into line behind his own candidacy. Federzoni suspected that Mussolini leaned toward a deal with Orlando.[10]

The confusion extended to relationships between Fascists and Nationalists. In Genoa, an accord for cooperation was signed between the ANI and PNF. In early October in Trento and Bolzano, the scene of the last great assault by the squads before the March on Rome, the blue-shirted Sempre Pronti participated. Still, just as in Taranto, resentment was likely to come to the fore. The Fascist paper *La Patria* complained that in Lazio (the area around Rome) anti-Fascists were using the association to conceal their activities. Shortly before the March on Rome, a conflict between local Fascists and Nationalists at Riomaggiore, near La Spezia, resulted in the death of one Nationalist and led to a bitter protest from the *Idea Nazionale.*[11]

On October 15, there was a meeting of the leaders of the Sempre Pronti from Milan, Bologna, Genoa, and Turin to decide on strategy in case the Fascists attempted a revolt. No decision seemed to have been taken at that meeting, but in a speech on the same day Federzoni set down the basic Nationalist position in favor of a national government, with no equivocation on the monarchy. Federzoni tentatively supported the Fascist call for new elections but emphasized that the real problem was to find a government capable of reforming the electoral laws to do away with proportional representation, which the Right viewed as an important factor in its decline after 1919.[12]

Politically, the Nationalists had relatively few options. They were stuck with the unattractive Salandra as their only candidate for the presidency of the council until the more-able Federzoni could build his following. Moreover, Mussolini seemed to treat Salandra's overtures as one might treat a salesman for some unwanted product. The conservative deputy Giuseppe De Capitani arranged for a meeting between Mussolini and Salandra on October 23, as the Fascist leader was passing through Rome on his way to the party congress in Naples. Federzoni had been working for such a meeting with Costanzo Ciano and De Vecchi. As it turned out, Mussolini used the occasion only to quiet his more conservative associates. The terms presented to Salandra, five ministries, including that of the interior, and Mussolini's own refusal to participate, showed that he did not want an understanding with the Right at that time.[13]

The Nationalists remained undiscouraged. During the congress of the PNF, Alfredo Rocco, who attended as a Nationalist observer, spent some time with Mussolini and returned to Rome with him on October 25. He reported on his discussions to Salandra and to Orlando. The difficulty still appeared to be that of winning over Mussolini to a Salandra-Mussolini or Salandra-Orlando-Mussolini combination. The Nationalists believed that they had made progress. According to Efrem Ferraris, a senior official at the Interior Ministry, a call was put through from the headquarters of the ANI during which the caller expressed the certainty that Facta would resign and that the Nationalists would enter the next government under Salandra.[14]

The Nationalists' hopes rested on their contacts in Rome. After Rocco reported on his talk with Mussolini to Salandra and Orlando, Salandra approached Facta to propose his own succession and to block a Giolitti-Mussolini combination. It was likely that the Fascist leadership around Mussolini saw no harm in allowing the Nationalists to push the Salandra-Orlando ministry to encourage Facta's resignation. Nevertheless, it also served the Nationalists' purposes to appear that they had Fascist backing. Both Ferraris, at the Interior Ministry, and Luigi Albertini, in Milan, were fairly certain that the Nationalists had no such support. Federzoni and Salandra did have assurances from Costanzo Ciano and Cesare Maria De Vecchi, two conservative Fascists who favored a Salandra government but who were not close to Mussolini.[15]

The March on Rome

On October 26, the crisis of the Facta government began when Salandra, accompanied by Riccio, saw the prime minister to give him the news of the Fascist mobilization and to announce Riccio's resignation from the ministry. The conservative move ended the stalemate which had become evident in the government. The cabinet had been divided between an antifascist group (Giovanni Amendola, Marcello Soleri, and Paolino Taddei) and conservatives like Vincenzo Riccio, who hoped to replace Facta with Salandra and Mussolini. Between the two groups stood Facta himself, who maneuvered ambiguously for the survival of his own ministry or for Giolitti. The Right faced the fact that time was working against the conservatives. The longer the Facta government lasted, the greater the possibility that Giolitti or one of the other liberal politicians would be able to work out a coalition with or against Mussolini. The Fascist mobilization was a godsend. The Nationalists and Salandra had no choice but to play their hand. Initially, at least, they were fortunate because none of the other major participants, except for Facta and his government, was in Rome, a fact which added greatly to the confusion during the hectic days of October 27–29. The Nationalists (except Rocco in Milan) Salandra, Facta, and his ministers were in Rome. The king was at his residence at San Rossore, near Pisa, and arrived only on the night of October 27–28. Mussolini resolutely refused to budge from Milan, where he had gone after the Fascist Congress of Naples. Giolitti was at his home in Piedmont and conducted his negotiations with Mussolini through Alfredo Lusignoli, the prefect of Milan. Thus, there was a possibility that a decisive series of moves from the capital might swing the crisis in favor of the Nationalists and Salandra. As the crisis unfolded from October 27 to October 29, the Right tried to use its position in the capital to thwart other contenders for power and to cajole Mussolini into an alliance with Salandra.

Almost immediately, Salandra and Mussolini tried to draw one another out. Mussolini called Salandra on October 27 in an effort to see if the conservative leader would accept the mandate for a new ministry. Salandra finessed by asking if Mussolini would come to Rome to be available for discussions on the formation of a rightist government. Mussolini refused to commit himself. However, as Renzo De Felice pointed out, the Nationalists and Salandra could never win at that game. Once they managed to cut out Giolitti and simultaneously refused to use force against the Fascists, Mussolini became the absolute arbiter of the situation simply by refusing to support

Salandra. Of course, the conservatives completely underestimated Mussolini's political skills, and, once they realized that he had beaten them at their own game, they frantically tried to regain their position in the new Fascist government.[16]

Publicly, the Nationalists responded favorably to the news of the Fascist military preparations, but their calculations, which certainly did not include a Fascist coup, prompted some cautionary countermeasures. Federzoni mentioned that the Sempre Pronti were mobilized on the night of October 27–28 to guard against unforeseen developments. Paolucci, the commander of the "blue shirts," agreed with Federzoni to put the militia at the disposition of the king. If Victor Emmanuel had signed the decree for martial law, the Sempre Pronti would probably have fought against the Fascists. Four thousand Nationalists had been armed by the military commander of Rome for that purpose. Paolucci also said that he had received assurances from De Vecchi, a Fascist commander of the March on Rome, that De Vecchi would not act against an order of the king.[17]

Much turned on what the king would do in the face of the Fascist threat. Victor Emmanuel had returned to Rome on the evening of October 27. During the night of October 27–28, Facta, urged on by Amendola and Taddei and with the backing of even the more conservative members of the government, who sought to use the Fascists but feared that they might run out of control, decided to present to the king a decree proclaiming martial law. Such a decree allowed the government to use troops against the Fascist insurrection. Facta visited the king during the early hours of October 28 to obtain the sovereign's consent. At 5:00 A.M., a meeting of the council of ministers was called as news of the Fascist revolt became more serious. An indication that even the extreme Right was preoccupied by the rapidity of events came when Riccio, on entering the meeting, was chided by Ferraris, who remarked that his friends were at the gate. Riccio resonded abruptly, "What friends?" and demanded stern measures against the Fascists.[18]

When the council of ministers agreed on the measures to be taken, Facta departed once more to see the king for his final consent. While Facta was in conference with the king, Federzoni and Forges Davanzati arrived at the Interior Ministry. They had been kept informed of the situation by Riccio. The exact role of the Nationalists during these hours was the subject of some controversy. To his dying day, Federzoni denied that he had played a major part. He recalled arriving with Forges at the ministry, shortly before the return of Facta. When the prime minister returned from his meeting with the king, he asked Federzoni to call Milan to make contact with Mussolini. Federzoni did so and stated that he simply reported the news of the king's refusal to sign the decree and of Facta's request that Mussolini come to Rome. Mussolini then asked Federzoni to call the Fascist command in Perugia to inform them of the news.[19]

Federzoni's version of his activities has been disputed by most other sources and, in fact, seems to have been much too modest. Forges and Federzoni did arrive at the ministry before Facta's return from seeing the king. It is likely that they already had a strong inkling that the king had refused to sign the decree. Rather than Facta, it was actually Federzoni who requested the call to Milan, and permission for the call was given by Taddei. From the transcript of Federzoni's call, subsequently published by Efrem Ferraris, it was his second of the morning, for he had already spoken with Emilio De Bono, another Fascist military leader. The call to Milan, made around 8:00 A.M., began with Federzoni explaining to Mussolini's lieutenant Aldo Finzi that the king might abdicate if the situation became worse. He reported that De Bono urged Mussolini to come to Rome and reinforced this request with his own appeal that Mussolini join the consultations in Rome to avoid the appearance of excessive pressure on the monarch. Finzi then put Mussolini on the line. Federzoni repeated the message received from De Bono, coupled with the request to come to Rome. Mussolini refused to be drawn to the capital. However, he asked that Federzoni make contact with the Perugia command.[20]

Federzoni then left the Interior Ministry and obtained an audience with the king. Shortly before 10:00 A.M., he was back at the ministry for another set of calls. The first was to Perugia, where he reached De Vecchi shortly before the Fascist commander left for Rome. De Vecchi had already spoken to General Cittadini, representing the king, who asked that the Fascist leader return to Rome for consultations on the crisis. Therefore De Vecchi already knew that the king had refused to sign the martial law decree. When Federzoni called, however, he still spoke as though the king might abdicate. It was a tactic which might have worked with De Vecchi, who was a staunch monarchist, if he had not already had assurances. De Vecchi warned Federzoni that he was being tricked, but Federzoni denied that that was the case.[21]

Around 10:00 A.M., Federzoni requested yet another call to Milan. This time he urged Mussolini to come to Rome as soon as possible. Mussolini asked if he had anything more to say. Federzoni told him that he would soon receive an invitation from the king to come to Rome. Federzoni then stated that he represented Salandra: "Look, I do not speak in my name. I am only an intermediary between you and Salandra, and I am trying to make clear the true situation here . . . I speak to you as a man of the Right must speak . . ." He went on to say that it was a pity that De Vecchi misunderstood his role.[22]

After speaking to Mussolini, Federzoni contacted Salandra, who also had been to see the king. Federzoni met with De Vecchi and Ciano and received assurances that they would support a Salandra government in which the Fascists would receive five ministries. At that point, events were proceeding according to calculation, with the exception of Mussolini's suspicious refusal to come to Rome to ratify the deal. Although the conspirators in Rome did not yet know it, Alfredo Rocco, who had traveled to Milan to deal directly with Mussolini, was aware that the vital consent from Mussolini would never come. He had already attempted to persuade the Fascist leader to accept Salandra. Mussolini cut him off by stating that it was already too late for that solution. Blissfully unaware of Mussolini's intransigence, Salandra and the Nationalists continued to orchestrate the crisis as they wished. In the afternoon, Salandra received his mandate from the king to form the new government. He accepted on the condition that the Fascists would participate. With Ciano's and De Vecchi's assurances to back him up, there did not seem to be insurmountable obstacles to the formation of the long-awaited conservative government. Since Mussolini's consent was still missing, a call was made to Milan around 3:00 P.M., during which Federzoni again tried to lure Mussolini to Rome. Again, he failed.[23]

Finally, Mussolini, by means of the prefect of Milan, made it clear that he would not come to Rome unless he was given the task of forming the new government. Rocco, who already knew this, consulted with Stefano Benni and Gino Olivetti, respectively president and secretary of the Confindustria, and then with Senators Ettore Conti, the head of an important electoral combine, and Silvio Crespi, owner of the *Corriere della Sera* and a textile magnate. Apparently these industrialists were equally concerned over Mussolini's decision. Just a few days earlier, they had made clear their preference for Giolitti, and although they had no objection to Fascist participation in the government, they certainly did not expect Mussolini to demand the presidency of the council. As they were about to persuade Mussolini to yield, a letter arrived for the prefect from the offices of the *Popolo d'Italia* with Mussolini's tentative list of members for his new government.[24]

The news of Mussolini's rejection of the Salandra presidency came as even more of a shock in Rome. The Fascist leaders present in Rome, De Vecchi, Grandi, Ciano, Giovanni Marinelli, Gaetano Polverelli, and Gaetano Postiglione met with Salandra and Federzoni until 1:00 A.M., on October 29 to try to work out ways to bring Mussolini around. At 1:25, Postiglione made the last call to Milan on that very long day. In the name of De Vecchi, Ciano, and the others he repeated Salandra's offer. Mussolini again flatly rejected this solution to the crisis, adding as a last indignity that he even preferred Giolitti to Salandra. At that point, the impasse in which the conservatives found themselves was apparent to all. By the dawn of October 29, hopes for Salandra's government dissipated like the morning mist. By midday, the news of the Fascist victory began to spread. Alfredo Misuri noted maliciously how the major Nationalist leaders frantically scrambled to adjust to the new situation. Yet the Fascists, who had taken most of Italy, were so weak in Rome that their celebration had to be delayed a day. The first demonstrations were joint Nationalist-Fascist affairs, with squads from both groups celebrating by attacking democratic, Socialist, and Communist papers.[25]

Until the papers of the House of Savoy are opened it will probably be impossible to determine whether the Nationalists had any part in the decision of the king to reject the martial law decree. It cannot be excluded that Federzoni helped influence the king. It must be remembered, however, that the king's refusal to sign the decree did not mean that Victor Emmanuel wished to appoint a Fascist government. Like the Nationalists, he thought that he was getting Salandra and needed no pressure from Federzoni to move in that direction. Probably a combination of factors, advice from military officers, fear of a civil war, and the existence of a right-wing alternative in the person of Salandra, brought the king around to rejecting the decree.[26]

After the decision to appoint Mussolini was made, the Nationalists occupied a rather difficult position. They had backed the wrong horse, and Federzoni had compounded that mistake by conducting the negotiations with the Fascists in a way which appeared extremely suspicious to Mussolini. It was apparent that the plans of the Fascist leader for his new government did not include a prominent place for the politicians of the conservative Right. Mussolini projected a much broader coalition, including elements of the Center and of the trade unions. Bruno Buozzi and Gino Baldesi of the General Confederation of Labor were given permission to negotiate with the new government. Only when Mussolini arrived at Civitavecchia on his way to Rome did the leaders of Tuscan fascism and the Nationalists board the train to dissuade him from any left-wing appointments. To an extent, they turned the tables on Mussolini. He had earlier rejected Salandra with the disparaging remark that the March on Rome was not worth the trouble if it only ended with a classic conservative. The conservatives now used the same logic to argue that too much had been accomplished to end with a Socialist minister in the government. However much success they had in blocking the labor representatives, neither Salandra nor the

Nationalists received very much from the new prime minister. Federzoni was named to the colonial ministry, but he had very much wanted foreign affairs, which Mussolini took for himself ad interim to block the Nationalist leader's aspirations. Alfredo Rocco became undersecretary at the treasury and Luigi Siciliani undersecretary in charge of arts at the Education Ministry. The other posts went to Fascists, Liberals, and Catholics. Shortly after the governmental nominations, Gelesio Caetani, another Nationalist deputy, received the ambassadorship to Washington, but only after Luigi Albertini had turned it down.[27]

The March on Rome presented a mixed result for the conservatives. While they had lost their battle to put Salandra in power and, as a result, held relatively unimportant posts in the new government, they had shown their ability to limit Mussolini's desire to experiment with a broader based government. More important, the Nationalists saw a party in power with which they had already undertaken a dialogue and over which they had some influence. The taming of the Fascist beast still remained to be done, but the last chapter was far from having been written.

Nine

The Nationalist-Fascist Merger

The Nationalists and the New Fascist Government

In October 1922 there was little agreement on what fascism meant. Conservatives, opportunists, former socialists, and syndicalists coexisted uneasily in the PNF. After 1920, the Fascist movement moved steadily to the Right, but the majority of conservative businessmen and politicians were still outside of the party. Mussolini's revolutionary past and the undefined ideology of the movement added to the confusion over the future course of the government. In a letter to Alberto Albertini, Oreste Rizzini, a journalist for the *Corriere della Sera*, wrote that Mussolini seemed the prisoner of the Nationalists and other conservatives, but he suspected that, as economic difficulties arose, the ministry was likely to slide toward the Left.[1]

The real aim of the new government was to stay in power. Toward the Chamber of Deputies, which potentially threatened his government with an adverse vote of confidence, Mussolini's tone was notably rougher than it was toward the conservative Senate. Above all, Mussolini wanted to avoid anything which would alienate moderate opinion until his power was consolidated.

With this in mind, the relationship between the ANI and the PNF took on greater importance. Although there was distrust on both sides, practical politics weighed in favor of an understanding. Because of their ties to the monarchy and to heavy industry, Nationalist approval of, and participation in, the government offered the kind of immediate reassurance to bourgeois opinion which Mussolini desired. On the Nationalist side, the attraction of political power was overwhelming. The Nationalists had always defined themselves as a governmental party. For the first time they could fill this role, and the moment could not be lost. Thus, mutual need outweighed suspicion, as discussions began once again for a fusion between the two movements.

The Nationalists were not totally satisfied with the situation in the days following the March on Rome. Their position in the new coalition was shaky. With the exception of Alfredo Rocco, the leaders of the ANI were not trusted by Mussolini and his inner circle. Mussolini acted firmly to curb Nationalist activity which tended to pressure or embarrass the government. On November 30, the prefects of Bari, Trieste, Venice, and Ancona were told to coordinate their efforts to stop any Nationalist or D'Annunzian provocation against Yugoslavia. As a result, the ANI's Fiume group was forced to suspend a demonstration set for November 17.[2]

Nationalist comment on the March on Rome emphasized the conservative and statist aspects of the Fascist take-over. Maraviglia defined it as an extra parliamentary solution for conservative ends. Nevertheless, the *Idea Nazionale* reacted with caution to the innovations of the regime, especially those dealing with the role of the party. The constitution of the Fascist militia as a legal arm of the state was accepted with extreme reluctance and only after it was clear that no threat to the position of the army was intended.[3]

Given the relationship between the two movements up to the moment of the March on Rome, the question of fusion was bound to arise. It had been amply discussed at the end of 1921. Cooperation, not fusion, was the watchword at that time. Once the Fascists were in power, the question of a merger reappeared. Fusion appealed to Fascist conservatives like De Vecchi, as well as to some younger, intelligent leaders like Giuseppe Bottai, who doubted the ability of early fascism to deal with the problems of governing Italy. Fusion with the ANI was an opening to a more cultured and technically competent elite. On the Nationalist side, Corradini, with his version of fascism as a more dynamic realization of the Nationalist ideal, was an enthusiastic proponent of a merger.[4]

More than ideological affinity, there was a practical issue which made discussions for fusion urgent. It was the astounding growth of both the PNF and the ANI in the south after October 1922. Fascism had developed slowly in the areas below Rome until shortly before the seizure of power. The original movement had been the product of class tensions in the Po Valley and in the northern industrial belt. Only in a few places, like Naples, was there an active southern movement which dated from the earliest days. Aurelio Padovani, the leader of Neapolitan fascism, was one of the most interesting and forceful figures to emerge from the postwar veterans' movement and from early fascism. His republicanism and hostility to traditional clienteles led him to reject alliances with parties like the ANI. Until Mussolini became prime minister, he seemed to sympathize with, or tolerate, Padovani, but, once in power, several factors combined to work for a reconciliation between Mussolini and the conservatives. Pressures to limit the syndical activities of Padovani and to make the Neapolitan situation conform to the national line grew in the months following October.[5]

In the south, the ANI had come to terms with the traditional power structure well before the March on Rome. Like the PNF, it experienced a rapid growth in 1922 and expanded especially rapidly after the March. A peculiar situation resulted. Normally, the first choice of opportunistic southerners was the local *fascio*, but where personal or political differences intervened to make adherence to the PNF impossible, the next choice became the conservative and safe Natonalist Association. Padovani greeted many of fascism's recent opportunistic recruits with hostility, whereas the Nationalists received them with enthusiasm. Reports of the prefects quite clearly described the scramble for position. For instance, in one town, in the province of Potenza, the mayor formed a Nationalist group as part of his electoral machine. In Tirolo, in the province of Catanzaro, the local Nationalist group took in former members of the Socialist administration. The prefect wrote that the ANI was made up of those who could not join the Fascist party.[6]

Of course, the most difficult situations arose around Naples, where the Nationalists opposed their own activism to that of Padovani. The leader of the ANI in the nearby province of Caserta was Paolo Greco. Ambitious and unscrupulous, Greco duplicated in the Nationalist squads the typical antisocialist and conservative weapon of agrarian fascism. Greco also appealed to those who had been alienated by Padovani's radicalism. His policy of taking over whatever elements were at hand inevitably led to conflicts with the Fascists, and these spilled over into national politics. Shortly after the March on Rome, Greco met with Michele Bianchi to request his intervention in working out an accord between local Nationalists and Fascists. Significantly, he was unable to approach Padovani directly. Bianchi promised to deal with Padovani, but little resulted from the effort. Incidents continued to pile up. On December 4, Greco's conservative squads attacked the local *fascio* at Qualiano, leaving four Fascists wounded. After the incidents, Francesco Turchi, the provincial secretary of the ANI, and Flaminio Orfei of the Neapolitan PNF declared themselves ready to fulfil the accords for cooperation. The *Idea Nazionale,* hinting broadly at Padovani's bad faith, demanded to know his position. Padovani refused any concessions, however, and dismissed an offer by the Nationalists for a meeting at Caserta. Greco and Paolucci had invited the political secretary of the PNF, Nicola Sansanelli, to speak, but Padovani vetoed the invitation and called his own meeting for December 19, at which cooperation with the Nationalists was rejected.[7]

Even more embarrassing was the outcome of a fight between Nationalists and Fascists at Afragola at the end of December, which led to a police raid on the offices of the ANI in Naples. The *Idea Nazionale* sarcastically commented that only Nitti dared to do a similar thing. Both Greco and Forges sought a meeting with Mussolini to clarify the situation. Mussolini was forced to telegraph the Neapolitan Fascist federation to demand an end to the incidents. Nonetheless, a few days later at Anversa, near Naples, 400 members of the Sempre Pronti and the ANI gathered for a march. The local Fascists responded by threatening a violent counterdemonstration. On January 22, in Caserta and Casaluce, fights broke out and shots were exchanged as the result of tension between the two parties. In Capua, the secretary of the ANI had earlier been expelled from the *fascio* by Padovani for bad conduct.

The prefect reported that tension would not let up until the man was also purged by the Nationalists. In another town, in the nearby province of Salerno, the Nationalists were forced by the prefect to abandon their organizational efforts because of the violent reaction of the Fascists.[8]

The growth of the ANI in the north and in Rome presented fewer problems. The secretary of the Turin group announced 2,000 members for the ANI and noted that two years earlier the only group in the whole province had been that of Turin. By 1922, new sections had been constituted throughout Piedmont. In contrast to this substantial growth, the prefect of Verona reported that the Nationalists had difficulty even holding meetings because of the smallness of their section. Although there are no statistics for total membership in the ANI, evidence indicates that the party was strongest in Rome. Elections to the council of the Roman group in 1922 showed the winning candidate with 4,538 votes, an indication of a rather large active membership. The labor branch of the ANI expanded during this same period. Mario Baratelli of the Labor Office reported 6,000 members and sixty sections, but most of these were in Rome among municipal and government workers.[9]

After October, the leadership of the ANI moved to consolidate recent growth. On November 12, the executive junta took a step toward conciliation with the PNF by calling on the regional and provincial secretaries to reject efforts of whole groups to pass *en bloc* into the ANI and to forbid the creation of new sections where one already existed. Party officials were also urged to examine prospective members for subversive or Masonic ties. Of course, these rules seem not to have been applied with any particular care. On November 30, an agreement was reached between the ANI and PNF to limit the formation of new sections where one "national" party already existed, but, once again, an agreement of that nature could not work when both sides still saw possibilities of rapid expansion in the virgin territory below Rome. Furthermore, expansion in the south was insurance for the Nationalists, who had no guarantee that Mussolini's government would last any longer than the other postwar coalitions.[10]

For those like Corradini who favored fusion between the two parties, continued friction acted as a spur to more rapid action. Some local Nationalists in Lazio even jumped the gun and began a process of merger on their own initiative. Nevertheless, most of the leaders of the ANI preferred to negotiate for the best possible terms. Federzoni cautiously stated the Nationalist position in a letter to Mussolini. He noted that all Nationalists were loyal to Mussolini but that fusion was a process which needed careful preparation. He suggested concessions from the Fascist side to ease tension in southern Italy, a meeting between Forges and Mussolini over the problems connected with the Nationalist militia, and the inclusion of Corradini and Foscari in the new list of senators to be named by the king.[11]

Federzoni was clearly reluctant to abandon outright the Sempre Pronti, but the legal situation of that organization of roughly 80,000 members was in doubt once the decision was taken to create an official Fascist National Militia and to dissolve the squads. The Nationalists accepted the decrees on the dissolution of the Sempre Pronti as an armed force but complained about the failure of a broader accord between the two parties. Paolucci was given the task of reorganizing the Nationalist squads. In reality, the Nationalists were in no hurry to make the transformation, and the Sempre Pronti remained as an armed force in many areas for some time after fusion.[12]

On January 1, 1923, Mussolini received Paolucci, Forges, and Maraviglia for discussions on the relationship between the two parties. Padovani, who had threatened his resignation as leader of the PNF in Naples, was asked to remain, and Mussolini instructed party officials to put an end to further conflict. Despite the conciliatory tone of the meeting, the Fascists were determined to demand an end to Nationalist expansion in the south as the price for improved relations. The Nationalist strategy was to insure that fusion would lay to rest the specter of any further leftward evolution of the Fascist movement, but it remained uncertain whether a total merger or simple federation would be the best way to maximize Nationalist influence and insure conservative control over fascism.[13]

On January 12 and 13, the Fascist Grand Council met to discuss the relationship between the two parties. One obstacle to fusion was removed when the Fascists accepted a motion of unquestioned loyalty to the monarchy. They also agreed to establish a mixed commission to continue negotiations with the Nationalists. The work of the commission proved to be extremely difficult, however. For the Fascists, it meant welcoming into their ranks a group of extremely able and dogmatic conservatives who had a reputation for trying to use the Fascist movement for their own purposes. In the past, Mussolini had always preferred to deal with the conservative establishment directly rather than through Nationalist mediation. For their part, the Nationalists had to calculate the relative advantages of independence over merger within a much larger political force. Initially, the two sides were rather far apart in their ideas on unity. In one of the earliest projects for federation, drawn up by Alfredo Rocco at the end of 1922, the ANI was to keep its own structure within the Fascist party and take charge of the education, planning, propaganda, and youth activities of the merged parties. One-third of each group's central committee would be made up of members of the other party. The Nationalists set their price extremely high, much higher, in fact, than the Fascists wished to pay. Fascist reluctance was all the stronger, since it was clear that the Nationalists would be followed by many other conservatives who had looked with favor on the Fascist victory but were waiting the outcome of the Nationalist-Fascist merger.[14]

On January 31, 1923, the fusion commission reported little progress, except for a broadly worded three-point agreement. First, the Nationalists were given credit for creating the ideology, the Fascists for creating the mass base. Second, the two parties agreed to work for the consolidation of the government. Finally, they agreed to set up a smaller committee to continue discussions. The situation after that limited agreement was still far from simple. The old problem of the relationship between the two parties in the south remained unresolved. To a certain extent, the expansion of both parties was beyond the control of the central leadership. A report from Paolo Di Tarsia, an inspector general in the Interior Ministry, summarized the situation perfectly. He noted that in

Basilicata there never existed anything which could truly be called fascism or nationalism: "Where there is a mayor, a communal administrator supported by the old clienteles, camouflaged as Nationalists, there arises fascism, or better, the other opposition clienteles dress themselves as Fascists, and the Fascist section is created." Even the old left-wing peasant leagues used this means to survive. (Mussolini wrote "*giusto*" [correct] in the margin.)[15]

The incident which led to Di Tarsia's report was extreme but typical enough. The local *fascio* had been formed by landowners in the region. This situation prompted leftists to use the Nationalist Association to cover their peasant organization. On January 31, 1923, the Fascists held a demonstration in Bernalda. Shots were fired from the ANI's headquarters, and the subsequent rampage by the black shirts left two Nationalists dead and the local headquarters in ruins. Di Tarsia called for the dissolution of several sections of both the PNF and the ANI. (The prefect later dissolved ten Nationalist groups and five *fasci*.) Ugo D'Andrea, sent by the Nationalists to carry out an investigation, presented a report to Di Tarsia which tended to confirm the picture of the use of the right-wing parties by men who could not carry out their political activities in any other way. The situation in the province of Salerno was not much different. The prefect noted that the Nationalist Association, once quite small, had been growing rapidly to reach thirty-two sections and 10,000 members. The inescapable conclusion was that the Nationalists were making a concerted effort to expand the ANI even after negotiations for fusion were well under way. The Fascists left no doubt that they expected the Nationalists to abandon a large part of their southern base. Sansanelli suggested that the Nationalists had already fulfilled their mission in the south and would be better off if they expanded less rapidly. Achille Starace, who later became secretary of the PNF, bluntly told the Nationalists that few of their sections would survive the fusion process. In reality, as Raffaele Colapietra showed in his study of Neapolitan fascism, the conservative oligarchy, represented in the Nationalist groups, managed to win out in all but name.[16]

Given the demands of national politics, the leaders of the ANI could not afford to let the southern problem become more than a bargaining counter. A second Rocco project on fusion made it clearer that the Nationalists were willing to concede on organizational questions if they could maintain their national influence. Rocco proposed a compromise which entailed the abandonment of independent political action on the part of the Nationalists. In return, the ANI would take charge of the cultural and propagandistic activities of the Fascist movement through control of newspapers, periodicals, and youth and technical study groups, receive formal recognition that Nationalist ideology would be the basis of the new party ideology, win seniority in the new party on the basis of service in the ANI, and obtain one-third of all positions on party organs.[17]

Mussolini's detailed and very negative critique of the Rocco draft emphasized the Nationalists' renunciation of independent political activity but rejected the almost exclusive hold on propaganda and cultural activities. Acceptance of Nationalists into the various organs of the PNF would be on the basis of need rather than on any numerical formula, and no promise was made that the entire membership of the ANI would be accepted into the PNF. In all, it was a very rigid response, which revealed Mussolini's instinctive caution toward the doctrinaire and tightly knit Nationalist elite. The Nationalists' willingness to trade off their mass base for influence on the highest level was apparent when they accepted a subcomission to study local problems between the two parties which was weighted in favor of the Fascist party.[18]

In mid-February, the Fascist Grand Council did make one conciliatory gesture toward the Nationalists by passing a motion against membership in Masonic organizations. Although many of the Fascists accepted it halfheartedly, the Nationalists seized on it as a major concession. The declaration on Freemasonry also helped precipitate events in Naples, where Padovani resigned from the Masonic lodge and also submitted his resignation as Fascist high commissioner in Naples. After a week's delay, the resignation was rejected, but orders were given to curb anti-Nationalist activities.[19]

The willingness of the Nationalists to abandon their members in the south made the work of the mixed commission easier. The *Popolo d'Italia* let drop that fusion was almost settled, with the sole remaining problem that of the continued existence of the ANI as a cultural organization. From February 23 to 27, there were a series of meetings between Mussolini, Federzoni, Giuriati, and Rocco to hammer out final details. Reporting on these negotiations, the conservative *Giornale d'Italia* seemed confident that an accord had been reached. On February 24, Federzoni gave an interview in which he accepted the Fascist argument that the ANI had been growing too rapidly in the south. The next day, the fusion pact was agreed on and was published on February 27. The ten-point accord followed closely the lines of Mussolini's earlier counterproposals:

(1) The association renounced all independent political activity, but an institute of Nationalist culture was to be established in Rome.

(2) The Nationalists, with some exceptions, would be allowed to pass *en bloc* into the PNF, with seniority based on service in the ANI.

(3) The Nationalists' worker organizations would merge into the Fascist corporations; Nationalists would be progressively integrated into the activities of the PNF on a one-by-one basis with no fixed percentages.

(4) An adequate representation for Nationalists on the Fascist Grand Council was promised, but Mussolini was given the right to determine the number.

(5) The Fascist militia would accept members of the Sempre Pronti, with previous service in the Nationalist formation to help determine rank in the Fascist militia.

(6) Provision was made for displaying Nationalist banners at public functions.

(7) Nationalist youth organizations would merge with those of the PNF.

(8) Parliamentary and local groups would merge.

(9) Banners of the ANI would be in the custody of the PNF.

(10) A mixed commission would remain in place to direct the process of fusion; Paolucci and Sansanelli were named to supervise the merger.[20]

First comments on the Nationalist side were enthusiastic, but the accord was far more popular with the Roman leadership than it was with the rank and file. Opposition developed in Bologna, Trieste, and Milan. Dino Alfieri succeeded in putting a motion through the Milanese group against fusion on the grounds that only the central committee of the ANI could decide the question. Both Ugo D'Andrea and Raffaele Paolucci reported on discontent among long-time members. The German ambassador reported to Berlin that many members of the ANI felt that they had been abandoned by their leaders. Maraviglia was sent to smooth out difficulties in Calabria, and Francesco D'Ayala went to Sicily in order to ease bruised feelings in the south. Not unexpectedly, Greco's application to join the PNF was blocked by Padovani, who continued to oppose Nationalist participation. Federzoni was forced to complain directly to Mussolini about the treatment meted out to the Nationalist Sempre Pronti as they were integrated into the Fascist militia. These difficulties were in contrast to the relatively smooth process of fusion in Rome, where the Roman group accepted the agreement on March 4. Two days later, the central committee of the ANI gave its assent "after long and exhaustive discussion." On March 7, Federzoni and Maraviglia officially became members of the Fascist Grand Council.[21]

The Consequences of Fusion

The absorption of the ANI by the Fascists was the first major step in the liquidation of the old Italian party structure. It was significant both for the way it was done and for the impact which it had on the PNF. The Nationalists emerged from the long and difficult fusion process far from being completely content. Still, close personal and political ties and the official recognition of their special status gave them much potential leverage. If Federzoni's estimate was correct, 100,000 Nationalists were eligible to join the PNF. In the province of Rome alone, 25,000 Nationalists were set to join. Even allowing for obvious exaggeration, it would be a massive influx of conservative members.[22]

A precedent was also set for the absorption of other conservatives into the PNF. In the short run, the Fascists were able to eliminate a strong rival for political power in the south, but only at the cost of moving more-traditional clienteles into the party. Nationalist participation became a guarantee for many that the regime would not embark on any radical social and political experiments. Both Salandra and the *Giornale d'Italia* began to push for an alliance of conservative and Catholic forces under the umbrella of the government, an updated version of the Destra Nazionale. Of course, the inclusion of such a large number of Nationalist members made it difficult to create a new Fascist political elite. The Nationalists were rarely party men. Their loyalty went to the monarchy and to the state rather than to the regime as such. How far this potential conservative influence would expand depended on Mussolini's ability to deal directly with the conservative establishment. As long as he could keep the Nationalists from injecting themselves as pivotal figures in the relationship between the government and the powerful institutional forces which sought to use fascism to control social unrest, Mussolini could afford to let the Nationalists come to him in their quest for political influence. Throughout 1923 and early 1924, he succeeded in minimizing the Nationalists' role. The brutal murder of the Socialist deputy Giacomo Matteotti reversed the balance of power and made way for the Nationalist penetration of the Fascist regime.[23]

Ten

The Nationalists and the Matteotti Crisis

UNTIL THE WATERSHED created by the murder of Matteotti, the Nationalists were able to move but slowly to consolidate their positions in the newly merged party and in the state. It was only when the government was badly shaken in June 1924, that they managed to gain what proved to be a very decisive influence. However, in the months after fusion their position was far from secure. Naples remained a sore point. On April 18, Padovani mobilized his followers to pass a motion condemning opportunists like Greco. Padovani's stand was part of a larger struggle by Fascist intransigents to stop what they saw as a drift to the Right. Fusion with the Nationalists and a movement within fascism itself, led by Massimo Rocca (a former Nationalist) and Giuseppe Bottai, which worked for an end to squadrism and a normalization of Fascist relations with the opposition, were both seen by the Fascist extremists as part of the same process of bringing the movement closer to established elites and thereby ending opportunities for rising through the party. These extremists, many of whom had earlier opposed Nationalist entry into the party, now acted against Rocca and Bottai and physically attacked the renegade Alfredo Misuri (who transferred his loyalties to the ANI and then joined Rocca and Bottai in the revisionist campaign).[1]

On April 29, Padovani appealed to Mussolini for support against Greco's Nationalists, noting that the failure to take sides only strengthened his enemies. He also complained to the head of the militia, General De Bono, that the Nationalists were attempting to take over many *fasci* around Naples. On May 17 and 18, Mussolini met with Padovani to offer him the command of the Bologna zone within the militia. Padovani refused. Mussolini then imposed a solution which allowed

Greco to control the political movement in the area around Naples, while Padovani limited himself to the militia. The next day, Padovani informed Mussolini that he refused any compromise short of full vindication. The prime minister then sent Italo Balbo to Naples to deal with the situation. The Nationalist-Fascist commission which supervised fusion urged Padovani's replacement. Corradini, Giuriati, Giuseppe Bastianini, and Michelangelo Zimolo were given the task of reorganizing Neapolitan fascism. Greco and Turchi received the news that, henceforth, the Nationalists would be accepted *en bloc* into fascism. Edmondo Forges Davanzati, Roberto's brother, along with Greco and Turchi, emerged to dispute the heritage of Neapolitan fascism after the fall of Padovani.[2]

During the "revisionist" crisis of 1923, the Nationalist leaders lent minimal support to those like Rocca and Bottai who wished to make fascism into the party of a new technical elite without totally rupturing ties with the old liberal constitutional order. When Alfredo Misuri called for the demobilization of the PNF, he was beaten up outside of parliament by Fascist toughs. Paolucci, Luiggi, and Suvich rallied to their colleague's support but received a reprimand from the directory of the PNF for their pains. Another prominent revisionist, Massimo Rocca, mentioned working on a project of constitutional reform with Alfredo Rocco in 1923, but when Rocca was expelled from the party in 1924, the *Idea Nazionale* expressed absolutely no sympathy for the person or the cause.[3]

The Elections of 1924

The major problem for the new government in 1923 and early 1924 revolved around its search for a stable parliamentary base. Even with the addition of the Nationalist contingent, the Fascists were far from having a majority in the Chamber of Deputies. Two tactics were used to reverse this dangerous situation. The Acerbo electoral reform, which gave two-thirds of the seats in the chamber to the party which won a plurality of at least 25 percent of the votes, was passed in 1923. To get this law approved (it condemned the existing parliament to death), the government had to resort to its second tactic. As the king refused to put the measure through by decree, the potential opposition to the law had to be coopted or broken. Conservative liberals were brought along by the promise of a return to the electoral system of single-member constituencies, as had existed before World War I. The Catholic party was subjected to extraordinary pressure from the Vatican and from the Fascist squads to go along with the reform.

With the Acerbo Law in place, the government called for new elections, set for the spring of 1924. These were the last relatively free elections until 1946, but they were held in a climate of extreme intimidation. Although the governmental list was assured of victory, Mussolini took no chances. He included on the Fascist ticket a number of conservative Liberals. The Nationalists enthusiastically supported this tactic as a step toward making the PNF into a truly national conservative party. The *Idea Nazionale* saw it as especially useful in the south, where the traditional clienteles could safely rally to fascism. The elections were another step toward the merger of the Right into a single party. Consequently, the Nationalists were extremely critical of those Liberals who refused to support the "national" list and preferred to run under the banner of the Liberal party.[4]

The results of the elections conformed both to the strategies of the Nationalists and of Mussolini. The most striking successes came in the south, where the PNF had only recently become strong. The pre-Fascist pattern of southern deputies providing governmental majorities was confirmed as fascism seemed destined to be swamped by the old order. Symbolically, in the area around Naples, Paolo Greco scored a personal triumph, and Padovani was long gone from the political scene. The Nationalists predictably viewed the elections as a victory for conservative normalization. The *Idea Nazionale* urged the Right to rally behind the government. Mussolini reacted in a somewhat different way. He reverted back to the earlier strategy of broadening his base to the Left by the inclusion of some labor representatives. The murder of Giacomo Matteotti totally upset his plan and changed the whole context of political maneuvering.[5]

THE RUPTURE WITH THE OPPOSITION AND THE TRIUMPH OF THE ANI

The reaction of the democratic and socialist opposition to the elections played havoc with the normalization plans. Understandably bitter over the violence used during the campaign, the anti-Fascists decided to make the opening of parliament an occasion to attack the government. Giacomo Matteotti, one of the brightest young leaders of the reformist Socialist party, denounced the numerous cases of fraud and illegitimate force, but the real purpose behind his attack was to draw a moral line between the Fascists and the opposition. On June 10, 1924, a few days after the speech, Matteotti disappeared. Although his body was not found until months later, the supposition on the part of both Fascists and the opposition was that he had been killed. The Democratic and Socialist deputies, joined by a few Liberals, withdrew from parliament in the so-called Aventine Secession.

Many of the former liberals and southern opportunists, who had only recently jumped on the bandwagon during the election, were likely to abandon the government if the scandal over Matteotti's disappearance and probable murder got out of hand. All they needed was a suitable alternative. The same was true of the king, the military, the Catholic Church, and big industry—institutional forces which had supported fascism only because they feared a reversion to the instability of the pre-1922 period. The security won through the electoral majority proved to be extremely transitory. Under those circumstances, the Nationalists played a pivotal role. Depending on the price Mussolini was willing to pay, they could either provide a cover for the Fascists with the traditional elites or offer their own candidate for power in the person of Luigi Federzoni.

Although as early as June 10 Raffaele Paolucci organized a protest over Matteotti's disappearance the Nationalist leadership moved much more cautiously. By June 12, pressure was building in parliament for a purge of the Interior Ministry and the appointment of Federzoni in place of Mussolini at that post. On June 13, Federzoni met with the ministers of justice and finance, Aldo Oviglio and Alberto De Stefani, on the need to purge both the government and the party of those involved in the Matteotti murder. About noon of the same day, there was a meeting with Mussolini at which Aldo Finzi and Giacomo Acerbo, both close associates of Mussolini and possible culprits, were present, to the annoyance of Federzoni. At that point, Mussolini still seemed willing to try to bluff it out, by assuring the critics that the guilty would be punished. As Finzi was seen to be one of those implicated because of his position as Mussolini's deputy at the Interior Ministry, the meeting was not very satisfactory. The rest of the day was spent plotting strategy with Forges Davanzati and Maraviglia at the offices of the *Idea Nazionale* and at Federzoni's office in the Colonial Ministry.[6]

June 14 proved to be a critical day in the resolution of the governmental crisis and in the long-range survival of the regime. Federzoni met with De Stefani and then proceeded to the Ministry of Public Instruction, where he saw Oviglio and Giovanni Gentile, Italy's leading philosopher after Benedetto Croce and the most important adherent to fascism from the world of culture. Federzoni, Oviglio, Gentile, and De Stefani agreed that the time had come to offer their resignations. At noon they met with Mussolini. Federzoni, Oviglio, and Gentile presented a letter with their resignations. Mussolini again tried to play for time. He argued that a reorganization of the governmental majority or the inclusion of Socialists or Catholics in the coalition at that moment would "neither be useful nor possible." He then told the four ministers that both Aldo Finzi and Cesare Rossi had been forced to resign. According to Federzoni's notes he then added: "Get to the bottom of it?

Fine, but to whom? To Mussolini? Not that!" De Stefani spoke of the double stain of corruption and murder, but Mussolini responded that it would be hard to prove and that the country was calm. At the end of the interview, Federzoni recalled that "we left little satisfied."[7]

Despite the brave words, Mussolini had already offered the heads of both Finzi and Rossi. General De Bono, the head of the militia, and Marinelli, a secretary of the PNF, were also singled out for a purge of the guilty. Federzoni's carefully orchestrated campaign to put maximum pressure on Mussolini picked up support from the war minister, General Antonino Di Giorgio, who saw the removal of top Fascists as an opportunity to deal a blow to the Fascist militia. Faced with this growing internal opposition, Mussolini buckled during the meeting of the Council of Ministers on June 16. Federzoni was appointed to the Interior Ministry and the prefect of Trieste, Crispo Moncada, a career civil servant, succeeded De Bono as head of the police.[8]

With Federzoni at the Interior Ministry and Roberto Forges Davanzati as one of the remaining secretaries of the PNF not implicated in the scandal, the Nationalists found themselves in a surprisingly strong position. This impression was reinforced by other governmental changes. Alessandro Casati, who took Gentile's place at the Ministry of Public Instruction; Gino Sarrocchi, who succeeded Gabriello Carnazza at the Ministry of Public Works; and Cesare Nava, the new minister of national economy, were either conservative allies of Salandra or, in Nava's case, a representative of the Catholic Right. Pietro Lanza Di Scalea was a former Nationalist, who kept the Colonial Ministry in the hands of the conservative Right, and two other undersecretaries, Roberto Cantalupo (Colonies) and Balbino Giuliano (Public Instruction), were also former Nationalists. Dino Grandi was put at the Interior Ministry to watch over Federzoni but rapidly became an ally of the Nationalist leader.[9]

The situation seemed to shift so radically in favor of the Right that Filippo Turati wrote to his friend Anna Kuliscioff that Federzoni seemed on the verge of edging out Mussolini. Other indications of conservative dissatisfaction with Mussolini and pleasure over the new government tended to confirm Turati's judgment. Ugo Ojetti, a journalist and attentive observer, of political trends, wrote in his notebook on June 26 that Corradini was quite critical of Mussolini, and Ojetti speculated on the motives behind the decision of the *Idea Nazionale* to give full coverage to a speech by Luigi Albertini, a leading critic of the goverment. Although Giovanni Amendola's *Il Mondo* felt that Federzoni was tied to the situation which led to Matteotti's disappearance, it did view the appointment of the Nationalist as a step in the right direction: "It seems therefore likely that Honorable Federzoni at the Interior Ministry may have the freedom and the willingness which would be indispensible to make the organs of the state function in the exclusive service of the law and in defense of all the citizens." The liberal press was almost unanimous in its praise of the Liberal and Nationalist appointments to the government.[10]

Why did not the Nationalists use their relative advantage to eliminate Mussolini and take over themselves? In answering this question, two things must be kept in mind. First, the Nationalist advantage demanded resolute action against the Fascist party. By late July, Mussolini began to regain a measure of initiative. Within the party itself, Forges Davanzati, an outsider, had no control over the provincial extremists, who threatened violence should Mussolini be removed from office. The second factor is more complex. The Nationalists, like the majority of conservatives, felt that time was on their side. A report to the Interior Ministry at the beginning of July mentioned that Vincenzo Riccio, Salandra's ally, refused to join the new government because of a prior commitment to Salandra who, it was said, expected to form a government by October. It was also rumored that the king favored Federzoni to form the next government. Therefore a Salandra-Federzoni combination was considered likely in the near future, although there is no indication that Federzoni personally desired that outcome. His later comments denied that he had any ties to the conservative antifascist plotting. Moreover, Maraviglia, in a very revealing article, expressed the fears of many conservatives when he said that the actions of Albertini and others to change the government were all well and good. But what then? Who or what would come after? He doubted how long a purely rightist government would last and felt that it was more likely to expect a reversion to the pre-1922 situation.[11]

Thus, the Nationalist strategy was not to bring down Mussolini but to hem him in by means of a series of conservative institutional and political checks. Federzoni's first actions at the Interior Ministry were certainly not those of a conspirator who wished to return to the constitutional liberal order. Although he began a purge of the most compromised Fascists and assured the bureaucracy that traditional practices of the civil service would henceforth be employed, Federzoni immediately used his position to issue a decree restricting freedom of the press (only applied fully after January 3, 1925, however). Federzoni defended his decree as a way of controlling both the opposition and the Fascist extremists. In fact, his instructions to the prefects, while striking at the Fascist intransigents, seemed to have been motivated by a desire to avoid incidents which would have made the moral position of the government even worse. The prefects were authorized to sequester the subversive papers, but persuasion and private pressure were to be used against the liberal-constitutional press. In a letter to Federzoni, Corradini commented that the press laws were the first steps to the revival of the government and toward "the state of the future, new, ours."[12]

To understand fully the pressures at work on the conservatives, the threat of retaliation by the provincial Fascist extremists must also be considered. Roberto Farinacci, the leader of Cremonese fascism, demanded that the government move to protect the Fascists who were involved in the Matteotti murder and to put an end to opposition attacks. Moreover, the intransigents were capable of acting against the conservatives, as well as the democrats and socialists. They were able to block the appointment of Raffaele Paolucci to the government. The former leader of the Fascist militia had become an outspoken opponent of Fascist squadrism.[13]

Another weakness of the conservative position was the lack of any cohesive principle between the Right and the various socialist and democratic opponents of the regime. Caught between their fears of a return to the pe-1922 political situation and the pressure from provincial Fascists, the Nationalists and their conservative allies embarked on what they saw as the safest course. They solidified their positions in the existing ministry and prepared to take over the government, if and when Mussolini stumbled badly. In their articles in the *Idea Nazionale* both Forges and Maraviglia continued to reject any normalization which ran the danger of a return to the old system or which would dismantle the strong government installed after the March on Rome. There could be no compromise with those who wished a system of mass parties and parliamentary politics. More cautiously, the *Giornale d'Italia* appealed for the restoration of control over the Fascist party and its squads, while praising the actions of Federzoni at the Interior Ministry.[14]

The Matteotti crisis moved into its final stage in November and December 1924. A series of events gave hope to the antifascists. On November 4, Giolitti withdrew his support from the government. He was soon joined by Orlando and Salandra. The opposition then presented a sworn statement by Cesare Rossi, formerly Mussolini's close aide, which revealed the extent of Fascist complicity in the murder. As the king made no move against Mussolini, Giuseppe Donati, the editor of the Catholic Popular party newspaper, charged General De Bono with involvment in the murder and demanded his trial before the Senate. The fact that Federzoni failed to use the press laws or even the range of private pressures to prevent the publication of this material enraged the Fascist extremists, who called for a "second wave" of the Fascist revolution.

Yet it was also clear that Federzoni would never move unless the situation became impossible or unless there was absolutely no danger. This caution kept the Nationalist leadership at arm's length from a plot against the government which involved Raffaele Paolucci. On December 15, he received a visit from Senator Campello, a high official in the royal household. Together they discussed a plan for a government of national emergency, with the participation of former prime ministers, including Mussolini. In order to give the king an excuse for dismissing Mussolini's government, Paolucci sought to unite the opposition and the dissident Fascists by setting conditions for a return to parliament of the Aventine deputies. On December 20, he met with forty-four Fascist deputies. This group, in turn, delegated Paolucci and three others to prepare a list of demands to present to Mussolini: an end to talk of a "second wave," respect for constitutional forces, and a return to the system of single-member constituencies. Paolucci related how all seemed ready. Both Salandra and Riccio were well disposed toward the idea, when suddenly on December 21 Mussolini himself offered to amend the electoral law to grant the key conservative demand of single-member constituencies. With that, the conservatives allowed themselves to be sidetracked, and nothing more came of the plot. The seriousness of this scheme is open to doubt, and, not surprisingly, there is no indication that the Nationalists gave any support to Paolucci. In a letter to Federzoni, written somewhat later, Alfredo Rocco was extremely critical of Giolitti and Orlando and used a visit to the king to counter any influence which Giolitti might have exercised.[15]

The impression that the Nationalist leadership had decided to stick with the government is reinforced by Federzoni's conduct during the last-minute maneuvers to pressure Mussolini to resign. The publication of the Rossi testimony increased demands that Mussolini step aside. On December 30, 1924, Luigi Albertini made such an appeal. The two Liberal ministers, Casati and Sarrocchi, argued the same thesis at a meeting of the Council of Ministers. They felt that Federzoni might support their move, but instead he joined with the military ministers in preventing the resignation of the government. Sensing the impotence of the opposition, Mussolini issued his famous challenge of January 3, 1925, by defying the Aventine deputies to replace him. On the same day, Federzoni instructed the prefects to repress any disorders and to inform the Fascists that there were to be no demonstrations. A second telegram ordered the dissolution of subversive organizations and surveillance of Communists. Going even further, he ordered full application of the press decrees which had been prepared in July. On January 6, the government was reorganized, with Alfredo Rocco becoming the new justice minister in place of Aldo Oviglio. Both Casati and Sarrocchi lost their positions to Fascists Pietro Fedele and Giovanni Giuriati. Federzoni stayed on at the Interior Ministry, where he and Crispo Moncada continued the policy of restoring the traditional relationship between the prefects and the central administration. An important turning point had been reached. The Nationalists would never again have a chance to replace Mussolini. Only on July 25, 1943, would Federzoni have another chance to act. It was a classic case of too little, too late.[16]

Eleven

The Legacy of Nationalism

The Nationalists and the Construction of the Fascist State

After January 3, 1925, the Nationalists held two key positions in Mussolini's government. Federzoni was interior minister and controlled the police and security apparatus; Rocco was justice minister in charge of establishing the new legal framework for the dictatorship. Together they gave to fascism its statist, authoritarian structures. In sharp contrast to Germany, where the conservatives progressively lost their positions, the emergence of the two Nationalist leaders just when the dictatorship began to consolidate itself is of the greatest importance. It helps explain why the repression was carried out within the framework of the traditional state bureaucracy and why party autonomy was reduced to a minimum. There was no equivalent in Italy of the Nazi S.S., a massive security force formally dependent on the party which gradually overwhelmed the state. That this did not happen under fascism resulted, in part, from the work of Federzoni and Rocco, and, in part, from the inclination of Mussolini, who supported the more traditional option of reinforcing state rather than party power. The Matteotti crisis proved to be a crucial turning point. Unlike Hitler, who unburdened himself of the conservative and nationalist politicians in 1933, Mussolini actually increased his dependence two years after taking power.

The greater leverage of the conservatives, just at the moment when the regime broke with the constitutional opposition and was forced to construct the apparatus of repression, influenced the outcome of the struggle between the radical Fascists of the "second wave" of the revolution and the conservatives who wished to preserve the authority and power of the traditional state institutions. Federzoni's eighteen months at the Interior Ministry bracketed the brief secretaryship of Roberto Farinacci, who ran the PNF from February 1925 to March 1926. Farinacci, the *ras*, or party chief, in Cremona, assumed office as the hero of the violent faction of the party and the squads. Many of his provincial supporters hoped for a purge of the state, a major role for the party, and the creation of a new political class. In fact, Mussolini, who was a technician of power rather than a man of principle, could never afford to consider the options offered by Farinacci and the Fascist party. He chose the safer way of compromise with the conservatives. Farinacci's authoritarian temperament was used to centralize and discipline the party, while on every important issue Mussolini bolstered the conservative position.

Both Federzoni and Rocco took advantage of their opportunity. Of the reforms which could be considered typical of Federzoni's contribution, both the press laws and the other reforms (which did away with elected officials in local governments and increased the power of the prefect as representative of state authority) diminished the ability of the party to undertake independent initiatives and made the state the chief instrument of repression.

Even more important in setting the basic direction of the Fascist state was Rocco. When he defined the new state as that which "realizes the legal organization of society to the fullest extent of its power and cohesion," he was merely restating ideas which had been set forth for years on the pages of the *Idea Nazionale*. He simply transferred the Nationalist conception of the state as the primary engine of political and social action into the institutional structure of fascism. Rocco believed that the liberal state was too inorganic to deal with large-scale economic and political activity, yet he was never very interested in the mass party.

The mission of both fascism and nationalism was to restructure the state so that it could cope with modern problems without revolutionary change. To accomplish this reorganization meant reinforcing the position of the executive and removing restraints on his power to control and manipulate the bureaucracy. The Law on the Powers of the Head of Government (1925) effectively ended the right of parliament to control the prime minister and gave the latter authority over the other ministers. The same year, a law was passed increasing the government's power over the bureaucracy through political tests for civil servants. In January 1926, a law granting to the government the right to issue decree laws was passed. The Law for the Defense of the State of November 1926 introduced the death penalty for attempts on the lives of major political figures, defined a new set of crimes against the regime, and established a special legal structure in the state bureaucracy to judge those crimes. The culmination of Rocco's legislation was the Law for the Judicial Settlement of Labor disputes of 1926, which achieved the aim first set forth in the Nationalist congress of 1914. Labor organizations were brought under the control of the state by extending legal recognition and by giving them the power to make legally binding contracts. The legislation insured the monopoly of representation to the Fascist unions by granting representative powers to only one recognized professional organization in every category of production. Even more important, Rocco's legislation made the state the primary guardian of the proletarian organizations.[1]

THE NATIONALISTS UNDER FASCISM: ALIENATION AND DISENCHANTMENT

The Nationalists were conservative elitists whose influence was exercised indirectly through other movements (Catholic, veteran, Fascist) which could develop a mass following. Until 1924, the leadership of the Nationalist Association revealed a high degree of cohesiveness, which increased its leverage. Once fascism consolidated its dictatorship, there was a parting of the ways. Forges Davanzati and Alfredo Rocco were much more at home in the regime than were Federzoni, Coppola, and Corradini. Except for Rocco, who remained in office until 1932, and Forges, who was a propagandist for the regime during the thirties, the major figures of nationalism were removed from the center of power by 1927.

The disappearance of the Nationalist leaders by no means meant the elimination of Nationalist influence, nor did it stop men whose intellectual formation took place within the Nationalist movement from playing key roles in the formation of Fascist cultural policy. Three ministers of education under fascism (G. Belluzzo, Balbino Giuliano, and Francesco Ercole) had a previous connection with the ANI. Former Nationalists played important roles in cultural organizations like the Dante Alighieri Society, which saw Dino Alfieri, Enzio Maria Gray, and Roberto Forges Davanzati enter the directing council. In 1928, when Mussolini created a Commission for Intellectual Cooperation to coordinate contacts abroad, that organization also passed under the influence of noted Nationalists.[2]

Moreover, the Nationalists managed to continue publication of their *Idea Nazonale* until 1925, when it merged with *La Tribuna*, and the merged paper remained under the direction of Roberto Forges Davanzati. Sonnino's old *Giornale d'Italia* also passed under Nationalist control in March 1926, when Corradini joined the administrative council and Virginio Gayda, another former Nationalist, became director. In addition, the journal *Politica*, under Francesco Coppola, remained essentially a Nationalist publication during the entire Fascist period.[3]

Of course, there was some attrition. Forges, whose fascination with the potential of the mass party and basically totalitarian outlook occasionally led him to stray from Nationalist orthodoxy, gave a different tone to the *Idea Nazionale-Tribuna* than could be found in the *Giornale d'Italia*. Although he was publicly optimistic, Corradini privately expressed reservations about the direction which the regime seemed to be taking. A series of aphorisms, which Corradini left among his papers, revealed this state of mind:

> One speaks too much of fascism and too little of Italy. . . . A personal regime does not produce a ruling class. . . . Dictatorship in a complex, modern state burdens itself with a mass of affairs above all human capacity. Consequently, numerous and extensive zones of national life remain outside of its vigilance and at the mercy of corruption. The result, the consequences of an absolute

> personal government are many and serious. First, an extraordinary development of an adulatory and courtesan mentality. Second, . . . it has the effect of disinteresting the citizens in public affairs and finishes by generating individualistic atomism, just about like the old regime . . .[4]

In a letter to Mussolini, written in 1925, Corradini noted the attacks of Croce against fascism and complained that he might be correct "to repeat that 'fascism is incapable of creating a new type of state', if we do not begin to contradict him with facts. In reality, fascism carried and still carries within itself a great historic mission for the state, but, as yet, we have not begun it."[5]

Some of Corradini's frustration stemmed from his feeling of being pushed aside by the new regime. Federzoni recalled that the Nationalist leader had little contact with Mussolini after 1927. Minor irritants also arose to increase Corradini's alienation. He felt that the regulation forcing journalists to be members of the Fascist press organization was aimed at his *Giornale d'Italia*. Having inherited the liberal paper, Corradini also had a staff which was not overwhelmingly fascist, nor entirely acceptable to the Fascist professional organization. To fire them meant paying large amounts in severance pay. Corradini saw it as an attempt by Telesio Interlandi, the racist editor of the Fascist *Il Tevere* and head of the Fascist Journalists' Association, to further his own publication at the expense of the older rival. Direct protests to Mussolini failed to clarify the matter, and Federzoni's diary notation indicated Corradini's discouraged state of mind: "He speaks of the Duce with affection and with a truly singular comprehension. I really believe that no one loves or understands him more than Corradini. But he detests the routine adulation and the abdication of all spiritual autonomy with which many *serve* the Duce but in reality betray him."[6]

If Corradini was personally unhappy, Francesco Coppola was preoccupied by both the ideological development of fascism and his own position in the regime. In early 1927, he complained to Federzoni that he felt "totally cut off from any possible participation in the life of the regime." He worried over "the psychological environment in which the moral education of the new generations is carried out" and cited "a tendency to rhetorical falsification and scorn for culture and intellectual effort, dangerous encouragement to the conquest of command posts without work, without preparation. . . . He thinks that the Duce, isolated and misled, does not have a clear idea of all that."[7] Coppola's *Politica* showed an increasing concern for the values of conservative Europe against the dangers coming from the Soviet Union and from Americanization and of the need to defend that Western culture against the new barbarians. Up to the early thirties, Coppola resisted both radical Fascist mysticism and the Nazi mentality. In 1932, he called Hitler a "dilettante" who would probably not leave a mark on history. The radical Fascists who showed enthusiasm for the Bolshevik example as an alternative to bourgeois society received no better treatment. For that conservative Nationalist, the fundamental split was between the West, with its Roman and Christian heritage, and the Jewish Bolshevik East. To defend the western world was not to defend social democracy, but the main lines of tradition and authority which were shared by the great states of Europe. Coppola did not believe that the corporative state represented a vast social experiment. Instead, it was the triumph of stability, hierarchy, and order.[8]

It took Luigi Federzoni longer than Coppola or Corradini to become disillusioned. His diary entries in 1927 reveal a consistent approval of Mussolini personally and of Fascist policy. His alienation seemed to have come in the 1930s and became more pronounced as Italy drew closer to Nazi Germany. By then, however, he had been shunted to the sidelines as president of the Senate and of the *Accademia d'Italia*.[9]

The Legacy of Nationalism

Although they were often personally frustrated, the Nationalists played a key role in making fascism both institutionally and ideologically conservative. Rocco and Federzoni used their increased influence during the Matteotti crisis to establish a regime which emphasized the importance of the state bureaucracy over the party or the Fascist unions. They joined with conservative industrialists to thwart social and economic innovations connected with the corporative state. Culturally, the Nationalists were proponents of a traditionalist outlook which impeded efforts by younger Fascists to create a new culture for the regime. They fully understood the value for the old order of hyphenated fascism, a system which lacked a common definition of what fascism meant and allowed each person to add a modifier to the term (Catholic-Fascist, Nationalist-Fascist, Syndicalist-Fascist).

Of equal importance was the fact that within the context of the regime the Nationalists offered a model toward which many of the most intelligent Fascists strove. Balbo and Grandi rapidly shed their early radicalism to become respectable monarchists and close friends of Federzoni. Symbols of success were not set by Farinacci or Achille Starace, but by the conservatives who still dominated the political and economic life of Fascist Italy. Even an innovative and dynamic Fascist politician like Giuseppe Bottai found Federzoni infinitely preferable to what he saw in the Fascist party leadership during the thirties.

To this extent, the gamble of the Nationalists paid off when they accepted fusion. They found in fascism both the mass base and the instruments of social control which they had been seeking since their revolt against liberal Italy. Yet their victory had dangers. They were authoritarian modernizers whose style and rhetoric has found a recent echo in some of the Third-World dictators, like the Shah of Iran, who use violence against the Left in their own country and speak of the revolt of "the proletarian nations" of the Third World. Conservative modernization is a difficult task because it implies a certain amount of mobilization of the masses, which the conservatives abhor. Fascism offered a way around this problem, but it did so by creating a system of all-pervasive political irresponsibility under the guise of an authoritarian dictatorship. Fascism was a world of private fiefdoms (Church, industry, army, party, corporations, universities) over which Mussolini acted as mediator. In such a situation, no one could revolutionize the social or economic order, but it was also true that no one could control Mussolini adequately or exercise political power except in the name of the Duce. Thus, when Italy embarked on the road to war or when the vicious racial campaign was begun, Federzoni, who disapproved of both, could do nothing about them, nor could Bottai, Balbo, or Grandi, who all protested loudly after the fact.[10]

The Nationalists' genius was in their ability to appropriate the political instruments, designed by others, to carry out their conservative modernization. In a moment of discouragement after the electoral disaster of 1919, Alfredo Rocco considered merging the Italian Nationalist Association into the Catholic Popular party in order to form its right-wing and thereby influence political developments. The emergence of fascism in 1920 provided a more direct way to realize his "national syndicalism." In the end, it was the mass nature of Fascist politics which made the movement unpedictable for the conservatives. Some thirty years later, after 1943, the Right finally took a more liberal option in the form of Christian Democracy. Any assessment of this more recent gamble falls in the realm of current events, but in Italy, where change is often illusion and where a good part of the Rocco legal codes are still in force, it is always difficult to determine who wins and who loses.

Notes

Introduction

1. For a discussion of the literature on the Nationalist Association, see the bibliographical essay at the end of this work.

2. The standard studies in English on the Action Française are Eugen Weber, *Action Française: Royalism and Reaction in Twentieth Century France* (Stanford: Stanford University Press, 1962), and E. H. Tannenbaum, *Action Francaise* (New York: Columbia University Press, 1962). The contribution of the Action Française to the rise of fascism has been analyzed by Ernst Nolte, *Three Faces of Fascism* (New York: Holt Rinehart and Winston, 1966).

3. The intellectual climate in France and in Italy at the turn of the century has been recreated by Paolo Vita Finzi, *Le delusioni della libertà* (Florence: Vallecchi Editore, 1961), pp. 16, 36–37, 49–50.

4. Differences between Italian and German political nationalism result from timing and political setting, but the function of the Italian Nationalist Association and of the DNVP was the same. The Italian Nationalists were, however, much more successful in influencing fascism. See Lewis Hertzman, *DNVP: Right-Wing Opposition in the Weimar Republic, 1918–1924* (Lincoln, Nebraska: University of Nebraska Press, 1963); George L. Mosse, *The Crisis of German Ideology: Intellectual Origins of the Third Reich* (New York: The Universal Library, Grosset and Dunlap, 1964); Fritz Stern, *The Politics of Cultural Despair: A Study in the Rise of the German Ideology* (Berkeley: University of California Press, 1961); George L. Mosse, "The Corporate State and the Conservative Revolution in Weimar Germany," in Receuils de la Société Jean Bodin, *Gouvernés et gouvernants*, vol. 24 *Période contemporaine* (Brussels: Éditions de la Librarie Encyclopédique, 1965), pp. 213–42.

Chapter One

1. Giovanni Papini, *Passato remoto, 1885–1914* (Florence: L'Arco, 1948), p. 132.

2. On Corradini, see Monique de Taeye-Henen, *Le nationalisme d'Enrico Corradini et les origines du fascisme dans la revue florentine "Il Regno" 1903–1906* (Paris: Didier, 1973), pp. 10–12; also Ugo D'An-

drea, *Corradini e il nazionalismo* (Rome: Augustea, 1928); P. L. Occhini, *Enrico Corradini e la nuova coscienza nazionale* (Florence: Rinascimento del Libro, 1933); Giacomo Pavoni, *Enrico Corradini nella vita nazionale e nel giornalismo* (Rome: Casa Editrice Pinciana, n.d.). Papini recalled that Corradini wrote clearly but with great effort. He would enter the *Regno* offices, read the newspapers, pace the room, write, pace again, until at a certain point, "he handed me a bundle of paper with an almost childlike smile as if to say, 'Once again, I pulled it out.' " (Papini, *Passato remoto*, pp. 132–35).

3. For the background to the *Regno*, see Occhini, *Corradini*, pp. 169, 193; M. Maffii, "Corradini e *Il Regno*," *Politica*, 18 (1937): 71. On the European background to the cultural transformation of the turn of the century, see H. Stuart Hughes, *Consciousness and Society: The Reorientation of European Social Thought, 1890–1930* (New York: Vintage, 1958), chap. 2. The Italian dimension is given in E. Garin, *Cronache della filosofia italiana del '900* (Bari: Laterza, 1966).

4. Mario Morasso, *L'imperialismo nel secolo XX* (Milan: Treves, 1905), pp. 13–15, 32. Idem, "I sovrani del nuovo regno," *Il Marzocco*, April 12, 1903 and *L'imperialismo nel secolo XX*, p. 46–48, 107, 241–44, 249–51, 295–97. Corradini estimated Morasso's importance in the following way: "Morasso is a follower, and I with him, of that political and individualist philosophy which combats democracy and the bourgeois ideal of progress. He follows that sincere philosophy which is based on nature and posits force as the means to the triumph of superior peoples and individuals." ("Imperialismo artistico," *Il Marzocco*, October 26, 1902).

5. On D'Annunzio's interest in the *Regno*, see G. D'Annunzio to E. Corradini, December 27, 1903 and March 19, 1904, in Archivio Federzoni-Argentieri, Rome. A full list of the *Regno*'s contributors is given in de Taeye-Henen, *Le nationalisme d'Enrico Corradini*, pp. 19ff. On Prezzolini and Papini during these years, see Delia Frigessi, ed., *La cultura italiana del '900 attraverso le riviste: "Il Leonardo," "Hermes," "Il Regno"* (Turin: Einaudi Editore, 1960), pp. 68–69; P. M. Arcari, *Le elaborazioni della dottrina politica nazionale fra l'unità e l'intervento*, 3 vols. (Florence: Marzocco, 1934–39), 2: 389–90; for the background of the Young Liberals, see F. Fonzi, *Crispi e lo stato di Milano* (Milan: Giuffrè, 1965), 121–23, and the articles by Giovanni Borelli, "Crispi," *Idea Liberale*, January 15, 1898; "Il giubeleo," ibid., February 28, 1898; "La logica delle cose," ibid., July 30, 1899.

6. See Corradini's articles, "Un biglietto sull'espansionismo," *Il Regno*, December 20, 1903; "Qualche altra parola," ibid., December 13, 1903; "La guerra," ibid., February 28, 1904; and "Solidarietà," in E. Corradini, *La vita nazionale* (Siena: Ditta I. Gatti, 1907), pp. 31ff. The Young Liberals rejected this stress on imperialism. See A.

Campodonico, "I risorgenti dell'oggi e i risorti di ieri," *Il Regno*, December 6, 1903.

7. The Nationalist admiration for foreign imperialism was evident in P. L. Occhini, "Re Joe," *Il Regno*, December 27, 1903; "Ancora Chamberlain," ibid., January 10, 1904; "Vittoria di T. R.," ibid., November 20, 1904. Corradini's enthusiasm for Japan can be seen in "Tra cecità e il sangue," ibid., March 31, 1905, and "Susumè," ibid., June 5, 1904. Corradini even judged the French Revolution positively because it galvanized the energies of the people to conquer most of Europe ("Che cos'è una nazione," *Idea Liberale*, June 26, 1904).

8. For a good summary of the irredentist question, see Giovanni Sabbatucci, "Il problema dell'irredentismo e le origini del movimento nazionalista in Italia," *Storia contemporanea* (1971): 53–106; John A. Thayer, *Italy and the Great War* (Madison, Wis.: University of Wisconsin Press, 1964), chap. 5. See "Nazionalismo e anticlericalismo," *Il Regno*, November 20, 1904; Occhini, "Il nostro compito," ibid., October 2, 1904; E. Peschioli, "La politica dell'Italia nella questione dell'Oriente," ibid., April 10, 1904; and on the conflict between Italian and German students, "Gaudiamus igitur," and R. Forster, "Dopo i fatti di Innsbruck," ibid., December 6, 1903.

9. Occhini, "Re Joe," ibid., December 27, 1903, and the liberal Mario Calderoni's protest, "Nazionalismo antiprotezionista," ibid., January 17, 1904. On economic policy in the Giolittian era, see Richard Webster, *L'imperialismo industriale italiano* (Turin: Einaudi, 1975), pp. 36–50; S. La Francesca, *La politica economica italiana dal 1900 al 1913* (Rome: Edizioni dell'Ateneo, 1971), pp. 9–40; and on Nationalist economic policy in particular, S. Bertelli, "Gli incunabili del nazionalismo," *Nord e Sud* 8 (1961): 83.

10. See by Corradini, "Per coloro che risorgono," *Il Regno*, November 29, 1903; "Qualche altra parola," ibid., December 13, 1903; "Realismo politico," ibid., January 24, 1904; "Tornando sul nostro programma," ibid., October 9 and 16, 1904; "Che cos'è una nazione," *Idea Liberale*, June 26, 1904.

11. For Prezzolini's position, see "I cenci vecchi del liberalismo," *Il Regno*, January 31, 1904; "Le due Italia," ibid., May 22, 1904; "A chi giova la lotta di classe," ibid., March 27, 1904; "La menzogna parlamentare," ibid., June 5, 1904; "La bottega socialista," *Idea Liberale*, August 21, 1904. See also Lucia Strappini, "Cultura e classe: Analisi di un mito," in L. Strappini, C. Micocci, and A. Abruzzese, *La classe dei colti: Intellettuali e società nel primo novecento italiano* (Bari: Laterza, 1970), p. 22.

12. V. Pareto to Prezzolini, December 17, 1903, cited in G. Prezzolini, *Il tempo della Voce* (Milan: Longanesi, 1960), p. 54; Pareto to *Il Regno*, cited as part of the article by Prezzolini, "La borghesia può

risorgere?" *Il Regno*, January 10, 1904; Prezzolini, "Aristocrazia dei briganti," ibid., December 13, 1903; idem, "Organizzazione borghese," cited in G. Papini and G. Prezzolini, *Vecchio e nuovo nazionalismo* (Milan: Studio Editoriale Lombardo, 1914), pp. 95–98.

13. "Fatti del mondo: La collaborazione dei cattolici," *Il Regno*, November 6, 1904.

14. "Nazionalismo e anticlericalismo," ibid., November 20, 1904; Corradini, "Il santo," ibid., December 2, 1905; idem, "Gregorio Magno," ibid., April 24, 1904. Writing of the compatibility between imperialism and Catholicism, G. A. Borgese remarked that the Church never let its principles interfere with "princes on the way to repression or the robust and vital nations on the road to conquest" (cited in Frigessi, *La cultura italiana*, pp. 433–34).

15. On the connection between economic crisis and the rise of the new nationalism, see R. Molinelli, "Per una storia del nazionalismo," *Rassegna storica del Risorgimento* 50 (July 1963): 391–406; V. Castronovo, *Economia e società in Piemonte dall'unità al 1914* (Milan: Banca commerciale Italiano, 1969), p. 332; Webster, *L'imperialismo italiano*, pp. 61–71.

16. Franco Catalano, "Milano tra liberalismo e nazionalismo," *Storia di Milano*, vol. 16 *Il principio del secolo 1901–1915* (Milan: Fondazione Treccani, 1962), pp. 99–101. Scipio Sighele, *Nationalismo e i partiti politici* (Milan: Treves, 1911), p. 2; G. Castellini, *Fasi e dottrine del nazionalismo italiano* (Milan: Quintieri, 1915), p. 5.

17. Webster, *L'imperialismo industriale italiano*, p. 111; and Roberto Michels, *L'imperialismo italiano* (Milan: Società Editrice Libreria, 1914), p. 5.

18. Carlo Salinari, "Le origini del nazionalismo e l'ideologia di Pascoli e di D'Annunzio," *Società* 14 (May 1958): 459–86, (especially pp. 481–82); Michels, *L'imperialismo italiano*, pp. 92–94. G. Pascoli, "In morte di Giosue Carducci," *Patria e umanità in Tutte le opere di Giovanni Pascoli; Prose*, vol. 1 (Milan: Mondadori, 1946), p. 407. In "Eroe italiano," Pascoli wrote that Italy "is the most menaced country in the world and at the same time the poorest" (ibid., p. 207). See also by Pascoli, "Una sagra," ibid., p. 170; "Nel cinquantennario della patria," ibid., p. 351. On the general subject of Pascoli's politics, see C. Varese, "Pascoli politico," in idem, *Pascoli politico e altri saggi* (Milan: Feltrinelli, 1961), p. 242.

19. Pascoli, "Enrico Panzacchi," *Prose*, p. 406.

20. Varese, "Pascoli politico," p. 242.

21. Pascoli, "La Grande Proletaria si è mossa," *Prose*, pp. 558–60.

22. Corradini, *Volere d'Italia* (Naples: F. Persella, 1911), pp. 51–75, 113, 136, 144–47; idem, "Nazionalismo e sindacalismo," *La Lupa*, October 16, 1910.

23. See by Corradini, "Sindacalismo, nazionalismo, imperialismo," in *Volere d'Italia*, pp. 24, 28–29; "La politica della vittoria," *Il Resto del Carlino*, August 3, 1910; "Il nazionalismo," ibid., July 9, 1910; *La patria lontana* (Milan: R. Quintieri, 1920), pp. 6, 200, 227, 243; G. Castellini, "Conversando con Enrico Corradini," *La Grande Italia*, March 20, 1910; G. De Frenzi, "Conversando con Enrico Corradini," *Giornale d'Italia*, July 10, 1910. On the formation of Corradini's national syndicalism, see Mario Isnenghi, *Il mito della Grande Guerra* (Bari: Laterza, 1970), pp. 10, 13, 16; and Francesco Perfetti, "Sindacalismo, nazionalismo, imperialismo," *La Destra* 2 (1972): 91.

24. On the cultural climate of the early years of the century, see Riccardo Del Giudice's introduction to Giuseppe Bottai, *Scritti* (Bologna: Cappelli, 1965), p. 19; Camillo Pellizzi, *Una rivoluzione mancata* (Milan: Longanesi, 1949); Lucia Strappini, "Cultura e classe: analisi di un mito." The most interesting example of the new electic outlook was Prezzolini's *La Voce*, which was a prolongation of his experiences with the *Leonardo* and the *Regno*. See G. Prezzolini, *L'italiano inutile* (Milan: Longanesi, 1963), pp. 107–8.

25. On Corradini's influence over the young imperialist nationalists, see "Il primo nazionalista d'Italia," *Il Tricolore*, April 3, 1909. The *Mare Nostro* of Venice also looked to Corradini as the leader of the movement (Gino Del Lago, "Enrico Corradini e il nazionalismo," *Mare Nostro*, August 1, 1910). On the *Tricolore* and Corradini, see Perfetti, "Sindacalismo, nazionalismo, imperialismo," pp. 83–95; A. Todisco, *Le origini del nazionalismo imperialista in Italia* (Rome: Giorgio Berlutti, Editore, 1925), p. 8; Mario Viana, *Lo sciopero generale e la guerra vittoriosa* (Turin: Stabilmento Tipografico Sella e Guala, 1910), pp. 10, 21; J. J. Roth, "Sorel and 'sorelismo,' " *Journal of Modern History* 39(1967): 30–45. Corradini counseled Viana to "watch closely the syndicalists. Their point of departure is from a certain point of view our own." (Corradini to Viana, April 1909, cited in Todisco, *Le origini*, p. 15).

26. T. Monicelli, "L'Italia di Lissa," *Il Viandante*, July 18, 1909; and "Confessioni," ibid., August 22, 1909, for fairly overt nationalist themes in syndicalism. Roberto Forges Davanzati (1880–1936) was born in Naples. After an early career as a socialist and syndicalist (including a stint as correspondent for the *Avanti*), Forges passed to nationalism and also became the Rome correspondent for the *Cor-*

riere della Sera of Milan (1907–14). From 1911, he was an editor of the *Idea Nazionale*. After the fusion between fascism and nationalism, Forges became a secretary of the Fascist party and then editor of the *Tribuna-Idea Nazionale*. Of all the major Nationalist leaders, he identified most closely with the totalitarian mentality of fascism. See Frater, *Roberto Forges Davanzati* (Milan: Editoriale Arte e Storia, 1939). Maurizio Maraviglia (1878–1955) was born in Pola. He too had a brief flirtation with socialism before becoming one of the founders of the Italian Nationalist Association. After the fusion with the PNF, he was a member of the Fascist Grand Council, vice-director of the *Tribuna* after 1925, and a senator in 1939.

27. For a sampling of the irredentist positions of *La Grande Italia*, see Arturo Colautti, "La porta aperta," April 17, 1909, and "La cambiale perpetua," May 16, 1909; G. Castellini, "I sei anni di Tommaso Tittoni," December 12, 1909; Italicus, "L'insidia pangermanista," May 9, 1909. Corradini wrote to Viana on April 9, 1909: "At this moment, there is in Italy a kind of sentimental imperialism: irredentism. Perhaps it is for the good that nationalism makes use of it as a means of propaganda." (cited in Perfetti, "Sindacalismo, nazionalismo, imperialismo," p. 90).

28. Picardi was the editor of the *Rassegna contemporanea* and became a founding member of the Italian Nationalist Association, only to withdraw along with other moderates in 1912. For a survey of the *Carroccio's* positions, see "Per cominciare," March 2, 1909; "Da Sonnino a Giolitti," December 19, 1909; on foreign policy, G. Bertolini, "Guerra di razze," June 15, 1909; L. B., "L'Italia e il panslavismo," April 15, 1909; S. Messina, "Nazionalismo economico," December 1, 1909; "Il Nazionalismo finanziario," April 15, 1910. F. Coppola, "Il nazionalismo in Italia," *La Tribuna*, December 3, 1910. Coppola was born in Naples in 1878. He was perhaps the closest of the Nationalists to the positions of the Action Française. Anti-Semitic, doctrinaire, and passionately interested in foreign policy, Coppola became editor of the review, *Politica*, in 1918. He supported the fusion with fascism in 1923, became a delegate to the League of Nations in the same year, a member of the Italian Academy in 1929, and a professor at the University of Perugia. As editor of *Politica*, he was the guardian of conservative nationalist purity during the fascist years.

29. On the relationship between the early Nationalist movement and the *Resto del Carlino*, see G. Carocci, *Giovanni Amendola nella crisi dello stato italiano* (Milan: Feltrinelli, 1956), pp. 21–22.

30. On Luigi Federzoni, see V. Cian, *Luigi Federzoni* (Piacenza: Società Tipografica Editoriale, 1934); and L. Federzoni, *L'Italia di ieri*

per la storia di domani (Milan: Mondadori, 1967). I would also like to thank Signora Elena Argentieri for placing at my disposition an unpublished manuscript by Federzoni on his early life and family history.

31. G. Castellini, "Conversando con Enrico Corradini," *Grande Italia*, March 20, 1910.

32. A copy of the invitation to the congress is in the Castellini papers, Fondazione Castellini, Museo del Risorgimento, Milan, cartella 5, fasc. 20306; on the tactic of the imperialist group at the congress, see Federzoni to Castellini, September 25, 1910, ibid.; also G. Castellini, ed., *Il nazionalismo italiano: Atti del congresso di Firenze* (Florence: A. Quattrini, 1911), pp. 8–9. (Hereafter cited as *Atti*.) Corradini's hopes for the *Tricolore* group are expressed in a letter to Castellini, undated but fall 1910, Fondazione Castellini, cartella 5, fasc. 20306.

33. G. De Frenzi (Federzoni) to Castellini, September 25 and November 10, 1910, Fondazione Castellini, cartella 5, fasc. 20306.

34. *Atti*, pp. 72–73; Arcari, *Le elaborazioni*, 2: 633–34.

35. Corradini, "Classi proletarie: socialismo; nazioni proletarie: nazionalismo," *Atti*, pp. 22–25; G. De Frenzi (Federzoni), "La politica delle alleanze," ibid., pp. 105–26; Sighele, "Irredentismo e nazionalismo," ibid., p. 80; cf. Corradini, "Classi proletarie," p. 21, and the debates, pp. 72–73. The final resolution is in Arcari, *Le elaborazioni*, 3: 4–5.

36. F. Carli, "La politica economica della Grande Italia," *Atti*, pp. 162–65; for the protests of the liberals, see ibid., pp. 62–64, 201–2. The final resolution is in Arcari, *Le elaborazioni*, 3:7.

37. See Maraviglia, "Il nazionalismo e i partiti politici," *Atti*, pp. 47–50; Arcari, *Le elaborazioni*, 3: 4.

38. For the debate on organization, *Atti*, pp. 218–22, 228–29.

39. For a survey of opinion: E. Flori, *Nazionalismo, determinismo e democrazia* (Milan: Tipografia della Perseveranza, 1911), pp. 12–13; Viana's interview with the *Tribuna*, December 7, 1910; Ugo Ojetti, "I nazionalisti in cerca del nazionalismo," *Corriere della Sera*, December 6, 1910; Corradini to Castellini, January 24, 1911, Fondazioni Castellini, cartella 5, fasc. 20306, in which he noted the moderate line on imperialism; Paolo Orano, "Il primo congresso nazionalista," *La Lupa*, December 11, 1910; G. Sergi, "A proposito del nazionalismo," ibid., December 25, 1910; L. Tancredi (M. Rocca), "Il neonazionalismo," in *Dieci anni di nazionalismo fra i sovversivi d'Italia* (Milan: Casa Editrice Rinascimento, 1918), pp. 29–30, and "Il nazionalismo," *La Lupa*, January 1, 1911; Sighele, *Nazionalismo e i partiti politici*, pp. 10, 13; V. Picardi, "Il congresso nazionalista di Firenze," idem, *Scritti politici*

e letterari (Rome: Libreria di Scienza e Lettere, 1922), pp. 73–76; D. Palazzoli, "Irredentismo catastrofico e politica nazionalista," *Grande Italia*, January 1, 1911.

CHAPTER TWO

1. Giovanni Giolitti, *Memoirs of My Life* (London: Chapman and Dodd, 1923), pp. 224–25.

2. Nino Valeri, *Da Giolitti a Mussolini* (Florence: Parenti, 1958), chap. 1; G. Carocci, *Giolitti e l'età giolittiana* (Turin: Piccola Biblioteca Einaudi, 1961), chaps. 1–2.

3. See the program in *Idea Nazionale*, March 1, 1911; "Il problema morale e il nazionalismo," ibid., August 31, 1911; Corradini, "Movimento nazionalista: dottrina e tattica," ibid., April 5, 1911. "La volontà e la forza della Germania," ibid., May 11, 1911; also "Il nazionalismo e la realtà politica," ibid., March 15, 1911; "Il rito della riforma," ibid., March 1, 1911.

4. "Il monopolio delle assicurazioni ovvero le delizie del riformismo," ibid., June 15, 1911; "Tradizioni liberali e il nazionalismo," ibid., July 1, 1911; "Da Camillo Cavour al nazionalismo," ibid., August 17, 1911.

5. "Movimento nazionalista," ibid., June 8 and September 28, 1911; also the letter of G. Limo and the comment of the editors, ibid., October 19, 1911.

6. William C. Askew, *Europe and Italy's Acquisition of Libya, 1911–1912* (Durham, N.C.: Duke University Press, 1942), pp. 15, 19–21; Augusto Torre, *La politica estera dell'Italia dal 1896 al 1914* (Bologna: Patron, 1960), pp. 155–57. On Italy's position and the role of the Banco di Roma, see Francesco Malgeri, *La guerra Libica* (Rome: Edizioni di Storia e letteratura, 1970), pp. 17–22; Carocci, *Giolitti e l'età giolittiana*, pp. 143–45; Torre, *La politica estera*, pp. 352–55. By 1911, the Banco di Roma pressured the government with the threat that it would sell its interests in Libya if Italy did not act. Marcella Pincherle, "La preparazione dell'opinione pubblica all'impresa di Libia," *Rassegna storica del Risorgimento* 56 (July 1969): 452–57; Askew, *Europe and Italy's Acquisition of Libya*, p. 36.

7. Giolitti, *Memoirs of My Life*, pp. 224–25, 249; Luigi Albertini, *Venti anni di vita politica*, pt. 1 *L'esperienza democratica italiana dal 1898 al 1914*, vol. 2 *1909–1914* (Bologna: Zanichelli, 1951), pp. 118–19; Malgeri, *La guerra libica*, pp. 60–61, 99–104.

8. Conflicting views on the importance of the ANI are given in Malgeri, *La guerra libica,* which emphasizes its role, and two articles by Marcella Pincherle, "La preparazione dell'opinione pubblica all'impresa di Libia," pp. 450–82, and her review of Malgeri's book in *Rassegna storica del Risorgimento,* 58 (1971): 111–19, which are cautious about attributing too much importance to the ANI. The debate is summarized in S. Bono, "La guerra libica: Considerazioni in margine di un recente libro," *Storia contemporanea* 3 (1972): 65–83. See also the very interesting article of Ronald Cunsolo, "Libya, Italian Nationalism and the Revolt against Giolitti," *Journal of Modern History* 37 (June 1965): 186–207. The ANI began its campaign in the *Idea Nazionale* with the article, "Il dovere di ricordare," March 1, 1911. By mid-March, the ANI called for an aggressive policy in Libya ("Movimento nazionalista," *Idea Nazionale,* March 15, 1911; "Quello che non s'è fatto e non si fa ora," ibid., April 5, 1911). See G. Bevione, *Come siamo andati a Tripoli* (Turin: Fratelli Bocca, 1912); on Bevione and the ANI, see Malgeri, *La guerra libica,* p. 50, and Pincherle, "La preparazione dell'opinione pubblica," p. 460–64. V. Castronovo, *La stampa italiana dall'unità al fascismo* (Bari: Laterza, 1970), pp. 192–94.

9. De Frenzi to Castellini, May 6, 1911, Fondazione Castellini, cartella 5, fasc. 20306.

10. See M. Panizza, "Per un'affermazione nazionalista anti-imperialista," *Grande Italia,* May 22, 1911; De Frenzi to Castellini, August 21, 1911, Fondazione Castellini, cartella 5, fasc. 20306; De Frenzi, "Tripoli e l'irredentismo," *Idea Nazionale,* June 1, 1911.

11. Corradini, "L'ora di Tripoli: La penetrazione pacifica degli altri," *Idea Nazionale,* August 24, 1911; "L'oggi e il domani di Tripoli," ibid., August 3, 1911; "A quanto è utile l'occupazione di Tripoli," ibid., September 21, 1911. On the exaggerations of the wealth of the colony, see Claudio G. Segrè, *Fourth Shore: The Italian Colonization of Libya* (Chicago: University of Chicago Press, 1974), pp. 23–25. On the syndicalist dimension to Corradini's appeals for intervention in Libya, see "Le nazioni proletarie e il nazionalismo," in Corradini, *Il nazionalismo italiano* (Milan: Treves, 1914), pp. 33–34 and idem, *Sopra le vie del nuovo impero* (Milan: Treves, 1912), pp. 16–18, 60, 226–28.

12. A. Labriola, "L'Europa contro l'Italia," *Idea Nazionale,* October 12, 1911; and "La prima impresa collettiva della nuova Italia," in A. O. Olivetti, ed., *Pro e contro la guerra di Tripoli* (Naples: Società Editrice Partenopea, 1912), pp. 48–53. Olivetti's book is a collection of articles from his *Pagine Libere* on the war. On the penetration of

nationalism into syndicalism, see Enzo Santarelli, *Le origini del fascismo* (Urbino: Argaglia, 1963), pp. 123–30. In fairness to Labriola, he later regretted his position in Libya, and it caused him some difficulties in the elections of 1913. See Dora Marucco, *Arturo Labriola e il sindacalismo rivoluzionario in Italia* (Turin: Fondazione Luigi Einaudi, 1970), pp. 203–7.

13. "Il nazionalismo nell'ora presente: La riunione del gruppo milanese," *Grande Italia*, November 12, 1911; "La nostra opera," *Idea Nazionale*, November 2, 1911; Corradini, "La morale della guerra," in *Discorsi politici* (Florence: Vallecchi, 1923), pp. 140–41.

14. "Fatti, non parole," *Idea Nazionale*, November 9, 1911. There was a feeling that nationalism might have burnt itself out in Libya. See Amendola to Prezzolini, December 27, 1911, in Prezzolini, *Il tempo della Voce*, p. 455, and N. M. Fovel, "Nazionalismo, democrazia, Tripolitania," *Giornale del Mattino*, December 21, 1911. "Alleate nemiche: La nostra debolezza nella Triplice," *Idea Nazionale*, June 13, 1912; Corradini, *Sopra le vie del nuovo impero*, pp. 192–99; "La pace mediocre e i pericoli balcanici," and "Il contrasto fra l'Italia e l'Austria," *Idea Nazionale*, October 17, 1912.

15. Sighele to Paolo Arcari, October 4, 1911, in P. M. Arcari, *Le elaborazioni*, 3: 128–29; Sighele, *Nazionalismo e i partiti politici*, pp. 23–24, 104–5.

16. Sighele, *Nazionalismo e i partiti politici*, pp. 114–25, 161–79, 186–87, 196–98; idem, *Pagine nazionaliste* (Milan: Treves, 1910), pp. 217–22; idem, *Ultime pagine nazionaliste* (Milan: Treves, 1912), pp. 76–77.

17. Coppola, "Nazionalismo e democrazia," *Idea Nazionale*, December 28, 1911; idem, "L'Israele contro l'Italia," ibid., November 16, 1911; for the protests of Levi and Musatti and the response of the editors, see ibid., November 23, 1911; Coppola, "Il mio antisemitismo," ibid., November 30, 1911. Sighele's rupture with the ANI came with the publication of his articles, "Le incertezze del nazionalismo," *La Tribuna*, April 17, 1912, and "Il partito dei reduci," ibid., April 13, 1912.

18. See the letters by Coppola and Corradini, *Idea Nazionale*, May 2, 1912.

19. On the position of the Catholics over Libya, see Malgeri, *La guerra libica*, pp. 236–54; G. De Rosa, *Storia politica dell'Azione Cattolica in Italia*, vol. 2 (Bari: Laterza, 1954), 329–37; G. Grilli, *La finanza vaticana in Italia* (Rome: Riuniti, 1961), pp. 39–40; G. Spadolini, *Giolitti e i cattolici* (Florence: Le Monnier, 1960), pp. 238, 244; A.

D'Alessandro, "Il Banco di Roma e la guerra di Libia," *Storia e politica* 7 (1968): 491–509; M. G. Rossi, "Movimento cattolico e capitale finanziario: Appunti sulla genesi del blocco clerico moderato," *Studi storici* 13 (1972): 249–88.

20. A. Zanetti, "Il Primo congresso," *Idea Nazionale*, November 30, 1911; "Movimento nazionalista," ibid., April 18, 1912; Mario Panizza, "Nazionalismo democratico e nazionalismo antidemocratico," *Grande Italia*, February 4, 1912; G. Turati, "L'azione democratica del nazionalismo," ibid., January 28, 1912; mm., "I partiti e la riforma elettorale," *Idea Nazionale*, May 16, 1912; Spadolini, *Giolitti e i cattolici*, chap. 7.

21. See Richard Webster, *The Cross and the Fasces: Christian Democracy and Fascism in Italy* (Stanford, Calif.: Stanford University Press, 1960), pp. 3–21; Carocci, *Giolitti e l'età giolittiana*, chap. 7.

22. F. Meda, "Il nazionalismo," *Corriere d'Italia*, August 12, 1912; idem, "Il problema della scuola: Il nazionalismo e la libertà d'insegnamento," ibid., August 14, 1912; idem, "La nostra risposta," ibid., September 1, 1912; for the Nationalist response, see "Il nostro anticlericalismo," *Idea Nazionale*, August 15, 1912, and "Nazionalisti contro clericali," ibid., September 5, 1912.

23. "Movimento nazionalista: Gruppo di Milano," *Grande Italia*, November 24, 1912; "I problemi vitali dell'Italia discussi dai gruppi nazionalisti," *Idea Nazionale*, November 21, 1912.

24. V. Leonardi, "L'azione del nazionalismo italiano," *Idea Nazionale*, December 5, and 18, 1912; "Le tendenze politiche del nazionalismo discusse dal Gruppo romano," ibid., December 18, 1912.

25. L. Valli, *L'Associazione Nazionalista* (Rome: Armani, 1912), pp. 16–17; Occhini to Arcari, December 4, 1912, in Arcari, *Le elaborazioni*, 3: 135.

26. Castellini, *Fasi e dottrine*, p. 24; Arcari, *Le elaborazioni*, 3: 16, 21–22; Associazione Nazionalista Italiana, Giunta Esecutiva, *L'educazione nazionale nella scuola secondaria* (Rome: Armani e Stein, 1912), pp. 4–9.

27. Corradini, "La condotta della guerra di Libia," *Idea Nazionale*, December 18, 1912; Arcari, *Le elaborazioni*, 3: 23.

28. The unhappiness of the moderates was evident in their comments on the Congress of Rome: P. Arcari, "Dopo il congresso nazionalista," *La Sera*, December 24–25, 1912; "Il congresso di Roma," *Grande Italia*, December 29, 1912; Sighele to Arcari, January 3, 1913, in Arcari, *Le elaborazioni*, 3: 132–33; L. Valli's Letter in *Idea Nazionale*, January 9, 1913. For the Nationalist counterattack, see

Coppola, "Tra i pensatori dell'*Asino* e i dottori dell'*Osservatore*," *Idea Nazionale*, January 9, 1913; Maraviglia, "La tendenza viva e la tendenza morta," ibid., January 2, 1913.

29. In a manuscript, written in 1914, Castellini recalled that the Congress of Rome set the future course for the ANI and marked the emergence of Federzoni as its political leader (Castelini, "Il nazionalismo nel 1914," MS, Fondazione Castellini, cartella 2, fasc. 18150).

Chapter Three

1. "Il contraddittorio fra nazionalisti e cattolici," *Idea Nazionale*, January 30, 1913. Livio Marchetti, "La mentalità economica del partito cattolico," ibid., February 20, 1913; F. Aquilanti, "La mentalità economica del partito cattolico: Risposta a Marchetti," ibid., February 27, 1913, De Rosa, *Storia politica dell'Azione Cattolica*, 2: 367–68.

2. Castronovo, *Economia e società*, pp. 328–29.

3. E. Conti, *Taccuino di un borghese* (Cremona: Garzanti, 1946), pp. 91–92, entry of September 2, 1913.

4. A. Caroncini, "Per un programma economico del nazionalismo," *Idea Nazionale*, June 19, 1913; I.N., "Il nostro punto di vista," ibid., June 19, 1913; "Il preteso dilemma economico," ibid., July 10, 1913; Corradini, "Nazionalismo e democrazia," speech of February 1913, in *Nazionalismo italiano*, pp. 153–57.

5. "Movimento nazionalista," *Idea Nazionale*, March 20 and April 17, 1913. The *Idea Nazionale*'s campaign against the Masons has been reprinted in L. Federzoni, *Paradossi di ieri* (Milan: Mondadori, 1926), pp. 149–231; Spadolini, *Giolitti e i cattolici*, pp. 293–305.

6. Sonnino to Bergamini, September 10, 1913, in Bergamini Archives, Biblioteca Comunale, San Giovanni in Persiceto. On the elections of 1913 in Rome, see Hartmut Ullrich, *Le elezioni del 1913 a Roma: I liberali fra massoneria e Vaticano* (Rome: Società Editrice Dante Alghieri, 1972).

7. Ullrich, *Le elezioni del 1913*, pp. 33, 35–36.

8. See Sonnino's letter to the electors of the College of San Casciano Val Di Pesa, February 20, 1909, in *Discorsi parlamentari di Sidney Sonnino, pubblicati per deliberazione della Camera dei Deputati*, vol. 3 (Rome: Tipografia della Camera dei Deputati, 1925), p. 287; "Il partito liberale e il suffragio univserale," *Nuova antologia*, September 16, 1911, cited in Sidney Sonnino, *Scritti e discorsi extraparlamentari*, ed. B. F. Brown, vol. 2 (Bari: Laterza, 1972), pp. 1576–93; Sonnino's

letter to the electors of the former college of San Casciano, October 18, 1913, *Scritti e discorsi extraparlamentari*, 2: 1613–25. Thanks to Professor Brown's exhaustive publications from the Sonnino Archives we have a better appreciation of the complexity of Sonnino's policies. Sonnino to Bergamini, September 10, 18, 20, and 30, 1913, Archivio Bergamini. Nationalist dislike for Leone Caetani was longstanding. He was mentioned unfavorably in Federzoni's speech to the Congress of Florence. Caetani was a noted expert on the Middle East, who opposed the Libyan War. See De Frenzi to Castellini, March 7, 1912, Fondazione Castellini, cartella 5, fasc. 20306; Giorgio Levi della Vida, *Fantasmi ritrovati* (Venice: Neri Pozza Editore, 1966), pp. 44–47. On Medici's Vatican connections, see Grilli, *La finanza vaticana in Italia*, pp. 43–45; on Foscari, see A. Odenigo, *Pietro Foscari: Una vita esemplare* (Bologna: Cappelli, 1959), pp. 93–95. Also for the Nationalists and the elections, see R. Molinelli, "Nazionalisti, cattolici, liberali," *Rassegna storica del Risorgimento* 52 (1965): 365; Castellini, *Fasi e dottrine del nazionalismo*, p. 28.

9. De Rosa, *Storia politica dell'Azione Cattolica*, 2: 341–42; Ullrich, *Le elezioni del 1913*, pp. 66–68. Albertini referred to Federzoni's letter in *Venti anni di vita politica*, 2: 251. Albertini's relatively favorable attitude toward nationalism is clear from his letter to Antonio Fradeletto, November 8, 1919, in Luigi Albertini, *Epistolario 1911–1926*, 4 vols. (Milan: Mondadori, 1968); 1: 215; the guarantee of Vatican support was mentioned in a conversation with Signora Luisa Federzoni, June 1976.

10. Corradini, "Il cimitero delle intenzioni," *Idea Nazionale*, October 2, 1913; and Maraviglia, "Giolitti e Sonnino," ibid. This unexpected kindness toward Giolitti might have resulted from the suspicious neutrality of *La Stampa* in the Borghese-Federzoni race (Ullrich, *Le elezioni del 1913*, p. 67). Federzoni's electoral program was presented in "Discorso programma del dott. Luigi Federzoni," *Idea Nazionale*, October 18, 1913. Reports of the questura (police headquarters) of Rome show a relatively hard-fought campaign with some foul play on both sides (Archivio Centrale dello Stato, Ministero Interno, Direzione Generale di Pubblica Sicurezza, Ufficio Affari generalie riservati), (1911–15), busta 68, fasc. 152 Rome, reports dated September 28 and October 2, 12, 13, 14).

11. S. William Salomone, *Italy in the Giolittian Era: Italian Democracy in the Making, 1900–1914* (Philadelphia: University of Pennsylvania Press, 1960), pp. 40–41; "Nazionalisti, liberali, cattolici," *Idea Nazionale*, November 13, 1913; "Nazionalisti e cattolici: Per la difesa dello stato e la grandezza della nazione," ibid., November 27, 1913; L. Federzoni, *L'Italia di ieri per una storia di domani* (Milan:

Mondadori, 1966), p. 15. The head of the Catholic Electoral Union singled out Federzoni's victory as especially satisfying.

12. Brunello Vigezzi gives an excellent summary of Salandra's ambitions in "Il suffragio universale e la 'crisi' del liberalismo in Italia," *Nuova rivista storica* 48 (1964): 530–34, 561–64.

13. The standard work on Alfredo Rocco is Paolo Ungari, *Alfredo Rocco e l'ideologia giuridica del fascismo* (Brescia: Morcelliana, 1963). Rocco was born on September 9, 1875 in Naples. After a successful academic career, he was elected to the Chamber of Deputies in 1921. He became an undersecretary at the Treasury in Mussolini's first ministry. Subsequently, he was president of the Chamber of Deputies (1924–25), minister of justice (1925–32), rector of the University of Rome (1932–35), and senator (1934–35). He died in Rome on August 28, 1935.

14. Rocco, "Come riorganizare il partito liberale," *La Tribuna*, November 10, 1913; Federzoni, "Il grande malato," *Idea Nazionale*, November 20, 1913; Rocco, "Il nazionalismo e i partiti: Questioni di tattica," ibid., January 1, 1914; Corradini, "Liberali e nazionalisti," and "Stato liberale e stato nazionale," cited in *Nazionalismo italiano*, pp. 100–4, 123–41.

15. Rocco, "Il problema economico italiano," *La Tribuna*, January 13–14, 1914, cited in *Opere di Alfredo Rocco*, 3 vols. (Milan: Giuffrè, 1938), 1: 14–19; see also Ulrico Aillaud, "La nostra politica sociale," *Idea Nazionale*, January 22, 1914, and "La politica sociale del nazionalismo," ibid., March 12, 1914.

16. Federzoni, "Principi di una nuova politica," ibid., December 18, 1913; "Il compromesso," ibid., March 19, 1914; and "Il voto dei nazionalisti per il ministero Salandra nella dichiarazione dell'on. Federzoni," ibid., April 9, 1914. On the possible appointment of a Nationalist to the government, see Gallenga to Salandra, March 23, 1914, cited in Vigezzi, "Il suffragio universale e la 'crisi' del liberalismo," pp. 570–71, note 49.

17. See "Movimento nazionalista," *Idea Nazionale*, March 12, 1914; Ungari, *Alfredo Rocco*, p. 24; ACS, Min. Int., Dir. gen P.S., Uff. aff. gen. e ris. (1911–15), busta 78, fasc. 185, sottof. 1, report of the prefect of Brescia, February 9, 1914.

18. Foges Davanzati to Albertini, April 4, 1914, in Albertini, *Epistolario*, 1: 236–38. Ferraris's holdings included the important armament works, the Società Italiana per la Fabbricazione di Proiettili, (Italian Society for the Production of Munitions) and the Fiat San Giorgio. A key Nationalist in the financial world was Carlo Marangoni, whose interests included the Società Anomina Finanziaria e Industriale Torinese (Turinese Financial and Industrial Corporation)

and the Società Italiana Trasporti Automobilistici (Italian Society for Auto Transport). The Bombrini family was important in Genovese industry and banking. See Castronovo, *Economia e società,* pp. 333–34, and Webster, *L'imperialismo industriale italiano,* pp. 156–58. On the composition of the board of directors of the Nationalist publishing company, see "Un giornale nazionalista," *Corriere della Sera,* May 19, 1914. An ally of Giolitti complained about the financial aid given the Nationalists by the "friends" in Turin. See E. Giovanelli to Giolitti, May 18, 1915, in *Quarant'anni di vita politica: Dalle carte di Giovanni Giolitti,* 3 vols. (Milan: Feltrinelli, 1962), 3: 169–70.

19. "Parole chiare per il nuovo giornale," *Idea Nazionale,* May 30, 1914. For convergences between industrialists and Nationalists, see Mario Abrate, *La lotta sindacale nella industrializzazione in Italia 1906–1926* (Turin: LIEDL'Impresa Edizioni, 1968), pp. 99–148; Webster, *L'imperialismo industriale italiano,* pp. 320–55, 437–542. The extent to which the *Idea Nazionale* outweighed the movement in importance can be seen in a letter, written by Federzoni as the *Idea Nazionale* was being reorganized, which complained that the association was almost out of funds and needed a registration fee for its congress (Federzoni to Castellini, May 8, 1914, Fondazione Castellini, cartella 5, fasc. 20306).

20. The critique of the ANI's majority by the liberals of the *Azione* can be seen in "Propositi," *Azione,* May 10, 1914; Caroncini, "Individualismo e nazionalismo," ibid., May 10, 1914; Amendola, "L'ordine italico," ibid., May 17, 1914.

21. Paolo Arcari, "Il nazionalismo italiano alla vigilia del terzo congresso," ibid., May 17, 1914; Amendola, "Alla vigilia del congresso nazionalista," *Il Resto del Carlino,* May 16, 1914; Federzoni and Maraviglia, "L'azione politica dei nazionalisti," *Idea Nazionale,* May 14, 1914.

22. Rocco and Carli, "I principi fondamentali del nazionalismo economico," in *Nazionalismo economico* (Bologna: Tipografia di Paolo Neri, 1914), pp. 5–15.

23. Ibid., pp. 19–22.

24. Ibid., pp. 25–40.

25. Ibid., pp. 54–59.

26. Rocco, "Politica e azione sociale," ibid., pp. 140–41.

27. Liberal opinion was hostile to the work of the congress. See "La movimentata giornata di chiusura del congresso nazionalista," *Corriere della Sera,* May 19, 1914; "Il congresso nazionalista," ibid.; V. Vettori, "La crisi del nazionalismo e le sue cause," *Giornale d'Italia,* May 26, 1914; Amendola, "Dissidio ideale," *Azione,* June 7, 1914; "Il congresso nazionalista," *La Perseveranza,* May 17–18, 1914. Albertini

intervened to tone down the impact of the *Corriere*'s attack: "Tell the truth, but do not offend them." (Albertini to Saverio Nasalli Rocca, May 20, 1914, *Epistolario,* 1: 241). For the final resolutions, see Arcari, *Le elaborazioni,* 3: 36. The rupture with the liberals did not extend to the city elections in Rome, where the ANI remained allied in the conservative coalition to bring down Ernesto Nathan. See "I costituzionali mantegono l'accordo con i nazionalisti," *Giornale d'Italia,* May 27, 1914; and "La lotta per il comune di Roma," *Idea Nazionale,* June 13, 1914. Nathan was ousted by the Right in 1914.

28. For Bevione's campaign, see Castronovo, *Economia e società,* pp. 335–37; Bevione to V. Cian, a letter published in *La Stampa,* May 23, 1914; "L'elezione politica di Torino: Liberali, nazionalisti e socialisti di fronte all'attuale momento politica," *Resto del Carlino,* June 19, 1914.

29. The growing political independence of the Catholics was reflected in the action of the Catholic University Students (F.U.C.I.) at their congress in 1914, which proclaimed the absolute incompatibility between Catholicism and nationalist ideology and forbade membership in the ANI (ACS, Min. Int., Dir. gen. P.S., Uff. aff. gen. e ris. 1911–15, busta 82, fasc. 208); De Rosa, *Storia politica dell'Azione Cattolica,* 2: 374–76; "Giudizi di deputati sul congresso nazionalista: Riserve dei cattolici," *Resto del Carlino,* May 21, 1914; Nello Quilici, "Collegi italiani: Marostica," *Azione,* June 7, 1914.

30. Luigi Lotti, *La settimana rossa* (Florence: Le Monnier, 1965), pp. 134–35, 149–50, 236–39. Nationalist activity was the subject of the article "Reazione popolare," *Idea Nazionale,* June 13, 1914. Additional information on the reaction is contained in the reports of the prefects: Milan, ACS, Min. Int., Dir. gen. P.S., Uff. aff. gen. e ris., 1911–15, busta 83, fasc. 186, part 3; Turin, June 10, 1914, ibid., busta 109, fasc. 238, part 2; Modena, June 11, 1914, ibid., busta 83, fasc. 186, part 3; Padua, June 12, 1914, ibid.; Brescia, June 12, 1914, ibid., busta 82, fasc. 186, part. 2; Venice, June 12 and 13, 1914, ibid., busta 84, fasc. 186, part 4; Florence, June 10, 1914, ibid., busta 83, fasc. 186, part 3; Report on the Disorders of June 1915, ibid., busta 82, fasc. 186, part 1; Rome, June 10, 1914, busta 109, fasc. 238, part 2; Palermo, ibid., busta 83, fasc. 186, part 3; Messina, June 10 and 14, 1914, ibid., busta 83, fasc. 186, part 3; Catania, June 13, 1914, ibid., busta 82, fasc. 186, part 2.

31. "Reazione popolare," *Idea Nazionale,* June 13, 1914; Rocco, "Dopo lo sciopero," *Dovere Nazionale,* June 13, 1914, cited in *Opere,* 1:111–13; "Legittima difesa," *Idea Nazionale,* June 13 and 19, 1914.

32. Rocco, "In piena pratica rivoluzionaria: Ostruzionismo, parlamentarismo, giolittismo," *Dovere Nazionale,* July 11, 1914, *Opere,*

1:115–18. The liberal-nationalists of the *Azione* took basically the same position. See "In balia di Malatesta," *Azione*, June 1, 1914; and W. Cesarini Sforza, "La lotta politica," ibid., June 21, 1914.

CHAPTER FOUR

1. See the accusation by Luigi Albertini, *Venti anni di vita politica*, part 2 *L'Italia nella guerra mondiale*, vol. 1 *La crisi del luglio 1914, la neutralità e l'intervento* (Bologna: Zanichelli, 1953), pp. 255–56. For the evolution of the Nationalist position on foreign policy, see "Alleate nemiche: La nostra debolezza nella Triplice," *Idea Nazionale*, June 13, 1912; and "Il contrasto fra l'Italia e l'Austria," ibid., October 17, 1912: Castellini to Albertini, November 12, 1912, *Epistolario*, 1:167; R., "La guerra balcanica e le terre irredente: I nuovi orrizonti dello slavismo," *Idea Nazionale*, November 7, 1912; on alternatives to total dependence on Austria, see Federzoni's remarks in "Gli avvenimenti nei Balcani discussi dal gruppo di Roma," ibid.; "Non facciamo i gendarmi dell'Austria," ibid., November 14, 1912; Forges, "Per orientarci di fronte alla nuova guerra balcanica," ibid., July 17, 1913. For an analysis of the anti-Slav tendencies in Italian nationalism, see E. Collotti, "L'irredentismo adriatico tra Slataper e Timeus," *Occidente* 11 (1955): 439.

2. On the initial pro-German reaction of some of the Nationalists, see "L'assemblea del gruppo romano," *Idea Nazionale*, July 31, 1914; Rocco, "Armiamo l'Italia per tenerla pronta agli eventi," *Dovere Nazionale*, August 1, 1914, in *Opere*, 1:131–33. On Pantaleoni, see R. De Felice, "Giovani Preziosi e le origini del fascismo," *Rivista storica del socialismo* 5 (1962): 493–555. Ruggero Fauro also lined up for Germany. See "L'Italia e la Germania nella crisi presente," *Dovere Nazionale*, August 1, 1914 in F. Gaeta, ed., *La stampa nazionalista* (Bologna: Cappelli, 1965), pp. 83–84. A more cautious view on the Triple Alliance can be found in "L'assemblea del gruppo romano," and Federzoni's motion "L'ordine del giorno della giunta executiva," *Idea Nazionale*, July 31, 1914; G. Bevione, "La condotta dell'Italia," ibid., August 6, 1914. Brunello Vigezzi noted the extremely important qualification which underlay Nationalist statements: that Italy obtain adequate compensation from Austria. See B. Vigezzi, *L'Italia neutrale* (Naples: Ricciardi, 1966), p. 169, note 1. Vigezzi cited many conservatives, including Luigi Albertini, who initially sided with Germany. See Vigezzi, *L'Italia neutrale*, p. 199. Sonnino had the same reaction (Sonnino to Bergamini, July 29, August 13, 16, and 29,

1914, in Archivio Bergamini). Austria was unwilling to make the concessions which the conservatives wanted. See Vigezzi, *L'Italia neutrale*, p. 189, note 1.

3. Corradini, "L'ora dell'azione, *Idea Nazionale*, August 20, 1914. Also Roberto Vivarelli, *Il dopoguerra in Italia 1918–1922*, vol. 1 *Dalla fine della guerra all'impresa di Fiume* (Naples: Ricciardi, 1967), pp. 88–89, 136–37; Vigezzi, *L'Italia neutrale*, chaps. 2, 3; Vittorio De Caprariis, "Partiti politici ed opinione pubblica durante la grande guerra," in Istituto per la Storia del Risorgimento Italiano, *Atti del XLI Congresso del Risorgimento italiano* (Rome: Istituto per la Storia del Risorgimento Italiano, 1965), p. 109, all show that Salandra, San Giuliano, and Sonnino considered neutrality to be temporary.

4. See R. De Felice, *Mussolini il rivoluzionario* (Turin: Einaudi, 1965), pp. 221–40; Leo Valiani, *Il partito socialista italiano nel periodo della neutralità* (Milan: Feltrinelli, 1963), pp. 7–12. On the development of "national" socialism during the war, see Santarelli, *Le origini del fascismo*, pp. 145–53. On Catholic opinion toward the war, see Vigezzi, *L'Italia neutrale*, pp. 200–4; De Caprariis, "Partiti politici ed opinione pubblica," pp. 105–8. The war caused a rupture in the Catholic-Nationalist rapprochement: see "I nazionalisti e la neutralità italiana," *Corriere d'Italia*, September 12, 1914; "Cattolici e nazionalisti," ibid., October 3, 1914. On the Nationalist side, see Rocco, "Disciplina nell'azione, non complicità nella rinuncia," *Dovere Nazionale*, September 5, 1914; Corradini, "I cattolici e la guerra," *Idea Nazionale*, December 19, 1914; and "Noi e i cattolici," ibid., March 31, 1915. For Giolitti's position, see the entries for November 3, 1914, February 12, March 9, and April, 1915, in O. Malagodi, *Conversazioni della guerra*, ed. B. Vigezzi, 2 vols. (Naples: Ricciardi, 1960), 1:24–28, 44–47, 53. For the growing conflict between Albertini and the Nationalists, see Vivarelli, *Il dopoguerra in Italia*, pp. 152–54.

5. Ferraris was involved, along with Diatto and Ernesto Rubino, in the Società Italiana per la Fabbricazione di Proiettili, the Società Italiana Prodotti Esplodenti (Italian Society for Munitions). See Castronovo, *Economia e società*, pp. 341, 350. Castronovo noted that the *Stampa* of Turin suffered a decline in circulation as a result of its lukewarm position on the war (Castronovo, *La stampa italiana*, pp. 215, 230). Typical of the Nationalist appeals to the industrialists were F. Carli, "I problemi economici della guerra e i mercati balcanici," *Idea Nazionale*, January 3, 1915; and "Le industrie e la politica economica nazionale," ibid., March 18, 1915.

6. Rocco, "Mentre dura la neutralità," *Dovere Nazionale*, August 29, 1914, in *Opere*, 1:163–66; Corradini, "L'Italia nella rivoluzione

europea," *Idea Nazionale*, November 24, 1914. For a contrast between the more traditional Sonnino and the ambitious Nationalist program, see S. Sonnino, *Diario 1914–1916* (Bari: Laterza, 1972), p. 49, entry for December 18, 1914; and Coppola, "L'offa del Trentino," *Idea Nazionale*, December 10, 1914; on empire building from Fiume to the Balkans, see R. Fauro, "Fiume deve essere italiana," ibid., April 30, 1915; Mario Alberti, "Il principio di nazionalità, la Russia e la Dalmazia," ibid., April 4, 1915; I.N., "Politica italiana nei Balcani o politica balcanica in Italia," ibid., November 15, 1914.

7. Coppola, "L'Italia e la Triplica Intesa," ibid., April 16, 1915; and "Noi e l'Intesa," ibid., April 2, 1915; Alberti, "I diritti dell'Italia sull'Asia Minore," ibid., April 29, 1915. On Salvemini's critique of the Nationalist program, see Vivarelli, *Il dopoguerra in Italia*, pp. 138–39.

8. See De Felice, *Musslini il rivoluzionario*, chap. 9; Valiani, *Il Partito socialista italiano*, pp. 10–14; the collection of Salvemini's articles from *L'Unità*, *La cultura italiana del '900 attraverso le riviste: L'Unità e la Voce Politica* (Turin: Einaudi, 1962), pp. 427–28. On Salandra's aims, see Vigezzi, *L'Italia neutrale*, pp. 128–31; De Caprariis, "Partiti politici ed opinione pubblica," p. 93; A. Salandra, *La neutralità italiana* (Milan: Mondadori, 1928), pp. 198–206, 214–15. Corradini to Albertini, February 25, 1915, in Albertini, *Epistolario*, 1:93; Coppola, "Per la democrazia o per l'Italia," *Idea Nazionale*, October 3, 1914; and "Si tradisce l'Italia," ibid., March 10, 1915; Corradini, "L'Italia e la guerra," ibid., February 22, 1915. See also De Caprariis, "Partiti politici ed opinione pubblica," p. 93.

9. Rocco, "Contro la politica dei dubbi, della incertezza, e della rinuncia vile," *Dovere Nazionale*, October 11, 1914.

10. "Oltre il parlamentarismo," *Idea Nazionale*, November 2, 1914; Corradini, "La nazione decide, il governo eseguisce," ibid., November 28, 1914; and "La corona e il governo," ibid., November 20, 1914. On Nationalist pressure against Sonnino, see F. Martini, *Diario 1914–1918* (Milan: Mondadori, 1966), p. 214, entry for November 6, 1914; and "Se sappiamo volere," *Idea Nazionale*, November 6, 1914.

11. Coppola, "L'offa del Trentino," *Idea Nazionale*, December 10, 1914; Fauro, "Contro l'inevitabile," ibid., December 18, 1914.

12. "Il giuoco dei giolittiani," ibid., January 12, 1915; "Il messaggio del dittatore," ibid., February 3, 1915. On Giolitti's letter, see Malagodi, *Conversazioni della guerra*, 1:41–42.

13. "Verso la ripresa parlamentare: Fuoco giolittiano sotto le ceneri," *Idea Nazionale*, February 11, 1915; Forges, "La congiura dei neutralisti," ibid., February 12, 1915; for Corradini's threat, see

Martini, *Diario*, pp. 321–22, entry for February 6, 1915. Federzoni, "Gli interventisti che non vorrebbero l'intervento," *Idea Nazionale*, April 13, 1915.

14. An example of the Nationalist tactic can be seen in Alfredo Rocco's conduct at the meeting of the Pro Patria group in Padua on February 6, 1915. He withdrew when the Republicans persisted in presenting a motion which called for revolution in the event that the government failed to go to war. The *Idea Nazionale* argued that every party had to abandon that part of its program which conflicted with the other parties' programs. See "Il convegno di Padova per la guerra," *Idea Nazionale*, February 9, 1915; report of the prefect of Padua, February 8, 1915, ACS, Min. Int., Dir. gen P.S., Uff. aff. gen. e ris., Conflagrazione europea, busta 4, fasc. Padova, sottof. Comitato Pro Patria. On contacts between Left and Right in irredentist groups, see S. Barzilai, *Luci ed ombre del passato* (Milan: Treves, 1937), pp. 138–39; E. Battisti, *Con Cesare Battisti attraverso l'Italia* (Milan: Fratelli Treves, 1938), pp. 180–81; Vigezzi, *L'Italia neutrale*, p. 378. The Nationalists also participated in plans for an expedition to Istria in the fall of 1914 to force the hand of the government (Barzilai, *Luci ed ombre*, pp. 138–40).

15. Battisti, *Con Cesare Battisti*, pp. 173, 197, 206–7. In yet another incident, the Nationalist deputy Gallenga was booed by Republicans at an interventionist meeting in Rome on October 25, 1914. Mussolini was also wary of associating too closely with the ANI. See De Caprariis, "Partiti politici ed opinione pubblica," p. 87.

16. Coppola, "Per la democrazia o per l'Italia," *Idea Nazionale*, October 3, 1914; Corradini, "L'Italia nella rivoluzione europea," ibid., November 20 and 24, 1914; and "Alea jacta est," ibid., December 7, 1914.

17. "La congiura tedesca," ibid., May 30, 1915; "Agire," ibid., May 12, 1915; M. Pantaleoni, "Avanti," ibid., May 15, 1915. On the May crisis, see B. Vigezzi, "Le radiose giornate di maggio 1915," *Nuova rivista storica* 48 (1959):341.

18. "Il Re," *Idea Nazionale*, May 13, 1915; "Chi tradisce il Re?" ibid., May 14, 1915.

CHAPTER FIVE

1. Christopher Seton Watson, *Italy from Liberalism to Fascism* (London: Methuen, 1967), pp. 453–54.

2. Rocco, "L'insufficienza dello stato," *Idea Nazionale*, January 17, 1916; "Prepariamoci per l'Italia di domani," ibid., October 15, 1915;

Corradini, *La marcia dei produttori* (Rome: L'Italiana, 1916), pp. iv–xi.

3. Coppola, *La crisi italiana* (Rome: L'Italiana, 1916), p. ix.

4. Rocco, "Perchè la guerra sia guerra," *Idea Nazionale*, August 8, 1916; Corradini, "La forza rivoluzionaria della guerra," ibid., April 4, 1917.

5. "Contro il tradimento socialista," ibid., May 23, 1915; "Grimm, Grimm," ibid., June 23, 1917; "Le fatali revisioni," ibid., July 1, 1917; "La vergogna denudata," ibid., December 23, 1917. The success of the Nationalist tactic can be measured by the letter of Albertini to Amendola, February 28, 1917, which mentioned favorably the *Idea Nazionale*'s attacks on the socialists (*Epistolario*, 2:689–90). On the general question of Nationalist exploitation of the socialist position, see Vivarelli, *Il dopoguerra in Italia*, p. 319; and G. Canepa, "Il congresso dell'Unione socialista," *Il Messaggero*, May 15–16, 1918.

6. "Parlamento e nazione," *Idea Nazionale*, October 22, 1915; "Concordia nazionale," ibid., July 7, 1915; "Responsabilità," ibid., September 24, 1915; "Esercito e parlamento," ibid., October 30, 1915.

7. "L'episcopato italiano e la guerra," ibid., July 28, 1915; Coppola, "Il Papa, la guerra, e l'Italia," ibid., June 25, 1915; "La portata politica del documento," ibid., August 18, 1917.

8. For an excellent treatment of Italy during the war, see Piero Melograni, *Storia politica della grande guerra* (Bari: Laterza, 1966). For the Nationalist attack on parliament, see "Il parlamento e noi," *Idea Nazionale*, December 5, 1915; Rocco, "L'insufficienza dello stato," ibid., January 17, 1916.

9. This parliamentary tactic found a strong critic in Mussolini: "We have entrusted the war to men who really do not think as we do. These men have immediately flaunted their separation from the interventionist *piazza* which brought them to power." See B. Mussolini, "Governo e nazione," *Popolo d'Italia*, September 7, 1917, in idem, *Opera omnia*, eds. E. and D. Susmel, 36 vols. (Florence: La Fenice: 1951–63), 9:165.

10. Salandra's rejection of cooperation from Turati and Claudio Treves was the subject of Piero Melograni, "I riformisti italiani," *Rivista storica del socialismo* 9 (1966):102–4.

11. "Il volto parlamentare del governo," *Idea Nazionale*, February 8, 1916; "Barzilai ministro," ibid., July 17, 1915; and "Il Partito repubblicano e la monarchia," ibid., July 18, 1915. For the Nationalist attitude on Sonnino, see "E dell'Italia?" ibid., April 17, 1916; "Sonnino e la nostra politica estera," ibid., June 15, 1916; "Il governo e le questioni del momento: Revisione e rinnovazione,"

ibid., June 11, 1917. See also Martini, *Diario*, pp. 674–75, 752, 878, entries for April 16 and July 5, 1916, and March 14, 1917; G. B. Gifuni, ed., *Il diario di Salandra* (Milan: Pan Editrice, 1969), p. 125, entry for April 24, 1917.

12. A. Salandra, *Discorsi della guerra* (Milan: Treves, 1922), pp. 98–102. See also Forges Davanzati, "La politica del silenzio," *Idea Nazionale*, February 3, 1916. Forges to Albertini, March 18, 1916, in Albertini, *Epistolario*, 2:573–75; Forges, "Per un caso di coscienza," *Idea Nazionale*, February 27, 1916.

13. Raffaele Colapietra, *Leonida Bissolati* (Milan: Feltrinelli, 1958), pp. 228; Albertini, *Venti anni di vita politica*, vol. 2, part 2, pp. 168–69: Martini, *Diario*, p. 653, entry for March 10, 1916. For the Nationalist reaction, see "Equivoco," *Idea Nazionale*, March 8, 1916; and "Virtù nazionale," ibid., March 17, 1916. The paper called Salandra's defense of his government "crippled and tired" ("Concordia parlamentare," ibid., March 21, 1916).

14. A. Salandra, *Memorie politiche* (Milan: Garzanti, 1951), pp. 5–6. Salandra told the king that he would refuse demands to enlarge his government. See also "Il ministro caduto," *Idea Nazionale*, June 12, 1916; the Roman Nationalist group called for a government composed of all interventionist parties, "L'Associazione nazionalista e la situazione politica," ibid., June 14, 1916.

15. "Il ministero nazionale," *Idea Nazionale*, June 19, 1916. For the growing hostility to Orlando, see "Necessità superore," ibid., September 4, 1917; "L'on. Orlando e il ministero nazionale," ibid., January 30, 1917; Colapietra, *Bissolati*, p. 243.

16. For the Nationalist-Cadorna relationship, see Melograni, *Storia politica della grande guerra*, pp. 21, 191, 345. Ugo Ojetti, then a journalist handling press relations for Cadorna, worked to win the support of the *Idea Nazionale*, when there was a rumor that Cadorna might be relaced by General Di Robillant. See Ojetti's letters to his wife, February 4, 5, 9, 29 and April 30, 1916, in Ugo Ojetti, *Lettere alla moglie* (Florence: Sansoni, 1964), pp. 194, 196–97, 226, 280. Ferdinando Martini related how Corradini returned in frustration from the front after his efforts to spread patriotic propaganda among the troops were rebuffed by Cadorna (Martini, *Diario*, p. 494, entry for July 10, 1915). The Nationalists seem to have thought in terms of a wartime dictator like Clemenceau ("Come si può disfare il disfattismo," *Idea Nazionale*, December 19, 1917).

17. "L'union dei partiti e il parlamento," *Idea Nazionale*, June 17, 1917.

18. On the Nationalist role within the *fascio,* see ACS, Min. Int., Dir. gen. P.S., Aff. gen. e ris., Conflagrazione Europea, busta 37, fasc. Roma, sottof. Comitato di difesa interna; Martini, *Diaro,* p. 653, entry for March 10, 1916; "L'assemblea annuale ordinaria del Gruppo nazionalista," *Idea Nazionale,* February 1, 1917, giving approval to the policy of working with the Left. In November 1916, the Nationalists joined in the formation of the Roman *fascio d'azione,* along with representatives of the Center and the Left (*Fronte Interno,* November 12, 1916). Also see, ACS, Min. Int., Dir. gen. P.S., Aff. ge. e ris., Conflagrazione europea, busta 30B, fasc. Roma, sottof. Congress interventista, report of July 6, 1917, detailing the Nationalists' threat to split the *fascio.* On the whole, however, Nationalist policy aimed to profit from the alliance, which the ANI hoped would continue ("Forze nuove sul fronte interno," *Idea Nazionale,* April 13, 1917).

19. On the Nationalist role in the financing and publication of the *Fronte Interno,* see ACS, Min. Int., Dir. gen. P.S., Uff. aff. gen. e ris., Conflagrazione europea, busta 30A, fasc. Roma, sottof. Fascio rivoluzionario, report entitled "Informazioni," November 14, 1915; ibid.; "Circa i progetti dei partiti repubblicano e socialista e la riunione degli interventisti;" Castronovo, *La stampa italiana,* pp. 243–49; ACS, Min. Int., Dir. gen. P.S., Uff. aff. gen. e ris., Stampa cessata 1894–1931, busta 25, fasc. Roma, sottof. *Fronte Interno;* De Felice, *Mussolini il rivoluzionario,* pp. 338–39; Vivarelli, *Il dopoguerra in Italia,* p. 95.

20. Earlier in the year Giolitti issued his first major public statement since 1915. See Albertini, *Venti anni di vita politica,* vol. 2, pt. 2, p. 585; Seton Watson, *Italy from Liberalism to Fascism,* p. 473.

21. Melograni, *Storia politica della grande guerra,* p. 465; Martini, *Diario,* pp. 1034, 1041–42, entries for November 6 and 9, 1917; ACS, Min. Int., Ufficio Centrale d'Investigazione. busta 31, fasc. 469, Interventisti. On the growth of the Fascio Parlamentare, see F. Pullè and G. Celesio, *Memorie del Fascio Parlamentare di Difesa Nazionale* (Bologna: Cappelli, 1932), pp. 102–4. Federzoni's efforts to make antisocialism a major issue can be seen in Pullè and Celesia, *Memorie del Fascio Parlamentare,* p. 122; *Martini,* Diario, p. 1085, entry for December 22, 1917. In September 1918, the Nationalist and anti-Orlando factions of the *fascio* triumphed over the moderates in Rome. See ACS., Min. Int., Dir. gen. P.S., Aff. gen. e ris., Conflagrazione europea, busta 73B, fasc. Convegni e congressi, report of May 31, 1918; and ibid., busta 30B, fasc. Roma, sottof. Fascio Interventista, reports of July 20, August 5, 8, 9, and September 9, 1918;

"La grande assemblea del fascio," *Fronte Interno,* September 10–11, 1918; "La crisi nel Fascio romano," *Idea Nazionale,* August 11, 1918.

22. Cited in Melograni, *Storia politica della grande guerra,* p. 439.

23. Albertini, *Venti anni di vita politica,* vol. 3, part 2, p. 33; Treves and Turati, "Proletariato e resistenza," *Il Messaggero,* November 10–11, 1917.

24. On the evolution of the Nationalist position during the battle of Caporetto, see Pio Mari, "L'offensive austro-tedesca," *Idea Nazionale,* October 25, 1917; "Dovere italiano," ibid., October 29, 1917; "Un programma di concordia," ibid., November 4, 1917; "I destini d'Italia," ibid., November 5, 1917; Rocco, "Dall'episodio alla storia," ibid., November 14, 1917.

25. Federzoni signed the Ciccotti project for some limited land reform, but opposition from within the ANI led the leadership to back off. See Federzoni, "Per i combattenti," *Idea Nazionale,* November 17, 1917; idem, "Per passare ai fatti," ibid., November 22, 1917; idem, "Uccidere la retorica," ibid., November 27, 1917. For a more cautious view on reform, P. Nonno, "Il progetto Ciccotti e le terre incolte," ibid., December 16, 1917.

26. Rocco, "La resistenza civile," ibid., November 21, 1917; I.N., "Il popolo e le sette," ibid., November 8, 1917.

27. For the Nationalist attck on the Commerciale, see "La banca tedesca," ibid., September 25, 1915; "L'A.E.G., la Banca Commerciale e il comm. Joel," ibid., October 30, 1915. Disagreements between Ferraris and the Nationalists began in September, when Corradini refused to stop the campaign against the bank. See also De Felice, "Giovanni Preziosi e le origini del fascismo," p. 9; and Castronovo, *La stampa italiana,* p. 246. The *Idea Nazionale* engaged in a duel with the *Tribuna,* which was backed by the Commerciale, see Martini, *Diario,* p. 607, entry for January 8, 1916.

28. Castronovo, *La stampa italiana,* pp. 246–47; ACS, Min. Int., Dir. gen. P.S., Aff. gen. e ris., Stampa cessata, busta 25, fasc. Roma, sottof. Affari generali, report of April 13, 1918, noting that the *Tribuna* lost 10 percent and the *Messaggero* 30 to 40 percent of their readership because of the same price increases.

29. When Corradini published his book, *La marcia dei produttori,* he wrote to Filippo Rejna of the Banca Italiana di Sconto that the book "is a lyrical outburst of the bourgeois doctrine of the producers. You should spread it around in industrial circles." See Castronovo, *La stampa italiana,* p. 247.

30. "Buon senso," *Idea Nazionale,* July 16, 1918; P. Nonno, "Il convegno degli agricoltori e industriali," ibid., July 21, 1918; G. L. Franchi, "Espansione e protezione," ibid., August 9, 1918; "I prob-

lemi della terra e l'Associazione per la Difesa dell'Agricoltura," ibid., April 21, 1918; "Per l'intesa fra agricoltori ed industriali," ibid., July 7, 1918.

31. Rocco, "Il problema del munizionamento," ibid., July 16, 1915: "Per la guerra e dopo," ibid., February 4, 1916; Pantaleoni, "Lo stato azionista," ibid., June 15, 1915; G. Valenti, "L'azione economica dello stato, ibid., May 3, 1916; idem, "Politica doganale: Per l'avvenire," ibid., May 13–14, 1916; "La mobilitazione della pace: Intervista con l'ing. Belluzzo," ibid., April 15, 1917; for the specific interests included in the Nationalist program, see "Costruire navi," ibid., September 18, 1918; and Franchi, "Autonomia economica," ibid., April 15, 1917. The *Idea Nazionale* was also hostile to high salaries and heavy taxes on profits: "Prepariamoci per l'Italia di domani," ibid., October 1, 1915; F. Carli, "La limitazione dei salari di guerra," ibid., October 15, 1915; Franchi, "Pilastri sulle nuovole," ibid., July 31, 1918, attacking the "soak the rich" ideas of the *Popolo d'Italia.*

32. Corradini's theories were given in two wartime books: *La marcia dei produttori* (Rome: L'Italiana, 1916) and *Il regime della borghesia produttiva* (Rome: L'Italiana, 1918), and in a series of articles: "Politica ed economia della nazione," *Discorsi politici 1902–1923* (Florence: Vallecchi, 1923), p. 376; "Diritti e doveri nazionale dei produttori," ibid., p. 350; "Per la formazione d'una coscienza politica degli industriali," *Idea Nazionale,* April 26, 1917; "Il programma nazionale dei produttori," ibid., July 24, 1917.

33. Corradini, "La fine dei demagoghi," *Idea Nazionale,* July 27, 1918; and "L'uomo della lotta di classe e l'uomo della lotta di nazione," ibid., October 23, 1915.

34. Corradini, "Politica ed economia della nazione," "La guerra e la lotta di classe," and "Diritti e doveri nazionali dei produttori," in *Discorsi politici,* pp. 352, 357–68, 375–89; "Considerazioni sull'passato e sull'avvenire," *Idea Nazionale,* August 16, 1916; *Il regime della borghesia produttiva,* pp. 33, 45–46.

35. Mussolini, "Il fucile e la vanga," *Popolo d'Italia,* May 1, 1918, *Opera omnia,* 11:35; "Novità," *Popolo d'Italia,* August 1, 1918, ibid., pp. 241–43; "Orientamenti e problemi," *Popolo d'Italia,* August 18, 1918, ibid., pp. 282–83. On the relationship between Mussolini and the Nationalists, see Vivarelli, *Il dopoguerra in Italia,* pp. 223–27, 235, 262–66; De Felice, *Mussolini il rivoluzionario,* pp. 409–12; N. Tranfaglia, *Dallo Stato liberale al Regime fascista* (Milan: Feltrinelli, 1973), pp. 74–78.

36. Mussolini, "Trincerocrazia," *Popolo d'Italia,* December 15, 1917, *Opera omnia,* 10: 140–41; "Orientamenti," *Popolo d'Italia,* June 12,

1918, *Opera omnia,* 11:117–19; "Novità," *Popolo d'Italia,* August 1, 1918, ibid., p. 243; "Divagazioni," *Popolo d'Italia,* September 1, 1918, ibid., p. 344; "Consensi," *Popolo d'Italia,* September 10, 1918, ibid., pp. 348–49.

37. Coppola, "La triplice alleanza," *Idea Nazionale,* July 20, 1915; Rocco, "Lo sforzo necessario," ibid., August 30, 1915; "Tra l'egomonia tedesca e l'equilibrio," ibid., August 14, 1915; Rocco, "Prepariamoci a tempi," ibid., August 31, 1915.

38. Federzoni, "I diritti d'Italia oltremare," ibid., January 27, 1917; Forges, "Non definire, ma fare," ibid., January 29, 1918. Fears that the allies were neglecting Italy's interests were evident in Coppola's exchange with the writers for the Action Française: "La questione dell'Austria: a Jacques Bainville," ibid., August 3, 1916; "La questione dell'Austria," ibid., July 12, 1916; "Austrofilia francese," ibid., July 13, 1916; "C'è anche l'Italia," ibid., July 15, 1916.

39. Forges, "Le formule e la storia," ibid., January 9, 1918; "La guerra dell'Intesa," ibid., January 8, 1918.

40. I.N., "Responsabilità," ibid., September 8, 1915; I.N., "Crisi di guerra," ibid., March 17, 1917; "Rivoluzione nazionale," ibid., April 1, 1917; I.N., "La crisi russa," ibid., May 16, 1917; "L'Intesa e la Russia," ibid., April 1, 1917.

41. "Kerensky," ibid., July 23, 1917; "Il soviet vuol salvare la Russia," ibid., August 13, 1917; Corradini, "Il pericolo russo e quello tedesco," ibid., August 12, 1917; Rocco, "L'attesa," ibid., September 13, 1917. Contrast with Mussolini's "Bandiere rosse," *Popolo d'Italia,* July 5, 1917, and "Viva Kerensky," *Popolo d'Italia,* July 26, 1917, in *Opera omnia,* 9:26–28, 78.

42. Corradini, "L'immenso Lenin," *Idea Nazionale,* December 27, 1917; "Inversioni," ibid., November 25, 1917; "Il leninismo," ibid., November 28, 1917; Corradini, "I buoni maestri fanno i buoni discepoli," ibid., December 3, 1917.

43. An indication of Mussolini's attitude can be seen in the headline from the *Popolo d'Italia* of November 2, 1917: "The New German Weapon is Called Lenin." See also "Nell'attesa," *Popolo d'Italia* (Roman ed.), November 4, 1917; Nor., "L'ora dell'intervento in Russia," ibid., July 11, 1918. The *Idea Nazionale* was, if anything, more ferocious: G. Miletti, "Necessità di agire," May 23, 1918; "Le necessità dell'azione," June 30, 1918; Corradini, "Il Kaiser e Lenin," September 9, 1918. Contrast with Labriola, "Kerensky e l'Intesa," *Il Messaggero,* December 29–30, 1917.

44. Forges, "C'è di mezzo il mare," *Idea Nazionale,* January 11,

1918; Corradini, "L'universalismo e l'Italia," ibid., April 8, 1917; "La parola all'Italia," ibid., January 15, 1918.

45. Federzoni, "L'Austria battuta in Albania," ibid., July 15, 1918; and "I diritti d'Italia oltremare," ibid., January 27, 1917; I.N., "Per i confini del nostro dominio nell'Oriente," ibid., February 13, 1917; "Etiopia," ibid., August 6, 1916. See also Albertini to Corradini, no date, *Epistolario,* 2:1043–44, note 224, in response to Corradini's letter of April 3, 1917 (ibid., p. 699).

46. I.N., "Il nuovo attentato jugoslavo: Il regno serbo-croato-sloveno," *Idea Nazionale,* August 5, 1917; "L'Italia e il patto di Corfu," ibid., August 7, 1917. For the position of the *Fronte Interno,* see Gianfranguerr, "Le questioni italiane all'estero," July 6, 1916; and "Criminose aberrazioni del prof. Salvemini," May 3, 1917.

47. Martini, *Diario,* p. 1108, entry for February 15, 1918; Malagodi, *Conversazioni della guerra,* 2:322, note 2; Colapietra, *Bissolati,* pp. 252–53; Vivarelli, *Il dopoguerra in Italia,* pp. 169–70; "Il convegno di Roma," *Idea Nazionale,* April 10, 1918.

48. I.N., "La guerra alle sue origini," *Idea Nazionale,* April 12, 1918; "Il gruppo nazionalista di Roma e il convegno delle nazionalità antiaustriache," ibid., April 22, 1918. For the *Corriere*'s critique, see "La politica antiaustraica in Inghilterra e in Italia," *Corriere della Sera,* August 17, 1918; "Le difese dell'on. Sonnino," ibid., August 20, 1918; "Gli S.U. e il patto di Londra," ibid., August 21, 1918.

49. For the reaction to the *Corriere*'s gambit, see "Note di politica estera," *Il Messaggero,* August 20, 1918; Rastignac, "Un po' di diffidenza," *La Tribuna,* August 26, 1918; I.N., "La politica antiaustraica dell'Italia: Il fondo del dissidio," *Idea Nazionale,* August 20, 1918; "Fuori degli equivoci," ibid., August 22, 1918; "Reciproca incomprensione," ibid., August 23, 1918; Malagodi, *Conversazioni della guerra,* 2:371, entry for August 20, 1918; Pullè and Celesia, *Memorie del Fascio parlamentare,* pp. 146–47.

50. "Le formule e la guerra," *Popolo d'Italia,* July 18, 1917, *Opera omnia,* 9:59–60; "Dov'è l'imperialismo," *Popolo d'Italia,* February 15, 1918, *Opera omnia,* 10:328; "Risultati," *Popolo d'Italia,* August 26, 1918, *Opera omnia,* 11:310–11. Corradini argued that Mussolini's slogans on the democratic war conflicted with his basic principles ("La verità della guerra," *Idea Nazionale,* April 8, 1918). See also De Felice, *Mussolini il rivoluzionario,* p. 344; and Vivarelli, *Il dopoguerra in Italia,* pp. 177–78, 235–42.

51. Salvemini's comment was cited in Strappini, "Cultura e classe: analisi di un mito," p. 122.

CHAPTER SIX

1. The weakness of the *fascio* and its probable dissolution was the subject of a report to the Interior Ministry, see ASC., Min. Int., Dir. gen. P.S., Aff. gen. e ris., Conflagrazione europea, busta 30B, fasc. Roma, sottof. Fascio Interventista, reports of November 13 and 19, 1918.

2. For a brief survey of postwar economic and political problems, see F. Chabod, *Italia contemporanea* (Turin, Piccola Biblioteca Einaudi, 1961), chaps. 1–3.

3. "La situazione politica attuale e i nazionalisti," *Idea Nazionale,* April 20, 1919; "La prima assemblea della sezione nazionalista barese dopo la guerra," ibid., April 16, 1919; "La ricostruzione del gruppo nazionalista a Venezia," ibid., May 22, 1919; "Il convegno nazionalista di ieri," ibid., December 16, 1919; "Movimento nazionalista," ibid., September 9 and 16, 1919. For the Sempre Pronti, see Romolo Ronzio, *La fusione del nazionalismo con il fascismo* (Rome: Edizioni Italiane, 1943), pp. 169–70; Gaeta, *Nationalismo italiano,* p. 201; Concetto Valente, "Vigilia elettorale a Bologna," *Idea Nazionale,* March 15, 1919.

4. ACS, Min. Int., Dir. gen. P.S., Aff. gen. e ris., Stampa cessata 1894–1931, busta 25, fasc. Roma, report of April 12, 1918; Castronovo, *La stampa italiana,* pp. 246–47, 273, 289–99; "Appunto sulla Società Editrice dell'*Idea Nazionale,*" September 28, 1920, in *Quarant'anni di vita politica: Dalle carte di Giovanni Giolitti,* 3:286–87. Corradini resigned from the editorship of the *Idea Nazionale* in June 1920 and was succeeded by Tommaso Monicelli. See *Idea Nazionale,* June 15, 1920.

5. Associazione Nazionalista Italiana, *Il nazionalismo e i problemi della scuola e del lavoro: Atti del secondo congresso di Roma* (Rome: L'Italiana, 1919), p. 4; "Reazione nazionalista," *Idea Nazionale,* December 14, 1919; "Movimento nazionalista," ibid., December 14, 1919.

6. "Manifesto," *Opere,* 2:529–44; Rocco, *Appunti di filosofia del diritto* (Padua: La Linotipo, Editrice Universitaria, 1918), pp. 27–29, 169–70, 185; Rocco, "Dalla vecchia alla nuova Italia," *Opere,* 2:545–67; Corradini, "La politica economica-sociale del nazionalismo," *Problemi della scuola e del lavoro,* p. 36.

7. "L'ultracarovivere," *Idea Nazionale,* July 6, 1919; "Nuovi parlamenti," ibid., February 25, 1919; Corradini, "Nazionalismo e internazionalismo," ibid., March 24, 1919; Rocco, "Ritorni del medioevo," *Politica* (1920):320.

8. Corradini, "La politica economica sociale del nazionalismo," *Problemi della scuola e del lavoro*, pp. 33–36.

9. Rocco, "Il programma politico dell'Associazione nazionalista," ibid., pp. 41–44, 98–111.

10. Rocco, "Il momento economico e politico," *Politica* (1919):83, 87–88; "Crisi dello stato e sindacati," *Opere* 2:631–45; F. Carli, "Sindacati e ricostruzione," *Politica* (1919):2–7.

11. "Gli industriali italiani per i problemi del dopoguerra," *Idea Nazionale*, December 12, 1918; Pio Perrone, "L'avvenire industriale dell'Italia," ibid., January 14, 1919; "Nitti e i produttori," ibid., January 15, 1919; Corradini, "Vecchio regime e nuove forze," ibid., February 2, 1919; M. Lombardi, "L'indirizzo di Bergamo," ibid., March 6, 1919; Corrado Marchi, "Il secondo convegno dei produttori," ibid., March 3, 1919. On the Nationalists and the agrarians, see P. Nonno, "Voci nuove nel mondo agrario," ibid., March 3, 1919; "Sabotaggio economico d'una politica bolscevica," ibid., February 26, 1919; "Volontà di creare," ibid., February 27, 1919; see also De Felice, *Mussolini il rivoluzionario*,pp. 440–41; and Gaeta, *Il nazionalismo italiano*, p. 157.

12. Agricola, "Realizzazioni bolsceviche nell'Emilia," *Idea Nazionale*, March 26, 1920. On the events in Rome, see G. A. Chiurco, *Storia della rivoluzione fascista* (Florence: Vallecchi, 1929), 1:118–19; Vivarelli, *Il dopoguerra in Italia*, p. 329. On the Nationalist opposition to the proletarian push, see "Il pericolo," *Idea Nazionale*, November 29, 1919; "L'appello ai cittadini," ibid., January 16, 1920; Corradini's important series, "La decomposizione dello stato nelle provincie," ibid., May 30, June 3, 6, 1920.

13. "L'Italia della vittoria," *Idea Nazionale*, April 17, 1919; O. Pedrazzi, "Una mirabile fine," ibid., April 18, 1919; "L'utile netto," ibid., April 19, 1919; De Felice, *Mussolini il rivoluzionario*, pp. 520–21.

14. O. Pedrazzi, "Fasci di combattimento," *Idea Nazionale*, March 25, 1919; Ronzio, *La fusione*, p. 170; Gaeta, *Il nazionalismo italiano*, pp. 208–9; R. Colapietra, *Napoli tra dopoguerra e fascismo* (Milan: Feltrinelli, 1962), pp. 57–59; Chiurco, *Storia della rivoluzione fascista*, 1:129. For a discussion of Nationalist-Fascist relations in this period, see Vivarelli, *Il dopoguerra in Italia*, pp. 326–27; De Felice, *Mussolini il rivoluzionario*, p. 528.

15. "Arditi e codardi," *Idea Nazionale*, May 18, 1919; "Arditi e nazionalisti contro i pussisti," ibid., June 17, 1919; Ronzio, *La fusione*, p. 170. On the role of the *Arditi*, see F. Cordova, *Arditi e legionari dannunziani* (Padua: Marsilio, 1969).

16. See Forges, "Per l'integrità del diritto italiano," *Idea Nazionale*, December 12, 1918; idem, "L'Italia in Africa," ibid., February 4,

1919; A. R., "Smirne," *Politica*, 1 (June 1919):288–89; Italicus, "Il problema adriatico e le aspirazioni italiane," *Idea Nazionale*, January 24, 1919; Forges, "Le date di Trieste e di Fiume," ibid., February 24, 1919; "L'unità dell'Adriatico," ibid., March 11, 1919. Forges rejected the right of the other allies to interfere in Italy's sphere: "La mostruosa inversione," ibid., January 17, 1919; and "Il trattato di Londra e il problema adriatico," ibid., February 5, 1919. On Mussolini's use of some of the same themes, see Vivarelli, *Il dopoguerra in Italia*, p. 249. Also see Gaeta, *Il nazionalismo italiano*, p. 148, for an acute judgment on Nationalist foreign policy.

17. On the rupture with Bissolati, see "L'Italia e l'umanità," *Idea Nazionale*, December 29, 1918; "Fuori della realtà a dano dell'Italia, ibid., December 30, 1918; "La crisi e il programma," ibid., January 2, 1919; "Milano impedisce a Bissolati di parlare contro i sacri diritti d'Italia," ibid., January 13, 1919; Pullè and Celesia, *Memorie del fascio parlamentare*, pp. 153–54.

18. Forges, "Strade buone e strade false," ibid., January 31, 1919; "Il trattato e la lega," ibid., January 23, 1919.

19. Forges, "L'Italia fa da se," ibid., April 23, 1919; Federzoni, "La sola pace giusta," ibid., April 16, 1919; and "Più forte perchè sola," ibid., April 25, 1919. For Nationalist activity, see ibid., April 26 and 28, 1919.

20. "La lega e il blocco latino," ibid., May 11, 1919; also "La conferenza contro l'alleanza," ibid., May 2–3, 1919; Cantalupo, "Cronaca di un ritorno," ibid., May 7, 1919.

21. "La conferenze delle beffe," ibid., May 18, 1919.

22. Corradini, "La nuova alleanza e l'Italia," ibid., May 13, 1919; "La realtà," ibid., June 12, 1919; "Il fascio all'opposizione," ibid., June 20, 1919.

23. Rocco, "La politica finanziaria," *Politica*, 1 (December 1918): 135.

24. E. Apih, *Fascismo e antifascismo nella Venezia Giulia* (Bari: Laterza, 1966), pp. 94–95, 101–3; Carlo Silvestri, "Una Repubblica delle Tre Venezie con presidente il Duca d'Aosta," *Trieste*, 7 (January 1960):25; Paolo Alatri, *Nitti, D'Annunzio e la questione adriatica* (Milan: Feltrinelli, 1959), p. 481.

25. Extremely useful background information on Fiume is given in Michael Ledeen, *D'Annunzio a Fiume* (Bari: Laterza, 1975), chap. 2.

26. On the role of the Trento-Trieste Society, see G. Giuriati, *Con D'Annunzio e Millo in difesa dell'Adriatico* (Florence: Sansoni, 1954), pp. 8–9; Apih, *Fascismo e antifascismo*, pp. 62–63, 90–92, 102; Alatri, *Nitti, D'Annunzio*, p. 190.

27. D'Annunzio to Corradini, December 27, 1918 and January 27, 1919, Archivio Federzoni-Argentieri (the letter of January 27, 1919 was also published in G. D'Annunzio, "Italia, in te sola: Lettere a Enrico Corradini," *Nuova antologia*, 427–28 (August 1943):144. D'Annunzio wrote in January: "I received this morning your letter about my collaboration. Before taking on any other obligations I want to see clearly my situation towards the other paper. My lawyer is working on it." In an undated but subsequent letter, he wrote: "Avv. Barduzzi [his lawyer], who takes care of my business affairs and knows my position vis-à-vis the *Corriere*, is here. Do you want to see him? Do you want to take him to see your Parisi?" (Archivio Federzoni-Argentieri.)

28. D'Annunzio to Corradini, February 15, 1919, Archivio Federzoni-Argentieri.

29. D'Annunzio to Corradini, March 15, 1919, in D'Annunzio, "Italia in te sola," pp. 145–46. When Federzoni published these letters he omitted the reference to Perrone. The original is in Archivio Federzoni-Argentieri.

30. Federzoni urged other Nationalist groups to coordinate their demonstration with those of Rome. Sinigaglia sent out similar telegrams (ACS., Min. Int., Dir. gen. P.S., Aff. gen. e ris, Agitazione Pro Fiume, busta 2, fasc. 6, sottof. 1, report of May 2, 1919). When D'Annunzio spoke in Rome on May 4, and for the anniversary of Italy's entry into the war on May 24, the ANI helped distribute tickets (Nicola D'Atri to Albertini, May 3, 1919, *Epistolario*, 3:1226; D'Annunzio to Corradini, May 25, 1919, in "Italia, in te sola," p. 147.

31. Apih, *Fascismo e antifascismo*, p. 89; Alatri, *Nitti, D'Annunzio*, pp. 121, 137, 159; Giuriati, *Con D'Annunzio*, pp. 11–12. Ledeen, *D'Annunzio a Fiume*, pp. 76–78; De Felice, *Mussolini il rivoluzionario*, p. 532; Giorgio Rochat, *L'esercito italiano da Vittorio Veneto a Mussolini* (Bari: Laterza, 1967), pp. 52–56; Salvemini, "Diario," *Il Mondo*, October 21, 1958, p. 12. For the Nationalist denial, see "Un altro complotto," *Idea Nazionale*, June 15, 1919. D'Annunzio admitted that an appeal to the king would be useless (D'Annunzio to Corradini, June 6, 1919, Archivio Federzoni-Argentieri).

32. D'Annunzio to Corradini, June 11, 1919, Archivio Federzoni-Argentieri.

33. ACS., Min. Int., Uff. Centrale d'Investigazione, busta 42, fasc. 901, report of July 3, 1919; on demonstrations against Nitti, see *Idea Nazionale*, June 22 and 23, 1919; Ledeen, *D'Annunzio a Fiume*, p. 78; Chiurco, *Storia della rivoluzione fascista*, 1:141, 143.

34. D'Annunzio to Corradini, August 18 and 19, 1919, Archivio Federzoni-Argentieri; Ledeen, *D'Annunzio a Fiume*, p. 87; Giuriati, *Con D'Annunzio*, pp. 11–12.

35. D'Annunzio to Corradini, September 11, 1919, announcing his move into Fiume. See Ledeen, *D'Annunzio a Fiume*, pp. 101–7, for reactions of the foreign powers.

36. On financing the Fiume venture, see De Felice, *Mussolini il rivoluzionario*, p. 549; Apih, *Fascismo e antifascismo*, p. 104. On the political maneuvering in Rome, see Turati to Kuliscioff, September 20 and 25, 1919; and Kuliscioff's response, September 27, 1919, in F. Turati and A. Kuliscioff, *Carteggio*, vol. 5 *Dopoguerra e fascismo 1919–1922* (Turin: Einaudi, 1953), pp. 147, 159, 165–66; Nitti to Albertini, September 21, 1919, *Epistolario*, 3:1290; Salvemini, "Diario," *Il Mondo*, October 21, 1958; Federzoni, *L'Italia di ieri*, pp. 48, 56; Alatri, *Nitti, D'Annunzio*, pp. 246, 279.

37. Nationalist activities in Fiume and elsewhere in support of D'Annunzio were detailed in Corradini, "L'avanguardia," *Idea Nazionale*, September 14, 1919; "I nazionalisti per Fiume," ibid., September 15, 1919; "Movimento nazionalista," ibid., October 2, 1919; on Zanetti's activities, see ACS. Min. Int., Dir. gen. P.S., Agitazione Pro Fiume, busta 2, fasc. 6, sottof. 2, reports of September 5 (Bologna), September 7 (Trieste), and September 13, 1919 (Ancona). Monicelli of the *Idea Nazionale* announced that he could receive news from Fiume without going through the Italian censor (ibid., busta 6, fasc. 6, report of the Questura of Rome, September 17, 1919). For the running attack on Nitti, see "Cinicismo cieco," *Idea Nazionale*, September 17, 1919; "Non si tratta con Nitti," *Vedetta d'Italia*, September 27, 1919; "Nuova intimidazione di Nitti: Le elezioni," *Idea Nazionale*, September 26, 1919; Forges, "Dov'è l'on. Tittoni," ibid., October 3, 1919.

38. ACS. Min. Int., Agitazione Pro Fiume, busta 3, fasc. 12, 15, 20, for rumor of plots and invasions. Plotting involving Nationalists is recounted in Giuriati, *Con D'Annunzio*, pp. 52–53, 58–59; Odenigo, *Piero Foscari*, p. 174; "Enrico Corradini e l'on. Foscari a Fiume," *Vedetta d'Italia*, October 10, 1919; Rocco, "Gli antecedenti, lo spirito le date della Marcia su Roma," *Idea Nazionale*, October 28, 1923; Vivarelli, *Il dopoguerra in Italia*, p. 539, note 249; for the Nationalist denials, Corradini, "Falsificazioni," *Idea Nazionale*, September 16, 1919; and "Fiume e l'Italia," *Vedetta d'Italia*, October 31, 1919.

39. Odenigo, *Piero Foscari*, p. 180; on Pedrazzi, see Alatri, *Nitti, D'Annunzio*, pp. 301–2; Pedrazzi, "Il trapano," *Vedetta d'Italia*, November 8, 1919.

40. Giuriati, *Con D'Annunzio*, pp. 97–99, 110–11, 208–14; Alatri, *Nitti, D'Annunzio*, p. 325.

41. "Responsabilità," *Vedetta d'Italia*, December 18, 1919. After this article the paper was attacked by demonstrators. Apih noted that conservative opinion favored a modus vivendi. See Apih, *Fascismo e antifascismo*, p. 107; Alatri, *Nitti, D'Annunzio*, pp. 344, 351–52; Giuriati, *Con D'Annunzio*, pp. 110–11; Odenigo, *Piero Foscari*, pp. 180–83.

42. On the situation preceding the elections, see "Incertezze e confusione in questa prima fase elettorale a Milano," *Idea Nazionale*, October 11, 1919; "I combattenti contro il ministero," ibid., October 12, 1919; "I combattenti torinesi di fronte ale elezioni," ibid.; for the situation in Rome, see "Come si delinea la lotta elettorale: La scissione del Partito liberale," and "Giù la maschera," ibid., October 8, 1919; "I proposti dei nazionalisti romani," ibid., October 15, 1919; "Parla l'on. Federzoni," ibid., November 12, 1919. The difficulties in forming lists was recounted in "Ai nazionalisti italiani," ibid., November 1, 1919; "I candidati nazionalisti," ibid., November 12, 1919; on the split in Rome, "La maggioranza dei liberali contro il blocco ministeriale," ibid., October 19, 1919. For comment on the results, see Forges, "Tra gride strainiere," ibid., November 20, 1919; "La nostra lota," ibid., November 19, 1919.

43. "La camera del 40%," ibid., November 19, 1919; "L'attivo della lotta," ibid., November 21, 1919; Federzoni, "Gruppi e partiti a Montecitorio," ibid., December 6, 1919. Federzoni recalled that during this period of pessimism Alfredo Rocco began to argue that the best Nationalist strategy would be to dissolve the ANI in order to merge with the Catholic Popular party and form its right wing (Federzoni, "Diario," entry for February 29, 1927, pp. 99–100, Archivio Federzoni-Argentieri).

CHAPTER SEVEN

1. Capece Minutolo di Bergnano to Giolitti, June 8, 1920, *Dalle carte di Giovanni Giolitti*, 3:272–73; telephone interception, Amendola to Albertini, June 12, 1920, ibid., p. 276; Rocco, "Fallimento, *Idea Nazionale*, February 1, 1920; "Tentativo accordo," ibid., March 9, 1920.

2. "L'ordine nazionale," ibid., June 13, 1920; Forges, "La nostra pregiudiziale," ibid., June 12, 1920.

3. "Noi e Giolitti," ibid., June 13, 1920; "I nazionalisti e il nuovo ministero," ibid., June 15, 1920; "Malignità," ibid., June 19, 1920.

4. "Per chi ha parlato il governo," ibid., June 26, 1920; "Metodo e programma," ibid., July 11, 1920; Zoli to Ambrosini, no date, in *Dalle carte di Giovanni Giolitti*, 3:273–74.

5. On Nationalist expectations, see "Il programma dell'Italia," *Idea Nazionale*, May 20, 1920; Coppola, "La liquidazione albanese," ibid., June 1, 1920; and "Revisione fatale per l'Oriente," ibid., June 20, 1920; A. Tamaro, "Il conflitto adriatico nel quadro balcanico," *Politica* 5 (August 1920):307–12. For the growing disappointment, see Coppola, "Valona," *Idea Nazionale*, August 5, 1920; Rocco, "La pace di Sevres," ibid., August 12, 1920.

6. Rocco, "Gli antecedenti, lo spirito, le date della Marcia su Roma," *Idea Nazionale*, October 28, 1923; A. Tamaro, *Venti anni di storia 1922–1943*, 3 vols. (Rome: Editrice Tiber, 1953–54), 1:94–95; Zanella to Giolitti, December 6, 1920, *Dalle carte di Giovanni Giolitti*, 3:309; Amendola to Albertini, October 27, 1920, *Epistolario*, 3:1430; for Nationalist denials, see "Il nostro colpo di stato," *Idea Nazionale*, October 26, 1920.

7. For the contrast between Mussolini and the Nationalists, see Mussolini, "Ciò che muore e ciò che verrà," *Popolo d'Italia*, November 13, 1920; "L'ultima parola non è detta," *Idea Nazionale*, November 12, 1920; Coppóla, "Il senso della vittoria," ibid., November 13, 1920; "La critica nazionalista dell'on. Federzoni al Trattato di Rapallo," ibid., November 27, 1920; "Al nostro posto," ibid., November 16, 1920; De Felice, *Mussolini il rivoluzionario*, pp. 637–55; G. Rumi, *Alle origini della politica estera fascista* (Bari: Laterza, 1968), pp. 142–44.

8. Forges, "Con la testa nel sacco," *Idea Nazionale*, December 4, 1920; Federzoni, "La sostanza del problema," ibid., December 9, 1920; Chiurco, *Storia della rivoluzione fascista*, 2:206.

9. On the background to the factory occupations, see P. Spriano, *L'occupazione delle fabbriche* (Turin: Piccola Biblioteca Einaudi, 1964).

10. "Patrigiano per impotenza," *Idea Nazionale*, September 17, 1920; Italo Minunni, "Punti fermi," ibid., September 7, 1920; "I nazionalisti contro il governo," ibid., October 13, 1920; Ronzio, *La fusione*, p. 101.

11. "Appello," *Idea Nazionale*, October 16, 1920.

12. "La verità e i falsi sermoni," ibid., October 21, 1920; "Il programma amministrativo della concentrazione nazionale di Roma," ibid., October 24, 1920; "Riscossa nazionale," ibid., November 2, 1920; De Felice, *Mussolini il rivoluzionario*, p. 608.

13. On the Nationalist reaction, see "Il Tricolore sul municipio," *Idea Nazionale*, November 5, 1920; "Per salvare il paese," ibid., November 23, 1920; Chiurco, *Storia della rivoluzione fascista*, 2:197–98.

14. On Nationalist actions against the socialists, see "Conflitti tra nazionalisti e leghisti bolognesi," *Idea Nazionale*, January 11, 1921; "Tragiche giornate a Bologna e a Modena," ibid., January 26, 1921; "Una spedizione di nazionalisti a Crevalcuore: La Camera del

Lavoro distrutto," ibid., April 19, 1921; Renzo De Felice, *Mussolini il fascista*, vol. 1 *La conquista del potere* (Turin: Einaudi, 1966): 5–6.

15. "Immunità parlamentare," *Idea Nazionale*, February 24, 1920; "L'Italia si salva da se," ibid., February 4, 1921; "Importante assemblea nazionalista a Torino," ibid., January 27, 1921. On the growth of the Sempre Pronti, see Raffaele Paolucci, *Il mio piccolo mondo perduto* (Bologna: Cappelli, 1947), p. 233. The growing Nationalist interest in fascism was reflected in "Nuovi orrizonti socialisti," *Idea Nazionale*, March 9, 1921.

16. "Le garanzie dei blocchi nazionali," *Idea Nazionale*, April 3, 1921; "Per lo stato," ibid., April 19, 1921; "L'opera e la fede del nazionalismo rivendicata nell'azione legislativa di Luigi Federzoni," ibid., May 12, 1921.

17. Umberto Fabbri to Umberto Pasella, October 23, 1919, ACS, Mostra della Rivoluzione Fascista, prima parte, busta 105, Carteggio del C.C. dei fasci, cartella 1 (Roma); report of D. Lettieri to the Central Council of the Fasci di Combattimento, March 12, 1920, ibid.; Fabbri to Pasella, April 18, 1920, ibid., cartella 2; for Pasella's remarks on the Nationalists, see "Fascio romano di combattimento: Assemblea generale del 9 giugno 1920," ibid.

18. The poor financial situation of the Roman *fascio* was the subject of a letter from Lettieri to Cesare Rossi, August 20, 1920, ibid., cartella 3. On the eviction of the Fascists, see U. Fraccia to C. Rossi, August 31, 1920, ibid. Cooperation during the elections continued, "La lista dell'Unione Nazionale," *Idea Nazionale*, April 20, 1921, but De Felice noted that many northern Fascists were hostile to such cooperation. See De Felice, *Mussolini il fascista*, 1:61, note 6.

19. "Le candidature nazionaliste," *Idea Nazionale*, April 28, 1921; "Liste nazionali-fasciste a Trieste," ibid., April 23, 1921; "La candidatura nazionalista milanese non riconosciuta," ibid., April 28, 1921; "Enrico Corradini," ibid.; "I nazionalisti e la lotta di Milano," ibid., April 29, 1921; Colapietra, *Napoli*, pp. 156–57.

20. Cesare Rossi to the Roman Fascio, copy of telegram, no date, ACS, Mostra della Rivoluzione Fascista, prima parte, busta 105, cartella 5 (Roma). The local Fascists wanted the *Popolo d'Italia* to express a preference for Vito Pellizzari over Federzoni. Federzoni headed the conservative list, Caetani was second, Rocco fifth, and Bottai seventh ("Il monito di Roma," *Idea Nazionale*, May 18, 1921).

21. "Un nuovo gruppo parlamentare," *Idea Nazionale*, June 17, 1921.

22. For the Nationalists who were also members of the Fascist movement, see Gaeta, *Il nazionalismo italiano*, p. 211; and "I nazionalisti milanesi per Fiume," *Idea Nazionale*, January 8, 1921, where

Massimo Rocca is listed under the name of Libero Tancredi. On the impact of Mussolini's remarks on the Republic, see "Si discute il regime?" and "La giunta esecutiva nazionalista e il nuovo orientamento del fascismo," ibid., May 26, 1921; Paolucci, *Piccolo mondo,* pp. 229–32; De Felice, *Mussolini il fascista,* 1:96–97; "Il gruppo nazionalista per il blocco di destra," *Idea Nazionale,* June 18, 1921.

23. Colapietra, *Napoli,* p. 165–66.

24. Federzoni, "La funzione della destra," *Idea Nazionale,* June 30, 1921; "I quattro punti della destra," ibid., July 2, 1921; Ronzio, *La fusione,* p. 129.

25. Albertini to Ruffini, July 8, 1921, *Epistolario,* 3:1484.

26. On the Pacification Pact, see "I termi dell'accordo," *Idea Nazionale,* July 22, 1921; De Felice, *Mussolini il fascista,* 1:145. On supporting dissidence within the Fascist movement, see Piero Marsich, "L'abdicazione dello stato," *Idea Nazionale,* July 22, 1921; "I fascisti contro la pacificazione," ibid., August 3, 1921; "Lo spirito del trattato per la pacificazione: l'on. Farinacci contrario," ibid., July 26, 1921; Emilio Gentile, *Le origini dell'ideologia fascista* (Bari: Laterza, 1975), p. 216. On the Nationalists' insistence on their elite status with respect to fascism, see, "L'unione delle forze nazionali," *Idea Nazionale,* August 13, 1921; Gaeta, *Il nazionalismo italiano,* p. 213.

27. "Viva impressione a Roma," *Popolo d'Italia,* August 18, 1921; Mussolini, "L'ora dei sermoni," ibid., August 19, 1921. For the Nationalist comment, see "La lotta delle tendenze nel fascismo," *Idea Nazionale,* August 20, 1921. Mussolini, "Una lettera aperta alla commissione esecutiva," *Popolo d'Italia,* September 16, 1921; Marsich, "Verso il partito?" ibid., September 21, 1921; Rocca, "Per una nuova destra," ibid., October 29, 1921; De Felice, *Mussolini il fascista,* 1:176.

28. Nationalist reaction to the Fascist congress was favorable: "L'opera della destra nazionale," *Idea Nazionale,* November 9, 1921; "Un servizio alla nazione," ibid.; "Le direttive dell'azione nazionalista discusse dal convegno dei delegati," ibid., November 6, 1921. A circular from the central committee of the ANI spoke of the progressive elimination of "pseudorevolutionary" elements from fascism (De Felice, *Mussolini il fascista,* 1:193). On the problem of dual membership, see M. Rocca, *come il fascismo divenne una dittatura* (Milan: Edizioni Librerie Italiane, 1952), p. 98.

29. "Il fascismo e i partiti nazionali in una intervista con l'on. De Vecchi," *Idea Nazionale,* November 16, 1921; Federzoni, "Nazionalismo e fascismo," ibid., November 17, 1921.

30. "Marsich risponde all'on. Federzoni," ibid., November 22, 1921; G. Bottai, "Integrazione nazionale," ibid., December 6, 1921; Dino Grandi, "Per intenderci," ibid., February 2, 1922. The indus-

trialist Ettore Conti shrewdly noted that the lack of mass support for the Nationalists would inevitably draw them closer to the Fascists in order to realize their program (Conti, *Taccuino,* p. 256, entry for December 10, 1921). On the debate, see De Felice, *Mussolini il fascista,* 1:195–97.

31. F. Ercole, "Contro un'affrettata fusione," *Idea Nazionale,* December 20, 1921. See also Antonio Pagano, "Fascismo, nazionalismo, sindacalismo," ibid., December 13, 1921; B. Giuliano, "Nazionalismo e fascismo," ibid., February 7, 1922; Rocco, "Il fascismo verso il nazionalismo," ibid., January 6, 1922.

32. Gaeta, *Il nazionalismo italiano,* p. 178. The crisis of the Banca di Sconto and of the Perrone interests was not as serious for the ANI as it might have been a few years earlier. After 1920, the Nationalists began to contract new alliances with the rival Banca Commerciale interests. See Adrian Lyttelton, *The Seizure of Power: Fascism in Italy 1919–1929* (New York: Scribners, 1973), p. 207; Danilio Veneruso, *La vigilia del fascismo: Il primo ministero Facta nella crisi dello Stato liberale in Italia* (Bologna: Il Mulino, 1968), pp. 272–74.

33. "La riunione di ieri del direttorio e del gruppo fascista," *Popolo d'Italia,* February 2, 1922; "L'equivoco della crisi," *Idea Nazionale,* February 3, 1922. The Fascists especially wanted to avoid an anti-Fascist outcome to the crisis (De Felice, *Mussolini il fascista,* 1:244). On the evolution of the crisis, see Veneruso, *La vigilia,* pp. 60, 117–18; Ronzio, *La fusione,* p. 189; Federzoni, *L'Italia di ieri,* p. 68; Salandra, *Memorie politiche,* pp. 12–13; "Il comitato centrale nazionalista contro il collaborazionismo socialista," *Idea Nazionale,* February 14, 1922.

34. "Il discorso di Federzoni per la Destra Nazionale," *Popolo d'Italia,* February 18, 1922; "Direttiva nazionale," *Idea Nazionale,* February 19, 1922; for the meetings of the Destra Nazionale, see the *Idea Nazionale* of February 21, 24, 25, 1922; and "La Destra Nazionale decide l'appoggio," *Popolo d'Italia,* February 26, 1922. On the conservative influence within the new coalition, see "Uomini," *Idea Nazionale,* February 28, 1922; "L'on. Federzoni eletto vice presidente della Camera," ibid., March 25, 1922; Veneruso, *La vigilia,* pp. 110–11, 119, 451.

35. Salandra, *Memorie politiche,* p. 14; Gifuni, *Il diario di Salandra,* pp. 261–63, entry for March 1922; Mussolini, "Da che parte va il mondo?" *Popolo d'Italia,* February 21, 1922.

36. On strains between Nationalists and Fascists and on the strengthening of the Nationalist militia, see "Le direttive dell'azione nazionalista discusse dal convegno dei delegati," *Idea Nazionale,* November 6, 1921; "I Sempre Pronti per la Patria e per il Re e la loro

organizzazione nazionale," ibid., December 27, 1921; Paolucci, *Piccolo mondo*, p. 233; "Le deliberazioni del comitato centrale nazionalista," *Idea Nazionale*, May 18, 1922. About this same period, the Nationalists began to organize public service workers into a National Labor Office (Ronzio, *La fusione*, pp. 156–57).

37. De Felice, *Mussolini il fascista*, 1:258–59, 263.

38. Ibid., pp. 196–97, Veneruso, *La vigilia*, pp. 264–65. For the Nationalist response, see "Pregiudiziale nazionalista," *Idea Nazionale*, April 18, 1922; and "Autonomia politica e azione nazionale," ibid., April 26, 1922. Nationalist interest in cooperating with the Fascists did not stop them from welcoming Alfredo Misuri into their ranks. Misuri had been elected as a Fascist but was expelled from the PNF. Mussolini specifically mentioned this case in his April 4 attack on the Nationalists. See Alfredo Misuri, *Ad Bestias! Memorie di un perseguiato* (Rome: no publisher, 1944), p. 66; and "L'on. Alfredo Misuri rientra nell'Associazione nazionalista," *Idea Nazionale*, April 6, 1922.

39. Mussolini, "Maschere e volto della Germania," *Popolo d'Italia*, April 19, 1922; Coppola, "La conferenza di Genova," *Politica* 12 (1922): 20–21, 24, 29–31. For the hardline position after Rapallo, see Mussolini, "Si può chiudere, signori," *Popolo d'Italia*, April 19, 1922; Veneruso, *La vigilia*, p. 147; Rumi, *Alle origini della politica estera fascista*, pp. 159–60.

40. Italo Balbo, *Diario 1922* (Milan: Mondadori, 1932), pp. 36, 38, entry for March 15, 1922; also Forges, "Lo stesso problema," and "L'aspro combattimento e la resa," *Idea Nazionale*, March 5, 1922; "I nazionalisti e i Sempre Pronti fiumiani all'avanguardia della riscossa nazionale," ibid., March 7, 1922.

CHAPTER EIGHT

1. Giuseppe Ottone and Gelesio Caetani, "La crisi economica e la politica demagogica," *Idea Nazionale*, January 18, 1922; Ottone, "Il congresso nazionalista, e la realtà nazionale: Programma economico," ibid., May 12, 1922; Corradini, "Le direttive della dottrina nazionalista," ibid., January 11, 1922; "Giornata nazionale," ibid., April 25, 1922. There was an appeal to conservative Catholics on the issue of aid to private schools as part of an effort to show that a conservative Church need not be represented by an uncontrollable democratic party.

2. Veneruso, *La vigilia*, pp. 469–70.

3. "La crisi finanziaria e i pericoli del collaborazionismo esaminata in un grande convegno indetto dai nazionalisti," *Idea Nazionale*, July 14, 1922; Giorgio Ghigi, "Il contenuto economico dei fatti di Bologna," ibid., June 8, 1922; Veneruso, *La vigilia*, pp. 197, note 250, Castronovo, *La stampa italiana*, pp. 316–17.

4. On the development of the crisis, see Veneruso, *La vigilia*, pp. 266, 454–55; the Nationalists were hostile to the Catholic party's strategy, "Un neonato già marcio," *Idea Nazionale*, June 18, 1922; whereas the Fascists seemed to seek a break with the Right, Bianchi, "La destra e il partito fascista," *Resto del Carlino*, July 22, 1922. Massimo Rocca recalled that Michele Bianchi hated the Nationalists (*Come il fascismo*, pp. 82–83). The initial mild Nationalist reaction changed after the Bianchi interview "Il collaborazionismo smascherato," *Idea Nazionale*, July 21, 1922; and "Rapporti artificiosi," ibid., July 23, 1922. Fascist superiority can be seen in Balbo, *Diario 1922*, pp. 94–95; and Efrem Ferraris, *La marcia su Roma veduta dal Viminale* (Rome: Edizioni Leonardo, 1946), p. 21, entry for July 4, 1922.

5. "L'atteggiamento dei liberali e dei nazionalisti," *Popolo d'Italia*, July 25, 1922; "Fuori dagli equivoci," *Idea Nazionale*, July 25, 1922; "Dal parlamento al paese," ibid., July 27, 1922; Veneruso, *La vigilia*, pp. 449–50. Ferraris noted that both the Nationalists and the Fascists were bothered by the presence of Taddei at the Interior (*La marcia su Roma*, p. 30).

6. Gaeta, *Il nazionalismo italiano*, p. 218; Rocca, *Come il fascismo*, p. 107.

7. On the Fascist-Nationalist reaction to the "legalitarian strike," see De Felice, *Mussolini il fascista*, 1:272–79; A. Rèpaci, *La marcia su Roma: Mito e realtà*, 2 vols. (Rome: Canesi, 1963), 1: 40–45, 75. For Nationalist activity, see "Supremo ricatto," *Idea Nazionale*, August 1, 1922; "Il crollo del socialismo," ibid., August 4, 1922. The *Idea Nazionale* of August 4 and 6, 1922 give detailed accounts of the Nationalist reaction.

8. On the growth of the ANI and Sempre Pronti, see *Idea Nazionale*, August 22, 25, 26, 29, 31, and September 7, 13, 17, 1922; Gaeta, *Il nazionalismo italiano*, p. 218; Paolucci, *Piccolo mondo*, p. 238.

9. "Conflitto fra nazionalisti e fascisti a Taranto," *Giornale di Roma*, September 19, 1922; "L'importante affermazione delle milizie azzurre tarantine," *Idea Nazionale*, September 20, 1922; Misuri, *Ad bestias!* pp. 68–71. Misuri was appointed inspector general of the Sempre Pronti soon after ("L'inteso sviluppo dell'orgaizzazione," *Idea Nazionale*, September 28, 1922). For the Nationalist reaction to Mussolini's Udine speech, see Forges, "Monarchia," ibid., September 22, 1922.

10. Ferraris, *La marcia su Roma*, p. 53, entry for September 16, 1922; De Felice, *Mussolini il fascista*, 1:367; Federzoni, *L'Italia di ieri*, pp. 70–71.

11. "Il patto di Genova fra nazionalisti e fascisti," *Idea Nazionale*, October 10, 1922; a similar accord was signed in Pisa, "Pieno accordo fra nazionalisti e fascisti in provincia di Pisa," ibid., October 18, 1922; Ronzio, *La fusione*, p. 209. On the conflicts, see Gaeta, *Il nazionalismo italiano*, p. 219; Rèpaci, *La marcia su Roma*, 1:273–74, for the citation from *La Patria*.

12. Gaeta, *Il nazionalismo italiano*, p. 218; Federzoni, *Presagi alla nazione* (Milan: Casa Editrice Imperia, 1924), p. 328; "Il discorso politico dell'on. Federzoni a Milano," *Idea Nazionale*, October 17, 1922. Umberto Guglielmotti recalled a meeting between Mussolini and Federzoni at the beginning of October at which the Nationalists asked and received assurances about the Fascist position on the dynasty in case of a coup (Memo, undated, in Archivio Federzoni-Argentieri, fasc. Il Gran Consiglio del Fascismo).

13. Salandra, *Memorie politiche*, pp. 18–19; Repaci, *La marcia su Roma*, 1:451.

14. Colapietra, *Napoli*, p. 207; Rocco, "Gli antecedenti, lo spirito, le date della marcia su Roma," *Idea Nazionale*, October 28, 1923; Ferraris, *La marcia su Roma*, p. 85.

15. Repaci, *La marcia su Roma*, 1:454. The Nationalists feared that Facta might succeed in gaining the support of D'Annunzio. See "Il mito e la speculazione," *Idea Nazionale*, October 24, 1922. On the maneuvering for a new government, see Ferraris, *La marcia su Roma*, pp. 81–82; Salandra, *Memorie politiche*, pp. 20–21.

16. Salandra, *Memorie politiche*, p. 21; Ferraris, *La marcia su Roma*, p. 91, for the Mussolini-Salandra call; De Felice, *Mussolini il fascista*, 1:263.

17. On the Nationalist reaction to the March, see Ferraris, *La marcia su Roma*, p. 93; Federzoni, *L'Italia di ieri*, p. 72; Rèpaci, *La marcia*, 2:405–6, testimony of Paolucci; Paolucci, *Piccolo mondo*, p. 240. Marcello Soleri mentioned a role for the Blue Shirts in the defense of Rome, and Alfredo Misuri noted plans to transport the Sempre Pronti squads to the south. See M. Soleri, *Memorie* (Turin: Einaudi, 1949), pp. 150–51; Misuri, *Ad bestias!* pp. 73–74.

18. Ferraris, *La marcia su Roma*, p. 99; Soleri, *Memorie*, p. 151; Rèpaci, *La marcia su Roma*, 2:398, Ferraris's statement.

19. De Felice, *Mussolini il fascista*, 1:369; Federzoni, *L'Italia di ieri*, pp. 72–75.

20. E. Ferraris, "Giolitti e il fascismo," *Risorgimento* 9 (September 1959):242; Repaci, *La marcia su Roma*, 1:525; De Felice, *Mussolini il fascista*, 1:369; Ferraris, *La marcia su Roma*, pp. 107–9.

21. Rèpaci, *La marcia su Roma*, 1:531–32. The call to De Vecchi caused some permanent resentment. In a letter to Federzoni of August 22, 1927, Forges remembered only the calls to Mussolini in Milan and to De Bono in Perugia and a violent discussion with General Pugliese about troop disposition at the royal palace. De Vecchi, however, believed that he spoke with Federzoni on October 28: "I have never given great importance to the telephone call received in Perugia and that I always believed to be yours. It had been preceded by the call from the sovereign and therefore only reflected my own anxiety . . . "Nevertheless, he recalled that several Fascists were present and all believed that Federzoni was speaking. See Forges to Federzoni, August 22, 1927; and De Vecchi to Federzoni, August 31, 1927, Archivio Federzoni-Argentieri.

22. Ferraris, *La Marcia su Roma*, pp. 111–13.

23. Federzoni, *L'Italia di ieri*, pp. 76–77; Tamaro, *Venti anni*, 1:266–67. Rocco, "Gli antecedenti, lo spirito, le date della marcia su Roma," *Idea Nazionale*, October 28, 1923; De Felice, *Mussolini il fascista*, 1:372; Ferraris, *La marcia su Roma*, p. 115; and "Giolitti e il fascismo," p. 243. According to Ferraris, Federzoni made a call around 11:00 A.M. when he spoke to an official at the Milanese prefecture.

24. Ferraris, *La marcia su Roma*, pp. 115–16; Rocco, "Gli antecedenti, lo spirito, le date della marcia su Roma," *Idea Nazionale*, October 28, 1923; on October 10, a group of industrialists told the prefect of Milan that Giolitti was the most suitable man to channel the fascist movement. See Roland Sarti, *Fascism and the Industrial Leadership in Italy 1919–1940* (Berkeley: University of California Press, 1971), pp. 35–37.

25. Ferraris, *La Marcia su Roma*, pp. 119–20; De Felice, *Mussolini il fascista*, 1:370 (who feels the last call was made by G. Postiglione); Federzoni, *L'Italia di ieri*, p. 77; Misuri, *Ad bestias!* p. 77; Salvemini, "Diario," *Il Mondo*, November 4, 1958, p. 11; Rèpaci, *La marcia su Roma*, 1:543.

26. Federzoni, *L'Italia di ieri*, pp. 73–75; "La verità sul decreto," *Idea Nazionale*, November 1, 1922; Rèpaci, *La marcia su Roma*, 1:511, 518; De Felice, *Mussolini il fascista*, 1:361 ff.

2. For a somewhat defensive tone to Nationalist comment, see "L'opera del nazionalismo nella giornata di sabato," *Idea Nazionale*, October 30, 1922; on possible socialist participation, see Carlo Silves-

tri, *Turati l'ha detto* (Milan: Rizzoli, 1947), pp. 68–69. De Felice, *Mussolini il fascista,* 1:375; Rèpaci, *La marcia su Roma,* 1:572. The Nationalists denied conflicts over the composition of the government. See "Elenco di menzogne," *Idea Nazionale,* October 31, 1922.

CHAPTER NINE

1. Oreste Rizzini to Alberto Albertini, November 20, 1922, *Epistolario,* 4:1651–52.

2. Rumi, *Alle origini della politica estera,* p. 230; "L'adunata di Fiume sospesa," *Idea Nazionale,* November 15, 1922.

3. "L'ordine interno," *Idea Nazionale,* December 30, 1922; Maraviglia, "La signorità dello stato e il compito del governo," ibid., January 5, 1923.

4. Rocco, *Come il fascismo,* p. 117; Corradini, "La rivoluzione del nazionalismo fascista," *Idea Nazionale,* December 8, 1922; Bottai, "Conversando con Enrico Corradini," *Giornale di Roma,* December 24, 1922; Corradini, "Nazionalismo e fascismo," *Idea Nazionale,* December 22, 1922.

5. Colapietra, *Napoli,* pp. 206–7, 213–14.

6. On friction between Nationalists and Fascists, see ACS, Min. Int., Dir. gen. P.S., Aff. gen. e ris., 1914–26, 1923, busta 62A, fasc. Potenza, where the prefect dissolved the local ANI group; ibid., busta 45, fasc. Associazione Nazionalista, sottof. Catanzaro, report of January 24, 1923. Here the prefect described the tension as the result of "personal rancors, divergences of an economic character, desires for local predominence."

7. On the situation around Naples, see ibid., busta 45, fasc. Associazione Nazionalista, sottof. Caserta, for a series of reports on the size and composition of the Nationalist groups; "La situazione in Terra del Lavoro," *Idea Nazionale,* November 12, 1922; "Per un leale accordo tra fascisti e nazionalisti in Campania," ibid., December 10, 1922; "Nobili parole dell'on. Paolucci ai Sempre Pronti napoletani," ibid., December 20, 1922; Colapietra, *Napoli,* pp. 193, 218–19.

8. "Un intollerabile arbitro," and "Nazionalismo e fascismo nel Mezzogiorno," *Idea Nazionale,* December 20, 1922; Mussolini to the Federazione Fascisti Napoli, December 31, 1922; ACS, Segr. part. del Duce, cart. ris., busta 5, fasc. 82r Federzoni. Further problems around Nales arose: ACS., Min. Int., Dir. gen. P.S., Aff. gen. e ris., 1914–26, 1923, busta 45, fasc. Associazione Nazionalista, sottof. Caserta, reports of January 22 and 25, 1923; ibid., sottof. Salerno,

report of January 31, 1923; "Un conflitto tra fascisti e nazionalisti," *Il Mattino*, January 24–25, 1923. Greco contended that the problems arose merely from local situations and that the ANI was eager for an accord ("Verso l'accordo nazional-fascista," *Il Mattino*, January 14–15, 1923). For problems elsewhere in the south, see ACS, Min. Int., Dir. gen. P.S., Aff. gen. e ris., 1914–26, 1923, busta 61b, fasc. Reggio Calabria, report of January 10, 1923; "Sanguinosa battaglia tra fascisti e nazionalisti," *Giornale d'Italia*, November 7, 1922, on events at Taranto.

9. On the growth of the ANI, see g.d.m., "I partiti politici in Piemonte: Il nazionalista," *Giornale di Roma*, December 15, 1922; ACS, Min. Int., Dir. gen. P.S., Aff. gen. e ris., 1914–26, 1923, busta 45, fasc. Associazione Nazionalista, sottof. Verona, report of January 29, 1923; "Il nuovo consiglio direttivo della Sezione Nazionalista Romana," *Idea Nazionale*, November 26, 1922; "I nazionalisti romani esaltano la vittoria della nuova Italia," ibid., November 17, 1922.

10. "Per la disciplina dell'organizzazione e del movimento nazionalista," ibid., November 12, 1922; Nicola Pascazio, "Michele Bianchi dice che Mussolini è un uomo nato per governare," *Giornale d'Italia*, November 16, 1922; "L'intesa tra fascisti e nazionalisti per impedire speculazioni e inquinamenti partigiani," *Idea Nazionale*, November 17, 1922; "L'accordo per le organizzazioni," ibid., December 1, 1922; Ronzio, *La fusione*, pp. 226–27.

11. "Tra nazionalisti e fascisti," *Giornale d'Italia*, December 31, 1922; "Tra nazionalisti e fascisti: Lettera di Enrico Corradini," ibid., January 2, 1923. Federzoni to Mussolini, December 24, 1922, ACS, Segr. part. del Duce, cart. ris., busta 5, fasc. 82r Federzoni.

12. De Felice, *Mussolini il fascista*, 1:434. On the size of the Sempre Pronti, see "Volontà nazionale," *Idea Nazionale*, January 24, 1923; "La trasformazione delle camicie azzurre," *Giornale d'Italia*, December 23, 1922.

13. "Nazionalismo e fascismo," *Idea Nazionale*, January 2, 1923; "Nazionalismo e fascismo," *Popolo d'Italia*, January 2, 1923; Mussolini to the Federazione Fascista di Napoli, December 31, 1922, ACS, Segr. part. del Duce, cart. ris., busta 5, fasc. 82r Federzoni; Colapietra, *Napoli*, p. 219; "I nuovi compiti dei Sempre Pronti," *Idea Nazionale*, January 3, 1923; "Dissensi fra nazionalisti per la fusione con i fascisti: Intervista con Umberto Guglielmotti," *Giornale d'Italia*, January 7, 1923; "I rapporti tra nazionalismo e fascismo," *Il Mattino*, January 7–8, 1923.

14. Ronzio, *La fusione*, pp. 230–31; De Felice, *Mussolini il fascista*, 1:434; for Federzoni's role in setting up the commission, see Federzoni's role in setting up the commission, see Federzoni to Mussolini,

January 13, 1923, ACS, Segr. part. del Duce, cart. ris, busta 5, fasc. 82r Federzoni. For the cautious comments of the two parties, see "Nazionalismo e fascismo," *Idea Nazionale,* January 14, 1923; and Arnaldo Mussolini, "Dopo il Gran Consiglio," *Popolo d'Italia,* January 16, 1923. See the first Rocco draft, ACS, Segr. part. del Duce, cart. ris, busta 5, fasc. 82r Federzoni. On the conservatives and fusion, see "I liberali e il fascismo," *Giornale d'Italia,* January 30, 1923; "I partiti nazionali," ibid., February 1, 1923.

15. "Compiti e rapporti nuovi," *Idea Nazionale,* February 1, 1923. Paolo Di Tarsia, "Relazione circa i conflitti tra fascisti e nazionalisti, provincia di Potenza, comune di Bernaldo, il 31 gennaio 1923," ACS, Min. Int., Dir. gen. P.S., Aff. gen. e ris., 1914–26, 1923, busta 61A, fasc. Potenza.

16. Ibid. Also "Associazione Nazionalista Italiana, Segreteria Regionale di Baslicata, Rapporti fra fascismo e nazionalismo: Memorandum per il comm. Paolo Di Tarsia." For an indication that the growth of the ANI resulted from refugees from older parties, see the report of the prefect of Catazaro, February 7, 1923, ibid., busta 45, fasc. Associazione Nazionalista, sottof. Catanzaro. The prefects' reports also gave an indication of the size of the ANI. A report from Lecce put the membership around 4,000 in twenty-one sections (ibid., sottof. Lecce, reports of January and February, 1923). On the occasion of the dissolution of the Sempre Pronti 24,938 members participated in the ceremonies (lower than the official Nationalist report). The largest group was almost 7,000 strong in Rome. See "Appunto per S.E. il direttore generale della P.S.," February 8, 1923, ibid. Fascist reaction was in "L'orientazione definitiva del fascismo nel pensiero dell'avv. Sansanelli," *Giornale d'Italia,* February 3, 1923; "Mussolini nel Mezzogiorno: Intervista con A. Starace," ibid., February 10, 1923. See also Colapietra, *Napoli,* p. 227.

17. For Rocco's second draft, see ACS, Segr. part. del Duce, cart. ris., busta 5, fasc. 82r Federzoni.

18. "Controproposte del Presidente del Consiglio," ibid.; "I lavori della commissione mista," *Idea Nazionale,* February 13, 1923; A Zanetti to Mussolini, February 15, 1923, ACS, Segr. part. del Duce, cart. ris., busta 5, fasc. 82r, Federzoni.

19. On the Masonic declaration, see Rocca, *Come il fascismo divenne una dittatura,* p. 235; "Un ordine del giorno dell'Associazione Nazionalista," *Popolo d'Italia,* February 16, 1923; "Il capitano Padovani esce dalla Loggia di Napoli e si dimette da Alto Commissario," *Giornale d'Italia,* February 18, 1923. See also the well-informed

article, "I tentativi per raggiungere la fusione tra fascisti e nazionalisti," *Il Mattino*, February 24–25, 1923.

20. On the final events leading to fusion, see "I rapporti tra fascisti e nazionalisti," *Popolo d'Italia*, February 23, 1923; "Per la fusione tra nazionalisti e fascisti," ibid., February 25, 1923. The secretary of the ANI for Lazio estimated that 25,000 Nationalists would join the PNF in Rome and its province ("Verso la fusione tra fascisti e nazionalisti," ibid., February 21, 1923); "Intervista con il ministro Federzoni sulla fusione tra nazionalisti e fascisti," *Giornale d'Italia*, February 25, 1923. Federzoni estimated that 100,000 Nationalists might join the PNF. The *Giornale d'Italia* viewed the projected accord as the first step toward the eventual merger of the conservatives, "Il piano di unificazione tra fascisti e nazionalisti," February 24, 1923. The text of the fusion accord was given in ACS, Segr. part. del Duce, cart. ris, busta 5, fasc. 82r Federzoni.

21. Official reaction to the accord was favorable: "Il valore dell'atto," *Idea Nazionale*, February 28, 1923; G. Polverelli, "Italia nazionale e fascista," *Popolo d'Italia*, February 28, 1923. There was, however, no comment by Arnaldo Mussolini. On signs of opposition, see Tamaro, *Venti anni*, 1:308; "Dissenso tra nazionalisti milanesi," *Giornale d'Italia*, February 28, 1923; ACS, Dir. gen. P.S., Aff. gen. e ris., 1914–26, 1923, busta 45, fasc. Associazione Nazionalista, sottof. Milano, report of March 8, 1923; "Impressioni a Montecitorio sulla fusione nazional-fascista: Intervista con l'on. Paolucci," *Giornale d'Italia*, February 28, 1923; Interview with Senator Ugo D'Andrea, Rome, February 1972; Von Neurath to Foreign Ministry, March 13, 1923, cited in Rumi, *Alle origini della politica estera fascista*, pp. 287–88. See Ronzio, *La fusione*, pp. 246–47. Many areas of the south were a problem. The Interior Ministry had to ban the wearing of blue shirts in demonstrations (telegrams to prefects of Catania, Girgenti, Messina, Palermo, Siracusa, Trapani, April 17, 1923, ACS, Min. Int., Dir. gen. P.S., Aff. gen. e ris., 1914–26, 1923, busta 45, fasc. Associazione Nazionalista). On Padovani, see Colapietra, *Napoli*, p. 228; and Salvemini, "Diario," *Il Mondo*, November 11, 1958, p. 12. Federzoni's protest is in an undated letter to Mussolini, "Milizia Nazionale," ACS, Segr. part. del Duce, cart. ris, busta 5, fasc. 82r Federzoni. See also "I nazionalisti romani approvano il patto di fusione," *Idea Nazionale*, March 4, 1923.

22. "Intervista con il ministro Federzoni," *Giornale d'Italia*, February 25, 1923; and "Verso la fusione fra fascisti e nazionalisti," *Popolo d'Italia*, February 21, 1923. Paolucci was both more realistic and

pessimistic when he told a reporter for the *Corriere della Sera* that of 63,000 Sempre Pronti, only 14,000 would join the Fascists (G. Emanule to Alberto Albertini, July 10, 1923, *Epistolario*, 4:1733–34).

23. "La situazione dei liberali dopo l'assorbimento dei nazionalisti nel fascismo," *Giornale d'Italia*, February 28, 1923; "Non fusione ma dissoluzione dei gruppi parlamentare: La revendicazione della Destra Liberale," ibid., March 7, 1923.

CHAPTER TEN

1. Colapietra, *Napoli*, 234–35. On revisionism, see A. De Grand, "Giuseppe Bottai e il fallimento del fascismo revisionista," *Storia contemporanea*, 6 (1975): 697–731.

2. Padovani to Mussolini, April 29, 1923 and May 19, 1923; and Padovani to Senator De Bono, May 1, 1923; "I Fascisti di Napoli" to Mussolini, August 17, 1924, ACS, Segr. part. del Duce, cart. ris, busta 44, fasc. 242r, Padovani. See also Colapietra, *Napoli*, pp. 237, 300. The Nationalists emerged in a strong position in Trieste (Apih, *Fascismo e antifascismo*, pp. 191–92) and in Rome, where Italo Foschi and Umberto Guglielmotti emerged for a time as important leaders. See Renzo De Felice, *Mussolini il fascista*, vol. 2 *L'organizzazione dello stato fascista 1925–1929* (Turin: Einaudi, 1968) p. 47.

3. Rocca, *Come il fascismo divenne una dittatura*, pp. 138–39; u.g., "Chiusura," *Idea Nazionale*, May 17, 1924.

4. R. Cantalupo, "Il dovere del Sud," *Idea Nazionale*, March 15, 1924; and "Il partito dei meridionali," ibid., April 10, 1924. On the need to support the National List, see Cantalupo, "La ricostruzione liberale," ibid., January 13, 1924; Forges, "Le querimonie dei partiti," ibid., March 24, 1924.

5. Maraviglia, "Normalizzazione," *Idea Nazionale*, April 18, 1924; Colapietra, *Napoli*, p. 282; De Felice, *Mussolini il fascista*, 1:600–18.

6. See the report by Sardi, "Crisi Matteotti," and the memo by Federzoni, "Affare Matteotti," in Archivio Federzoni-Argentieri.

7. A copy of the collective letter to Mussolini of June 14, 1924, ibid.

8. Tamaro, *Venti anni*, 1:432; De Felice, *Mussolini il fascista*, 1:650.

9. Federzoni, *L'Italia di ieri*, p. 100.

10. Turati to Kuliscioff, June 17, 19, 21, 1924, *Carteggio*, 6:209, 214, 220; Ojetti, *Taccuini*, p. 146, entry for June 26, 1924. "Responsabilità," *Il Mondo*, June 18, 1924; "Sulla buona strade," *Giornale d'Italia*, June 18, 1924; Rastignac, "Governare il paese," *Il Tribuna*, June 18, 1924; "Dalla rivoluzione alla restaurazione," *Resto del Carlino*, June 19, 1924.

11. Federzoni wrote: "I would like to know how Turati could attribute a thought . . . that I might associate myself with elements, even moderate, of the Aventine opposition. I aimed instead openly and energetically to purge fascism of all reckless and dangerous elements which brought it to the serious test of 1924." See Federzoni, "Giornale di un viaggiatore senza importanza," entry for April 22, 1947, pp. 272–73, Archivio Federzoni-Argentieri. For contemporary fears of the "post-Mussolini," see Maraviglia, "Il concerto degli oppositori," *Idea Nazionale,* July 5, 1924.

12. On Federzoni's press law, which put extra legal pressure on the *gerente responsabile* (responsible official of the paper, see Castronovo, *La stampa italiana,* p. 351. In a telegram to the prefects on September 18, 1924, Federzoni stated: "For some time, certain Fascist papers insist on naming specifically the principal adversaries for reprisals or punitive actions. Such publications have taken on by now an intolerable tone which could render them politically dangerous because eventual acts could involve the moral responsibility of the Fascist party and even the government which tolerated such publications." (Archivio Federzoni-Argentieri.) Also Corradini to Federzoni, July 9, 1924, ibid.

13. See A. Lyttelton, "Fascism in Italy: the Second Wave," in G. Mosse and Walter Lacqueur, eds., *International Fascism* (New York: Harper Torchbook, 1966), pp. 75–100; Paolucci, *Piccolo mondo,* p. 248.

14. Forges, "Sisignori! Fascismo non è liberalismo," *Idea Nazionale,* August 6, 1924; Maraviglia, "Problemi di orientamento," ibid., August 3, 1924; "Lo spirito liberale che anela il paese," *Giornale d'Italia,* August 1, 1924.

15. Paolucci, *Piccolo mondo,* p. 256; Rocco to Federzoni, January 18, 1924 (probably 1925), Archivio Federzoni-Argentieri.

16. Giuseppe Rossini, ed., *Il delitto Matteotti* (Bologna: Il Mulino, 1966), pp. 148–49; Tamaro, *Venti anni,* 2:57; De Felice, *Mussolini il fascista,* 1:702–10. For the order to enforce the press decrees more fully, see A. Aquarone, *L'organizzazione dello stato totalitario* (Turin: Einaudi, 1965), pp. 347–49.

CHAPTER ELEVEN

1. Alfredo Rocco, *La trasformazione dello stato* (Rome: La Voce, 1927), pp. 36, 333, 415–17. The efforts by the Nationalists (Rocco and his brother Arturo, Coppola, and Fulvio Suvich) to thwart the Fascist syndicalists has been analyzed by Bruno Uva, *La nascita dello stato corporativo e sindacale fascista* (Assisi: Beniamino Carucci Editore,

no date), pp. 3–79. Much of the maneuvering took place on the Commission of eighteen, a study committee which had been set up in 1925 to plan for the corporative state. The Nationalists formed a very aggressive minority in their fight against an independent role for the unions. It should also be noted in dealing with Rocco's contribution to the Fascist regime that he had a major role in the negotiations for the Lateran Treaty between church and state. See Francesco Margiotta Broglio, *Italia e la Santa Sede dalla Grande guerra alla Conciliazione* (Bari: Laterza, 1966), pp. 141–51.

2. Philip Cannistraro, *La fabbrica del consenso: Fascismo e mass media* (Bari: Tempi Nuovi Laterza, 1975), pp. 14, 28, 49.

3. See the *Tribuna*, December 27, 1925; and the *Giornale d'Italia*, March 30, 1926.

4. Corradini's aphorisms are in Federzoni, *L'Italia di ieri*, pp. 17–19. Examples of Forges's more totalitarian attitude can be seen in his call for a purge of cultural life. See R. Forges Davanzati, *Fascismo e cultura* (Florence: R. Bemporad, 1927), pp. 8,18–19.

5. See Corradini to Mussolini, July 10, no year, Archivio Federzoni-Argentieri.

6. Federzoni, "Diario," entries of February 18 and March 3, 1927, Archivio Federzoni-Argentieri.

7. Ibid., entries of January 22 and February 19, 1927.

8. See by Coppola, "La crisi dell'Europa e la sua cultura," *Politica*, 37 (1932–33): 43–74; "Roma e antiroma," *La Tribuna*, June 21, 1927; "Idee che debbono essere chiare," ibid., June 23, 1927; "Dalla filosofia della storia e della realtà," ibid., June 25, 1927. For the remarks on Hitler, see "Postilla: la lotta politica in Germania," *Politica*, 34 (1932):306–13. Of course, Coppola's own anti-Semitism acted as a bridge for an eventual reconciliation with the Nazis.

9. Federzoni's diary entries in 1927 were uniformly favorable to Mussolini and revealed little sympathy with the complaints of his Nationalist friends. His disillusionment grew throughout the 1930s. (Conversation with Signora Elena Argentieri and with Signora Luisa Federzoni, June 1976).

10. The climate of political irresponsibility has been analyzed by Giuseppe Bottai, *Venti anni e un giorno* (Milan: Garzanti, 1949).

Bibliographical Essay

THIS ESSAY is designed to give an indication of those sources which have been most useful in the preparation of this study. More specific references can be found in the notes to the chapters.

PRIMARY SOURCES

One of the problems in dealing with the Italian Nationalist Association is the lack of records for the ANI itself. Membership rolls and the files of the secretariat are unavailable. The most important source of documentation are the holdings of the Direzione Generale di Pubblica Sicurezza of the Interior Ministry and the Segreteria Particolare del Duce in the Archivio Centrale dello Stato in Rome. The most useful private archive is that of Luigi Federzoni, also in Rome. The bulk of Federzoni's papers were either lost or stolen after the fall of fascism, and what remains must be just a small part of the materials which Federzoni was known to have collected during the Fascist years. There is also a diary for the first months of 1927, when he was colonial minister. An important source for the early history of the Nationalist movement is the Fondazione Castellini, Museo del Risorgimento, Milan. The Bergamini Archive in the Biblioteca Communale, San Giovanni in Persiceto, is extremely well organized and its director, Dott. Gandini, very helpful. Professor Francesco Perfetti of Rome very kindly offered to put at my disposition materials from the papers of Mario Viana which are in his possession.

Even more important than the letters and other private and official documents are the newspapers and reviews of the movement: the *Regno* of Florence, the *Tricolore* of Turin, the *Grande Italia* of Milan, and the *Idea Nazionale* and *Politica* of Rome. Franco Gaeta has published a useful anthology of the Nationalist press: *La stampa nazionalista* (Rocca San Casciano:

Cappelli, 1965), and Delia Frigessi did the same for the *Regno* in *La cultura italiana del '900 attraverso le riviste: "Leonardo," "Hermes," "Il Regno"* (Turin: Einaudi, 1960).

SECONDARY SOURCES

The only complete history of the Italian Nationalist Association is Franco Gaeta's brief but well done *Nazionalismo italiano* (Naples: Edizioni Scientifiche Italiane, 1965). Still useful, but somewhat dated by its pro-Fascist bias, is Paola Maria Arcari's, *Le elaborazioni della dottrina politica nazionale fra l'unità e l'intervento, 1870–1914* (3 vols., Florence: Casa Editrice Marzocco, 1934–39), which contains a wealth of documentation from her father's (Paolo Arcari) papers. Salvatore Saladino's contribution on Italian nationalism in Hans Rogger and Eugen Weber, *The European Right: An Historical Profile* (Berkeley: University of California Press, 1965) is a good introduction to the subject in English.

The Nationalists have received extended treatment in Renzo De Felice's monumental biography of Mussolini: *Mussolini il rivoluzionario* (Turin: Einaudi, 1965) and *Mussolini il fascista*, vol. 1 *La conquista del potere* (Turin: Einaudi, 1966) and vol. 2 *L'organizzazione dello stato fascista* (Turin: Einaudi, 1968). A somewhat different picture of Mussolini's evolution to the Right and of Nationalist influence is presented in Roberto Vivarelli, *Il dopoguerra in Italia: Dalla fine della guerra all'impresa di Fiume* (Naples: Ricciardi, 1967). A semiofficial history of fascism from the Nationalist point of view is Attilio Tamaro's, *Venti anni di storia 1922–1943* (3 vols., Rome: Editrice Tiber, 1953–54).

On specific periods of Nationalist activity, the following contain much useful information: John A. Thayer, *Italy and the Great War* (Madison: University of Wisconsin Press, 1964) and Raffaele Molinelli's articles in the *Rassegna storica del Risorgimento*: "Per una storia del nazionalismo italiano," 50 (July 1963):391–406; "Nazionalisti, cattolici e liberali," 52 (July 1965): 354–78; "Il nazionalismo italiano e l'impresa di Libia," 53

(April 1966): 295–318, for the period before the war; on the Nationalists in World War I, B. Vigezzi, *L'Italia neutrale* (Naples: Ricciardi, 1966) and Piero Melograni, *Storia politica della Grande Guerra* (Bari: Laterza: 1969). For the postwar era, apart from the volumes of De Felice and Vivarelli, an extremely useful study is Danilo Veneruso's, *La vigilia del fascismo: Il primo ministero Facta nella crisi dello stato liberale in Italia* (Bologna: Il Mulino, 1968). A work with a decidedly Fascist point of view but with a good deal of information nonetheless is Romolo Ronzio's *La fusione del nazionalismo con il fascismo* (Rome: Edizioni italiane, 1943).

The Nationalists themselves have left little behind in the way of retrospective justifications. Most books by and about the Nationalists date from the Fascist era. Two exceptions are works on Enrico Corradini and Alfredo Rocco. Corradini's contribution to nationalism was the subject of Monique de Taeye Henen's *Le nationalisme d'Enrico Corradini et les origines du fascisme dans la revue florentine "Il Regno" 1903–1906* (Paris: Didier, 1973). Mario Isnenghi's *Il mito della grande guerra da Marinetti a Malaparte* (Bari: Laterza, 1970) also has some interesting sections on Corradini. Paolo Ungari's brilliant study of Alfredo Rocco, *Alfredo Rocco e l'ideologia giuridica del fascismo* (Brescia: Morcelliana, 1963) is an all-too-brief introduction to the career of one of the most influential jurists of the twentieth century. A third exception is the memoir of Luigi Federzoni, *L'Italia di ieri per la storia di domani* (Milan: Mondadori, 1967), which contains a detailed account of the July 25, 1943 meeting of the Fascist Grand council (Mussolini's fall from power) but is much more general for other periods.

Index